BEHIND THE MASKS

IN THE FOOTSTEPS OF THE EARLY
GREEK DRAMATISTS

JILL DUDLEY

Published by
Orpington Publishers

Origination by
Creeds Design & Print Ltd.,
Bridport, Dorset
01308 423411

Cover design
Creeds Design & Print Ltd.

© Jill Dudley 2020

ISBN: 978-0-9955781-2-8

CONTENTS

	Page
Prologue	v

PART ONE: FIRST TRIP

Chapter 1	Athens The Evolution of Drama from its Religious Roots Aristophanes – *Clouds, Frogs*	3
Chapter 2	Island of Salamis Euripides – *Cyclops, Trojan Women* Sophocles – *Ajax*	13
Chapter 3	Troezen Euripides – *Hippolytus*	27
Chapter 4	Epidaurus Aeschylus – *Agamemnon, Libation Bearers, Eumenides*	37
Chapter 5	Corinth Euripides – *Medea*	49
Chapter 6	Eleusis Aeschylus – *Persians* Aristophanes – *Plutus, Women of the Thesmophoria*	59
Chapter 7	Island of Aegina Aristophanes – *Wasps, Birds*	69

PART TWO: SECOND TRIP

Chapter 8   Aulis   85
    Euripides – *Iphigenia at Aulis, Iphigenia in Tauris*

Chapter 9   Thebes   99
    Sophocles – *Oedipus Tyrannus*
    Aeschylus – *Seven Against Thebes*

Chapter 10 Colonus   113
    Sophocles – *Oedipus Colonus*

PART THREE: THIRD TRIP

Chapter 11 Macedonia: Pella & Aigai   125
    Euripides – *Helen*

Chapter 12 Dion   137
    Euripides – *Bacchae*

Chapter 13 Mt. Olympus   147
    Euripides – *Alcestis*
    Aristophanes – *Peace*

Epilogue   157

ADDENDA

The following dramas may be of interest. The first includes the legendary story of Prometheus as well as the myth of Io (a priestess of Hera) of whom Zeus was enamoured. The second continues with the legendary descendants of Io and Zeus. The third and fourth reveal the importance of burial rites. The fifth is about the tragic madness of the hero, Heracles.

Aeschylus – *Prometheus Bound*	163
Aeschylus – *Suppliants*	169
Sophocles – *Antigone*	173
Euripides – *Suppliant Women*	177
Euripides – *Madness of Heracles*	183
Extant Dramas	189
Translations	191
Bibliography	193
Glossary	195
Index	209

PROLOGUE

To go to the theatre brings me all the tragedy that I want in life. It puts in front of me the mirror image of what could be, and I come away enthralled by other people's troubles, not my own, enriched by the words and action which have kept me glued to my seat.

The idea for *Behind the Masks* began when I was half-way through writing *Gods & Heroes*. Having written about the fall of Troy I began to wonder what had happened to the survivors of the war, and the unfortunate women of the Trojan royal household who became the captive slaves of the victorious Greeks. Their fate, I discovered, was to be found in the tragedies written by the fifth century B.C. dramatists.

The more I read, the more absorbed I became until I found myself caught up in the whole project of Greek drama, and how it first evolved. It was a vast canvas but I thought I could narrow it down by concentrating on the fifth century dramatists only, their thinking and what influenced them.

Besides writing about the survivors of the Trojan War, they wrote also about such famous legendary and mythological figures as Theseus, Oedipus, Heracles and Prometheus.

There was the comic dramatist Aristophanes too who wrote, not about the historic and legendary past, but about contemporary political and social issues. He lampooned public figures and, in his crazy, imaginative way, drew attention to the idiocy of war, political corruption and social injustices.

At times I was surprised to come across lines of dialogue which reminded me of passages in the New Testament written over four centuries later. I draw attention to them, questioning whether the early Christians were themselves influenced by Greek texts from those early dramas.

This book is essentially a travelogue about the places where the early dramatists lived and worked, and where the famous legendary figures in their tragedies originated. It is an easy introduction to early drama for those who don't want scholarly brain-demanding insights into the structure of the plays. I am not writing for scholars, or joining in debates about the exact meaning of a Greek text. Nor am I discussing remote subjects such as iambic pentameters, dactyls, strophes, hexameters, stasimons, anapaests – what are they? As I'm not writing for those who want to know, it doesn't matter.

Travelling around Greece and visiting the locations where these playwrights lived and wrote has taken time. I only hope that those who read *Behind the Masks* will enjoy it as much as I've had in researching, travelling and writing it.

The works of these first dramatists are masterpieces of western literature. The fact that some are still staged today, two and a half thousand years on, must surely be their greatest recommendation.

PART ONE
FIRST TRIP

CHAPTER 1

ATHENS

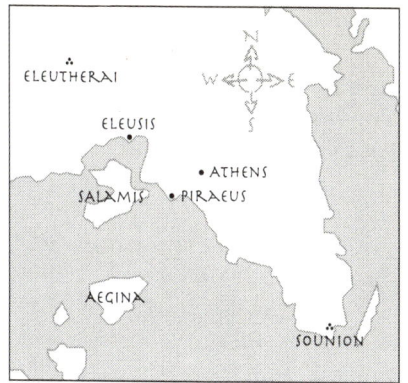

When I told Harry, my dear husband and stalwart travelling companion, that I needed to return to Greece yet again to see where the early dramatists lived and worked, he dug in his heels. He was too old to travel any more, he said; for God's sake find other younger people to come with me, he implored; all he wanted was a quiet life, to potter in his vegetable garden and walk the dog. His emphatic 'no more travelling' was, in fact, proving to be a blessing in disguise. If Harry wasn't there with me in person, he was certainly still there with me in spirit – and to be 'in spirit' saved a fortune (his words).

So there I was in Athens with two new travelling companions on a warm and sunny morning in June. We were seated on one of the tiered seats in the small gem of an amphitheatre, the theatre of Dionysos Eleuthereus, tucked below the south-east side of the Acropolis. Beyond the site, bottle-green cypress trees rose spear-like, breaking the grey monotony of the city streets and buildings. In the far, far distance was a stretch of glittering sea and the busy port of Piraeus; and beyond that still, a hazy outline of the island of Aegina where the comic playwright Aristophanes had spent his adolescent years – an island high on my itinerary of places to be visited.

"So, come on, remind us who Dionysos was?" Hilary, the elder of my two new companions asked. She was an ex-nun who'd jumped the wall some thirty years back when her natural curiosity had caused her to think about things logically. Harry was happy she was accompanying me as he hoped some of her discipline and piety would rub off on me.

"He was god of wine and drama," I answered.

She was silent a moment, then said: "I suppose that makes sense. I mean, too much wine and there's bound to be drama, don't you see?"

Her gentle blue eyes fixed on me enquiringly.

"Or you could say too much drama and you need that bottle of wine," Fiona, her younger friend, quipped with a short laugh. I'd noticed the evening before that she certainly hadn't stinted on the drink – celebrating, she'd said. I suspected Fiona's interest in ancient Greece was stricly limited; sea, sun and relaxation were what she'd come for.

She looked stylish in a panama hat perched jauntily on her head. Being tall and slender she could have been a model had she wanted to. I wasn't surprised when she suddenly got up and said: "Sorry, folk, but I can't sit here on this hard seat a moment longer. I'll wait for you down there." She indicated a bench in the shade of a pine tree.

Hilary murmured: "I've promised her we'll explore Plaka before it gets too hot. But meanwhile –" She pointed to a sculpted marble screen on which were panels depicting scenes from the life of Dionysos; it ran along the back of the theatre on a narrow platform known as the *bema*. One of the panels portrayed the birth of Dionysos.

"Isn't there some strange myth about his birth?" Hilary asked.

I told her the best known story: Zeus, supreme god of the ancient world, fell in love with Semele, the daughter of King Cadmus of Thebes. Unfortunately, Zeus' wife Hera, in understandable fury at her husband's extra-marital fling, persuaded Semele to ask Zeus one night to reveal himself to her in his full glory as a god. This she did and, as Hera well knew would happen, the blaze of Zeus' divinity reduced the poor girl to a cinder. Zeus, however, rescued the embryo of his unborn child and placed it in his thigh till the infant was ready to be born.

"Such a strange story!" Hilary remarked. "You wouldn't think anyone could make it up, would you?" Her amazement and curiosity showed on her face. "Do you think they really believed that in those days? I mean Roman Catholics insist on the perpetual virginity of Mary even though she later had several children by Joseph. It makes no sense, does it? But that's what they say. Sorry, I'm going off track. Go on about Dionysos. What happened when he was born?"

I explained how he was given to Ino, Semele's sister, till Hera, in a fit of jealous fury, drove her mad, and Dionysos was handed over to nymphs who cared for him. He was then taught by Silenus, a Satyr. Satyrs were lascivious creatures, upright like men but also with the tails of a horse and often with the legs of a goat. They were fond of revelry and were devoted followers of Dionysos. Silenus, though a Satyr, had a reputation for wisdom. Vase paintings portrayed him as ugly with a snub-nose, a pot-belly, and the ears and tail of a horse.

I pointed out the sculpted Satyr at the centre of the marble screen and told Hilary that Silenus would have looked something like that. Hilary's interest in Greek mythology was genuine, but she was noticing Fiona under the pine tree, and remembering her promise to explore Plaka with her. Fiona was on her mobile checking for text messages – she was very much into internet-dating which kept her amused and endlessly optimistic.

I told Hilary not to stay on my behalf and that, in fact, I'd quite like to have time on my own while seated here in this small theatre.

I watched Hilary descend to the paved area around the semi-circular stage – or *orchestra* to give it its correct name, from the Greek verb *chorevo*, meaning 'to dance'. It was where singing and dancing had taken place. The word 'theatre' also came from the Greek *theatron* implying 'watching place'. And from where I sat I was watching. I saw Hilary join Fiona and say something to which Fiona's face lit up. She looked up at me on my hard stone seat and gave me a cheery wave. The two made their way to the exit where they turned and waved again.

With them gone, I focused on the purpose of my visit. I saw in my note-book where I'd jotted down things I needed to remember, that I had the name Peisistratus scribbled down. This first theatre of Dionysos Eleuthereus had been founded by Peisistratus, a sixth century B.C. ruler of Athens. He'd brought a wooden image of the god to the city (on the instructions of the Delphic oracle, or so it was claimed) from a temple of Dionysos at a place named Eleutherai in the mountains near Thebes. He'd done this for political reasons in order to bind the Boeotian city of Eleutherai to Athens for greater security. The word Eleutherai means 'liberty' or 'freedom'.

Dionysos was frequently portrayed carrying a thyrsus (a pine-cone-topped staff) and a drinking cup or bunches of grapes, and wore an ivy wreath on his head. Pine-cones were a symbol of fertility and his festivals were caught up with the idea of renewal, not only of agriculture but also the reproduction of the human race. They were wild and joyous occasions, often with erect phalloi strapped to the bodies of the revellers.

It was this Peisistratus who'd instituted what had come to be known as the Great Dionysia festival in Athens, sometimes called the 'City Dionysia'. It had taken place annually at the end of March or beginning of April, a time when seafaring resumed after the winter months, making it easy for visitors to come from all the far reaches of

Greece, her islands and colonies.

There'd been other Dionysos festivals in Athens: the Lenaia which had been held in late January, a less important festival than the Great Dionysia; it had probably been at the Lenaia that new unknown playwrights had first tried out their work. There had also been the Anthesteria, a three-day event held in mid-February when wine-casks had been opened and the new wine tasted.

In those days gods and goddesses had been honoured at fixed annual festivals when people would enjoy a break from their work and daily routine, and the festivals of Dionysos were no exception.

"Much more fun," I'd said to Harry when I'd been reading about Greek religion at home one day. "Their religious festivals were a communal jolly, not a holier-than-thou gathering. Nobody was expected to believe with faith impossible-to-believe doctrines."

"Ah, but Christianity is a proper religion, unlike your ridiculous pagan gods," was Harry's predictable comment.

Maybe it was because they were ridiculous that I found the old Olympian gods entertaining and amusing. The Olympian gods were always laughing, or so the ancients liked to claim, which of course was not altogether true, as they had often squabbled and been really nasty to each other. Wild, imaginative stories about them had been passed down through the generations, but nobody had been expected to take them literally; there'd been no sacred book said to have been the holy word of Zeus.

I found it really interesting that, after the conquest of Palestine by Alexander the Great in the fourth century B.C., there had been an attempt to Hellenize the Jews, and certainly the Greek gods had been introduced and worshipped alongside Yahweh.

Harry had always dismissed any Christian parallels I might raise. However, it was a fact that at the time of Christ there had been many Gentiles in Galilee who worshipped the Greek gods. There was every chance that many were devotees of Dionysos, or Bacchus as he was known by the Romans. There was a Roman amphitheatre at Sepphoris, only a few miles from Nazareth, where Jesus' maternal grandparents lived, and where ancient Greek tragedies might well have been staged. Why wouldn't Jesus, who didn't start his ministry till he was thirty, have visited the theatre? He may well have seen the *Bacchae* by Euripides in which King Pentheus of Thebes pooh-poohed the claim by Dionysos that he was divine, resulting in Pentheus' violent death. In one translation of the first line in the drama spoken by the god was:

Behold God's Son is come into this land... a curiously Christian concept.

According to the evangelist John in the Gospel of St. John, Jesus said: "I am the true vine..." (John 15:1) True vine! Why did he say that? Was he implying that there was no truth in Dionysos with his bunches of grapes? When I'd mentioned this to Harry one day, he'd shrugged and said, "No connection whatever!" But when I'd suggested it to Hilary at supper, she'd immediately said: "I wonder if there's a connection – a link of some sort? I mean, Jesus took a cup of wine at the Last Supper, and said it was the cup of the new covenant in his blood. Christians drink sacramental wine, the blood of Christ, don't you see?"

To get back to Dionysos and the Great Dionysia festival. It began with a colourful procession; the wooden image of the god was borne on a chariot followed by his ecstatic women devotees known as Maenads, together with men dressed up as Satyrs dancing and singing. The procession was accompanied by pipes, and those following abandoned themselves to a wild state of liberation – a form of union with Dionysos Eleuthereus.

The Maenads (also known as Bacchantes) was the name for the women worshippers of Dionysos. Often, in celebrating his rites, they'd run into the nearby forested mountains possessed by a frenzied ecstasy. In that state they were capable of great physical strength enabling them to catch, tear apart and devour whatever animals crossed their path. Harry, of course, said they were crazy demented women let loose from their home chores, and it was as well that Christianity had come along and put an end to all that nonsense!

After the return of the god's wooden image to his temple, a contest was held for the best dithyramb (a somewhat wild choric hymn). It consisted of music and dancing performed by competing Choruses.

The area where the dithyrambs were staged was in the *orchéstra*, at that time a flattened circular space at the centre of which was an altar of Dionysos. Here the *orchéstra* was now paved with grey and cream marble slabs.

The dithyrambs would have been watched by spectators seated on the sloping ground, not on a tiered stone seat as I was that day. It was from those raw beginnings that the first dramas had evolved.

It was believed that the playwright Aeschylus (525-456 B.C.) had been the founder of drama when, in addition to the Chorus, he'd introduced an actor, and then two actors making dialogue possible. The Chorus remained useful for such things as describing action in the past, for moving things on covering a span of time, or for explaining what was going on offstage. The actors and Chorus all wore masks requiring good diction if they were to be heard clearly by the audience of fourteen thousand. Mask-making had been a thriving industry at the time, and small-part actors would be cast in several roles, only having to change their mask and costume to assume a new identity, male or female. Women at the time were never part of a theatrical production.

Gradually, as drama developed, a *skene* was introduced – from which our word 'scenery' comes. In those days a *skene* was a wooden structure, a façade with three entrances through which actors could enter and leave. Various props were developed to suit whatever was required, such as the *mechane* ('machine'), a type of crane to bring the gods down from the sky; or a contraption on wheels known as an *ekklyma* which could be rolled into view showing some secondary action taking place. High-backed marble seats along the front row were reserved for dignitaries, and a larger one centrally placed was where the priest of Dionysos sat.

To qualify here at the Great Dionysia festival, each playwright had to enter three tragedies followed by a Satyr play. A Satyr play was not satirical, but so-named because it always had Satyrs in the cast. Euripides' *Cyclops* was the only one to survive of its kind, revealing that the great tragedian was also capable of comedy (see Chapter 2).

In the fifth century, at the time of the three great dramatists, nearly all the tragedies were based on myth or legend; there were none with original fictional plots. Many were also about the family of King Agamemnon, commander-in-chief of the Greek army in the Trojan War, or the return of the victorious Greek warriors from that war, or the Trojan women of the royal household who had become their captive slaves. Some had been about legendary figures such as the indomitable Heracles, or Prometheus who stole fire from heaven for the benefit of mankind.

Evolving as they had from the dithyramb contests, those early fifth century B.C. dramas needed expert direction and choreography. To produce a play required substantial financial backing, which was provided by a man known as a *choregós*. A *choregós* was an Athenian citizen of some standing with sufficient wealth to afford to put on a good performance. To be appointed *choregós* was looked upon as a privilege and honour. When a drama won first prize, the *choregós* was awarded a gilded cauldron on a tripod and his initials were inscribed on its marble base. It was then displayed alongside the other tripod winners which, in time, were so numerous that they could no longer be contained within the sanctuary of Dionysos and overflowed into what was to become known as the Street of the Tripods. Hilary and Fiona would be walking along that same street to get to Plaka, the old part of Athens, now a rabbit-warren of tavernas and souvenir shops.

High up this south-east corner of the Acropolis was a cave. In 320 B.C. a *choregós* named Thrasyllos had won the coveted prize, and had erected a monument at the mouth of the cave with his tripod prominently displayed. That day work was being undertaken, and I could see white marble pilasters flanking the cave mouth. Were they, I wondered, restoring the Thrasyllos monument?

After the three days of tragedies, the comic playwrights had their turn. The greatest comic dramatist had undoubtedly been Aristophanes (c.445-c.375 B.C.) Unlike the tragedians, however, he never wrote about ancient myth and past historical events, but applied himself to topical subjects, frequently poking fun at the public figures of the day. If any writer had a wild imagination and the capability of being a buffoon, it was Aristophanes. It must have been tough for Euripides (480-406 B.C.) when he'd been lampooned by this young and rising star of a playwright over thirty years his junior. Aristophanes' repetitive joke had been that Euripides' mother sold green vegetables in the market. In fact, Euripides' parents had been respected, well-to-do citizens. But possibly he'd drawn some comfort from the fact that his friend, the great philosopher Socrates, had also been ridiculed. Socrates had accepted any criticism with equanimity, remarking that, if what Aristophanes had said about him was just, then he would try to reform himself, and if not, then it really didn't matter.

If Aristophanes' humour had often been schoolboyishly lavatorial, his imaginative turn of mind had catapulted him to the forefront of all other comic playwrights. The plot of *Clouds*, for example, revolved around a father who despaired of his son whose life was spent gambling. Debts had accumulated and the father was determined to visit what Aristophanes called the Thinkery where Socrates, as a Sophist, would instruct him how to outwit his creditors who were clamouring for payment. Sophists were trained in the art of persuasion, of being able to make an obvious lie appear as truth.

For a brief summary, out of the Thinkery come two characters called Right and Wrong, known collectively as the Arguments. Wrong is confident he can persuade any Right-thinking citizen that he,

Wrong, is the superior of the two.

In the play, Socrates swings into view by means of the *mechane* and descends from the clouds in a basket – he's been studying the sun, and the stars, and declares that the clouds you see are the true gods, not those that are worshipped in Athens; that it is the clouds that produce rain, not Zeus (frequently referred to as the cloud-gatherer); and they, the clouds, also cause thunder, not Zeus – such truths spoken in jest! Aristophanes' spoof, though entertaining, might well have contributed to Socrates' later prosecution for impiety and his eventual execution.

In fact, many of the fifth century B.C. intellectuals had questioned the truth of the gods of their day; some thought of them as unseen forces that permeated and directed the lives of men, though not always for the good. Why, they wondered, did they never come up to man's expectation of them? At best they seemed unable to help when asked, at worst they just didn't care, or didn't exist at all. Yet tradition demanded that the gods receive due worship and respect for fear of angering them; divine vengeance could be terrible. Towards the end of his life Socrates had tended towards a monotheistic view, the belief in a universal Mind that guided human action.

Like Socrates, much of Euripides' thinking had been ahead of his time. They'd both believed women should be given a voice in society, that they had hidden capabilities and untapped talents which could be beneficial to the city. In those days, a woman's role had been to care for the home and family and keep out of the limelight – the general opinion was that the best women were only those who were never talked about.

Euripides had a great understanding of women; his women were not just cardboard cut-outs, they were characters to be contended with; they had thoughts, emotions and towering passions.

Aristophanes (also a friend of Socrates) wrote several spoofs where women took the dominant role and showed themselves as powerful influences over men as, for instance, in his comedy *Lysistrata* 411 B.C. In it the women of Athens decide to go on a sex strike until men cease their pointless wars. Or with his *Assembly Women* c.393 B.C. in which he has women taking over the role of men in Athens because men have made such a botched job of things.

It was interesting to compare the work of these first tragedians. In Aristophanes' undoubted masterpiece *Frogs*, he does just that. It was written just after the death of Euripides in 406 B.C, and was staged the following year. In it Aristophanes jokingly has Dionysos (since he

ATHENS 11

is god of drama) having a great longing to get Euripides back from the dead.

Giving full vent to fantasy, Aristophanes has Dionysos disguised as Heracles (to give himself courage and to strike fear in those he might meet). He descends into the darkness of Hades, accompanied by his slave Xanthus.

After many terrors, with a great deal of slapstick as Dionysos and his slave go ever deeper down into the underworld, they eventually find themselves before the palace of Hades (king of the underworld). There a heated argument is taking place between Aeschylus and Euripides as to which of them in their lifetime was the better playwright. Aeschylus is annoyed that the newly deceased Euripides has arrived, because up till now, as the best playwright in his profession, he's had the honour of having his dinners in the Great Hall seated close to Pluto (Hades). Now, with the arrival of Euripides, he risks losing his seat. Such an honour taken from him? Certainly not! It is a privilege he is determined to retain. He taunts Euripides with the fact that his own tragedies have survived his death, whereas those of Euripides will, no doubt, die with him.

The argument then turns on whose plays have made the citizens of Athens better people. Euripides claims: *I taught them to see, to observe, to interpret; to twist, to contrive; suspect the worst, take nothing at its face value. (957-958.)* He explains how he's taught the audience to use its brains. People have learnt from him how to think, how to run their own households, to ask questions, such as *Why is this so? What do we mean by that? (975.)*

Aeschylus in his turn defends his characters: *Fine, stalwart characters, larger than life, men who didn't shirk their responsibilities. My heroes weren't like these market-place loafers, swindlers, and rogues they write about nowadays: they were real heroes, breathing spears and lances, white-plumed helmets, breastplates and greaves; heroes with hearts of good solid ox-leather, seven hides thick. (1041-1047.)*

It is decided that Dionysos himself must judge which of them is the better. Dionysos suggests they weigh the words of each; both must speak a line from one of his plays and whichever line proves the weightier will be pronounced the winner. They try this out and the pan containing the sentences by Aeschylus continuously weighs heavier than the lines by Euripides. Dionysos, however, remains uncertain, and finally says: *You know I like them both so much, I don't know how to judge between them. I don't want to make an enemy of either. One of them is so clever, and the other is so good, don't you think? (1413-1416.)*

Pluto (Hades) tells Dionysos that there's no point in him coming down to his kingdom if he returns without taking one of the two back with him, and Euripides asks why he wants to take one of them back anyway? After pondering the matter, Dionysos points out that without dramatists there can be no ...*drama festivals, and then where shall I be? (1425-1426.)* A decision has to be reached, and Dionysos eventually settles on Aeschylus.

If Aristophanes in his comedy has Aeschylus claiming his plays are the best because they have survived his death, in reality only seven of his ninety plays are around today compared to seventeen manuscripts of Euripides' ninety. In the following chapters the reader can decide for himself.

Tomorrow from Athens we're sailing off to the island of Salamis, a fifteen minute journey by ferry-boat from Piraeus, the port of Athens. Salamis is where Euripides was born and lived much of his life. It is popularly believed that he wrote many of his tragedies in an isolated cave on the southern tip of the island – a cave I'm very much hoping to climb up to.

CHAPTER 2

THE ISLAND OF SALAMIS

It was mid-morning when we set off for the port of Perama. Hilary was the self-appointed driver, and Fiona the destination-finder. As I was the only one who had a fixed itinerary I was accepted as overall boss and sat on the back seat where I had nothing to do till we got to our destination, which suited me just fine.

We'd started out late because early that morning before breakfast we'd gone up the Acropolis to see the raising of the Greek flag. While paying our respects to the Parthenon, gloriously majestic in the early-morning light, half a dozen raw recruits, shouldering their rifles, marched up the marble steps with their commanding officer, through the *Propylaia* (the great entranceway); they'd crossed the rock and marble terrain to the belvedere at the eastern end, where they'd stood to attention and sung the Greek National Anthem – a raucous rendering as though a good night out had been enjoyed by all. We'd watched as the flag had been raised till it fluttered in the light breeze against the amber-coloured early-morning sky.

The young recruits had then stood statue-like, rifles upright before them on the ground, chins in the air and eyes closed for a minute's silence.

Back at our hotel I'd asked the receptionist why they'd had that minute's silence with their eyes closed, and was told they were committing themselves to the defence of their families and country; they were, he said, recalling past wars and those who'd given their lives in the name of freedom.

Since then I've read that in World War II the Nazis flew the swastika from the Acropolis. The silent fervour of those young recruits had been an expression of the human need for freedom, an ideal which had been expressed by the fifth century B.C. dramatists.

We reached Perama, and Fiona said we needed to ask the way to the right departure gate for Salamis. We turned up a side street, parked the car, and I crossed the road to consult a bearded fellow lounging against the wall of a chemist shop. "Perama?" I asked. "Ferry-boat – *yia Salamis – Salamina?*" The island was called by either name. The man replied so fast I wasn't smart enough to pick up on his words – it was something Greeks were well aware of with foreigners who spoke halting Greek.

The shop owner emerged who spoke English, and Fiona joined us. She knew no Greek but was much better than I was at getting the gist of what was being said in broken English and, more importantly, remembering the directions given.

"Salamina?" the man queried and, to my surprise, immediately added: "The Battle of Salamis!" And he launched into the miraculous Athenian victory over the Persian fleet in 480 B.C. He banged his clenched fists together to indicate the sinking of ships. "Many, many ships lost – down!" He went on to explain how it was hoped one day that Greece would get funding so archaeologists could explore the sea-bed and recover ancient artefacts from the sunken ships. We listened briefly to his ambitious hopes, but we were anxious to get going as the hotel on Salamis where we were to stay was on the far side of the island.

Astonishingly, and with no difficulty at all, we found our way as instructed, drew alongside a kiosk where Hilary had only to stick her arm out of the window to buy our ferry tickets for the island. We barely knew we were on board as we lined up behind a car ahead which had come to a standstill; immediately we heard the grinding sound of the ramp being winched up behind us. We were on our way.

It was only a fifteen minute journey, and we went up on deck to watch as we approached the port of Paloukia; I tried to visualize the great Battle of Salamis; it was somewhere in this strikingly blue sea with its ships, yachts and small boats moored and docked in an orderly manner, that the Greek warships (Aeschylus had been on one of them) had instilled blind panic in the Persian fleet. It had been a deliberate strategy and, in the chaos, the Persian ships had rammed and sunk each other. (For a stark description of the event see Aeschylus' *Persians*, Chapter 6.)

Sailing into port that day, however, was peaceful and the sea was sparklingly calm in the afternoon sunshine. I felt a surge of excitement at the moment of arrival. We descended to the hold and got ready to disembark.

With the deafening rattle of chains the ramp was lowered again, and we waited patiently as motorbikes weaved and worked their way forward to get away first and roar off in a cloud of exhaust fumes.

So there we were at last on the island favoured by Euripides. Ugly and polluted? Some guide-books said so, but to me that sunny afternoon as we drove across the island to the coastal town of Eantio, it was beautiful and mountainous.

★

When we reached Eantio we faced a major hitch in our plans. Never mind the dramas of Euripides, we suddenly found ourselves at the centre of our own. We searched for the hotel along the sea-front but couldn't find it. "Ask someone," I said.

Hilary and Fiona were curiously reluctant to admit they were defeated; they were always convinced that our destination could be found on the map or with the SatNav. After another scouring of the town's sea-front we asked a woman with a shopping-bag. We told her the name of the hotel and at first she looked puzzled. Suddenly her brow cleared and she pointed along the road to a skeleton construction swathed in sack-cloth.

What?

The woman told us of one other hotel at the other end of Eantio where we might find accommodation. We adjusted to our unfortunate situation and headed back through the town.

We arrived at a dazzlingly bright hotel set back behind a high metal gate. We pressed the bell hopefully and were soon greeted by a pleasant smiling, lean and stooping elderly man. He said nothing but gestured to us to follow him down marble steps to a swimming-pool, and what looked like a small banqueting hall at the back. He waved us forward to a half-asleep fellow seated at a table who regarded us with considerable boredom, sneezed, blew his nose, huffed and puffed until I commiserated and asked him if he had a cold? Hilary came to the point and said we wanted rooms. The man cogitated over an open tome and pretended he was full, though we'd seen no guests or parked cars. Eventually he handed us two keys to adjoining rooms with sea-views and balconies. It was cheaper than our non-existent hotel and, what was more, breakfast was included. We now considered ourselves fortunate.

The deaf-mute carried our luggage and was very happy-faced when I gave him a tip, and put his hand to his heart in gratitude before withdrawing. In time we learned he was perfectly well able to speak and could hear what was said, he just didn't speak to newcomers not knowing what language to use.

So at last we were installed. Tomorrow we planned to drive to Peristeria, a small seaside town some fifteen kilometres away on the south-east tip of the island. It was from there that the cave of Euripides could be reached – the cave where the great dramatist composed his dramas.

★

We set off before nine for Peristeria, and somehow missed all the landmarks given to us by the hotel, so Fiona was thrown back on her SatNav.

It was said that Euripides was born here on the island on the very day of the great naval Battle of Salamis 480 B.C. But it was also claimed that he was born in a small village in the heart of Attica where there were several temples, including one of Dionysos. Because of the constant threat from Persia, it was believed his family had left the mainland for the greater safety of Salamis.

It is believed that Euripides had been married twice, and had three sons and a daughter; he is reported to have been of a slightly morose temperament, but that he'd been interested in philosophy, and possessed an extensive library. Socrates had thought highly of his work and, whenever possible, had attended every new Euripidean drama entered for the Great Dionysia.

Maybe it was because it was on Salamis that Euripides wrote many of his great tragedies that I felt a certain affinity with the island. Yes, I knew the north of it looked across the narrow straits to the sprawling industrial suburbs of Athens with its heavy industry; but what I had seen of the island so far I'd found surprisingly picturesque.

We drove down into Peristeria and, as we passd through the small seaside town, we came to a narrow street: the Street of Euripides. A moment later we saw a notice-board with an arrow pointing right to Euripides' Cave. Several hundred yards up a dirt-track we reached a wide parking area from which a foot-path with graduated steps wound up through trees and undergrowth. There was no time to lose as already the sun was hot. Grasping my trekking-stick, with my eyes to the ground, I set off purposefully followed by the others.

And so we climbed the mountainside. After fifteen minutes hard slog we arrived at a levelled area where there was a small sanctuary of Dionysos. The ruins of this sanctuary were surrounded by a high wire-mesh fence. A notice-board informed us the sanctuary was third century B.C., built in celebration of Euripides – it was nice to think of the god of drama honouring the playwright, rather than the other way about. Trees provided welcome shade, and I sat on an oblong block of white marble for a short respite from what for me had been a fairly arduous climb – some of the stone steps up the track had been much more than a foot in depth up which I'd had to be hoisted. But the words 'no problem!' still rang reassuringly in my ears – they'd been spoken by a young aspiring Olympic Games sprinter at our taverna the evening before when I'd asked if the cave was difficult to get to. He must have seen I was no spring chicken, and could easily have shown misgivings but, no, he'd been encouraging and had used those two words 'no problem' unhesitatingly.

To sit for longer than five minutes would be fatal as energy would ebb away. Another steep hundred metres or so and at last before us in the rockface we saw the low, arched cave entrance flanked by large boulders. So this was it! We found ourselves on a wide shelf of flat ground on one side of which was a slope of scrub and undergrowth falling precipitously away with a few trees clinging precariously to it. We turned to the rockface with its cave and low-level arched entrance, then turned again to look out towards the distant sea glinting serenely in the midday sun. A great oil tanker sailed slowly into view from around a headland.

It was my moment of triumph – the moment I'd been planning for and looking forward to all winter. Such is the human mind with its capacity to see into the future, to plan an event and bring it to reality in the present moment. Euripides' cave and here I was! A chorus of cicadas sang their greetings.

Hilary and I crouched down and took a few tentative steps into the cave interior. It is not easy to explore a cave bent double, and there were many jagged corners. Foolishly I'd left my torch down in the car. The cave ceiling was black, marbled with white streaks; the black wasn't from smoke but was the bare rock itself.

I was hopelessly cautious, but Hilary was adventurous and continued on, calling back to tell me of her progress as she found the corridor she was creeping along becoming narrower. Eventually she shouted she was standing upright. But it was too dark for me to venture on, and soon I was outside again. I had read that the cave was forty-seven metres deep and had twelve small chambers.

I was content with just being there. Euripides would surely have worked outside the cave? The sheer isolation and the views to the sea would have been inspirational with the continual trilling of the cicadas. By now ten oil tankers had sailed into view. In Euripides' day these would have been triremes with billowing sails. Two low islets lay offshore and, looking eastwards, there was a hazy landmass which I thought must be the tip of the peninsula beyond Athens where the great temple of Poseidon at Sounion stood supreme. Looking south, we thought we could see the island of Aegina where Aristophanes had spent his childhood. To the west was the Peloponnese where we would be heading in a few days. Euripides would have drawn inspiration from these same landmarks we were gazing at.

What plays had he written up here, I wondered? His satyr *Cyclops* would surely have flowed naturally from him in such a place? Or his several tragedies regarding the women survivors of the Trojan War?

★

The plot of Euripides' *Cyclops* begins with Silenus and his Satyrs who, in pursuit of Dionysos, who has been seized by pirates, find themselves the captives of a Cyclops named Polyphemus, a one-eyed giant and son of Poseidon, god of the sea. Homer wrote vividly about Polyphemus and the Cyclopes in his *Odyssey*.

The story is as follows: Polyphemus lives in a great cave near Mt. Etna in Sicily, and rears sheep. One day Silenus and his Satyrs arrive, are taken prisoner, and forced to do all the menial tasks such as milking the ewes, cleaning out the cave and so on. One day Odysseus and his crew, who are on their way back from the Trojan War, also come ashore. Polyphemus is out in the fields, and Odysseus offers Silenus wine in return for food, as he has run out and he and his men are starving. Silenus is delighted to drink wine again, and gets happily tipsy. They are interrupted by the return of Polyphemus who, bored with eating nothing but lamb and mutton, is very partial to human flesh, and fixes his one eye on Odysseus and his crew.

Odysseus, who is renowned for his cunning, knows that if he can get Polyphemus drunk then, with the help of the Satyrs, he can

THE ISLAND OF SALAMIS

gouge out the Cyclops' one eye with a burning olive-wood stake, and so escape.

There is much burlesque as the Satyrs lose courage and, instead of helping, retreat to a safe distance from which they pretend they've become suddenly lame; they have ash in their eyes and can't see, and suchlike.

In the end Odysseus is assisted by his crew. When Polyphemus springs up in agony, yelling out that Nobody has blinded him, there is a great play on the word 'Nobody', a name by which the cunning Odysseus has said he is called. Nobody has blinded him – therefore he is not blind. Where is Nobody so he can be punished? – Nobody is nowhere, and so it goes on.

The Satyr ends with the Chorus singing that Odysseus and his crew, who have by this time escaped, will from now on serve Dionysos and so live happily ever afterwards. The Satyrs, no doubt, set off to find their abducted god, Dionysos.

The story of the abduction of Dionysos by pirates is a well-known one from Homer's *Hymn to Dionysos*. In it the handsome young god is spotted by them on the shores of a headland and they take him to be a wealthy young prince. They capture and take him on board their vessel and sail away. To their dismay their prisoner frees himself from his bonds, and the deck begins to flood with wine. Soon a vine twines itself around the mast and becomes laden with bunches of grapes, and the boat begins to founder. When their so-called prince turns into a roaring lion they all jump overboard, except for the helmsman whom Dionysos orders to sail to the Aegean island of Naxos. It is there that Dionysos finds the beautiful Ariadne, daughter of the king of Crete, who's run off with Theseus, famed for having killed the Minotaur. Whether Silenus and the Satyrs ever arrived on Naxos I do not know. What is known, however, is that Dionysos introduced his vine to the island and, while there, fell in love with Ariadne and married her, having first got Theseus out of the way by reminding him of his royal duties. He returned to his native Athens – but maybe by then Theseus had grown tired of Ariadne because he was later to marry her sister Phaedra.

★

In sharp contrast to Euripides' humorous *Cyclops* is his tragedy *Trojan Women*. In it Queen Hecuba, widow of King Priam of Troy, has become the slave-woman of Odysseus. She laments the outcome of the ten-year war, the loss of her sons and husband, and the total destruction of her city. Her husband has been brutally murdered by Neoptolemus (Achilles' son), and her widowed daughter-in-law Andromache has become Neoptolemus' slave, and has now to obey his every command as well as share his bed. Euripides does not spare the spectators as he draws his audience into the raw emotions of war.

Despite the hopelessness of their situation, Hecuba advises Andromache to accept her fate, to submit to Neoptolemus, and even to try to endear herself to him; in this way she will at least see her infant son Astyanax grow up and maybe rebuild Troy. It is all she can offer as a crumb of comfort to her daughter-in-law ...*honour then thy present lord* (Neoptolemus) *and with thy gentle manners win his soul...* (696-700.)

As Hecuba speaks, a Greek officer arrives with an urgent message. He sympathises with the stricken women, but is himself compelled to obey orders. On the command of Odysseus, Andromache's young son is now to die. He dreads delivering this news and, seeing the two women's renewed outburst of utter despair and their lamentations, he consoles them with the only hope left, by saying that if they accept it quietly they will at least be allowed to give the infant his due burial rites.

Before the murder of the small child, Andromache is ordered to board Neoptolemus' ship to be taken back to his kingdom, and it is left to Hecuba, the grandmother, to mourn over her young grandson.

The body is brought to her laid out on his dead father Hector's shield. His corpse has been carefully washed in the river Scamander by the Greek messenger who is anxious to spare the grieving queen more distress than is necessary – the child has been brutally flung down to his death from Troy's citadel.

Harry and I had once seen the Scamander and had paddled in its clear shallow waters. That day the swift-flowing river had been peaceful and idyllic, its banks overhung with willows and alders. Over three millennia had passed since it had been clogged with the bodies of the dead and wounded in the Trojan War, and since the small mutilated body of the child Astyanax had been washed in its waters which, when we were there, were gently swirling over and around large dark boulders.

Euripides makes the suffering of Queen Hecuba all too vivid as she mourns her grandson: ...*O ye Argives, was your spear keen, and your*

THE ISLAND OF SALAMIS

hearts so low and cold, to fear this babe? 'Twas a strange murder for brave men! For fear this babe some day might raise again his fallen land! Had ye so little pride? While Hector fought, and thousands at his side, ye smote us, and we perished; and now, now, when all are dead and Ilion lieth low, ye dread this innocent!... (1158-1167.)

Hecuba cradles the dead body, and compares the infant with his father, her own dead son Hector whom she'd once held in her arms at the same age: *...Poor little child! Was it our ancient wall, the circuit built by loving gods, so savagely hath rent thy curls, these little flowers innocent that were thy mother's garden, where she laid her kisses; here, just where the crushed bones show white – ah heaven!...Ye tender arms, the same dear mould have ye as his; how from the shoulder loose ye drop and weak! And dear proud lips, so full of hope and closed for ever! What false words ye said at daybreak, when creeping to my bed, called me kind names, and promised: 'Grandmother, when thou art dead, I will cut close my hair, and lead out all the captains to ride by thy tomb.' Why didst thou cheat me so?...*

Dear God, the pattering welcomes of thy feet, the nursing in my lap; and oh, the sweet falling asleep together! All is gone. How should a poet carve the funeral stone to tell thy story true? 'There lieth here a babe whom the Greeks feared, and in their fear slew him.'... (1177-1194.)

And so the poor woman, now cast down to the lowest depths of desolation, performs the funeral rites over the mutilated body of her small grandson, tenderly wiping the blood from the torn skin. *I make thee whole; I bind thy wounds, oh, little vanished soul this wound and this I heal with linen white...Yet let the rite be spoken...Nay, not I, but he, thy father far away shall comfort thee! (1229-1234.)*

The tragedy ends with the sound of what remains of the walls of Troy crashing to the ground, and the trumpet blasts from the victorious Greeks as they prepare to sail for home.

With this tragedy Euripides might well have struck a sensitive chord with his Athenian audience. It is a graphic example of the horrors of war and Euripides' violent aversion to it. It was written during the Peloponnesian War when Athens and her colonies were on and off at war with Sparta from 431-404 B.C. In it he drew attention to the sheer savagery of the Athenians towards the inhabitants of the island of Melos the year before. On that occasion they'd failed to persuade the authorities on the island to surrender, and so had brutally massacred its entire male population and enslaved the women.

"What are you dreaming about out here," Hilary had emerged from the cave and was standing by me.

"The horrors of war," I replied. "The actual realities that war and defeat bring. Euripides' *Trojan Women*, to be exact. It brings home to you the tragic lives of the widowed survivors of the Trojan War, who were subjected to slavery and obedience to their victorious masters."

"Somebody has to suffer if you want Greek tragedy," Fiona said airily.

I eyed her for a moment. "That's exactly what Harry would say," I told her.

"Your Harry is a lamb – a man after my own heart. Takes those Greek stories with a pinch of salt."

"But some people do lead tragic lives," Hilary remarked.

"What I want to know," Fiona said, "is why your great man wanted to climb all the way up here to write his dramas?"

I had no answer for her, except that every writer has to have his or her quiet sanctuary to work in. Would he have worked up here in wild weather? Did he creep into his cave and light a fire to warm himself? Or sit at the mouth of it and stare out at the distant storm-tossed sea through driving rain? Or did he use it only as a summer retreat? Scholars only agree that here was where he came for quiet solitude, while the Muses wove their spell about him, and powerful language flowed from his stylo. To see what he saw in this his favoured spot where he wrote many of his masterpieces, had been an honour and a privilege, and for the time being I felt quietly triumphant.

★

There was a second reason why I'd come to Salamis – also to do with the Trojan War. The second was because of the warrior Ajax, son of Telamon, king of Salamis, who'd sent ships to join the Greek armada.

We drove off along the coastal road and headed up into the hills till we came to a notice-board with an arrow pointing to a large round tower which crowned a promontory. This was Kolones where four ancient tombs had been found and, astonishingly, a temple of Ajax.

Because he'd shown remarkable strength, courage and endurance when under attack in the Trojan War, he had, apparently, been evoked by the Greeks in the Battle of Salamis. His bravery had been shown in the tenth and final year of the Trojan War when the Trojans were setting fire to the Greek ships and the army was in great jeopardy. Ajax fought on, keeping the Trojans with their firebrands at bay, he prevented them from advancing closer by wielding a heavy ten-metre long pike or pole and, taking giant strides from ship to ship, had successfully warded off the enemy.

Although a hero of the Trojan War, Ajax* had later suffered from what today would be diagnosed as 'post traumatic stress syndrome'. After the death of his friend Achilles, he'd asked to be allowed to have his armour. But Odysseus (whose fame and daring outshone Ajax's) had also demanded it and, when it was finally awarded to him, Ajax had exploded with rage; his earlier respect for Odysseus turned to such savage hatred that he was hell-bent on killing him together with King Agamemnon (commander-in-chief of the Greek army) and his brother Menelaus. The goddess Athena, seeing the danger to Odysseus (whom she favoured), intervened and cast a fit of madness over Ajax. The result was that, instead of murdering his intended victims, Ajax turned his wrath on a flock of sheep and herd of cattle; in blind rage, he killed the beasts and dragged their carcasses back to his hut.

After the slaughter of the animals, Athena lifted the veil of madness from him, and he was aghast at what he'd done. In despair he took himself off along the seashore, plunged a sword deep into the pale soft sand point up, and threw himself on it. A search-party set out to look for him, and he was found by his slave-girl impaled on the sword of Hector.

When Harry and I were ourselves in Beşik bay, a beautiful crescent of white sand which fringed the Trojan plain, I hadn't given a thought to the madness of Ajax, only to his heroism, and never to the fact that he was soon to lose the high regard in which he was held. To attain esteem and the respect of one's fellow beings was all important in those days; the word was *kleos*. To gain *kleos* was the aim of all Greek warriors; to die gloriously was, well, a glorious end.

We approached Kolones, the round towerlike structure of massive blocks of stone. It had an impresssive entrance-way with a great stone lintel. The whole was surrounded by a high wire-mesh fence preventing entry to the fallen blocks inside the tower. Its large dimensions on this headland made it clearly visible from land and sea. I walked through the tangled undergrowth following a goat-track which circled the Cyclopean monument.

Hilary, who'd been standing in front of a notice-board, said: "It doesn't say who the tombs are dedicated to apart from Ajax. Do you

*The storyline of Sophocles' tragedy *Ajax* follows, but it is unknown for which competition it was entered.

think Ajax's bones were brought back here for burial?"

"I think I've read somewhere that his body was cremated and his ashes were put into a golden urn and taken to the Hellespont," I said.

"But there was a temple here dedicated to him. I wonder why they built him a temple?" Her blue eyes turned to me enquiringly.

"I really don't know," I said. "I do know though that a festival was founded here in his honour."

"A temple and a festival, how curious!"

"As for his half-brother Teucer, Ajax's father Telamon was so angry that Ajax's body hadn't been brought back from Troy (or at least his bones), that he banished Teucer from Salamis. He ended up in Cyprus where he founded the ancient city-state of Salamis. So now you know why there's a Salamis on Cyprus," I said.

I had done more than I'd ever expected that day, and the thought of a late siesta was appealing. The following day was set aside to visit the Archaeological Museum of Salamis where I hoped to find out more about the island's ancient history.

★

We were on the east side of the island following a tarmac road on a gentle gradient heading for the highest point of a headland. Seated as usual on the back seat of the car, I caught occasional glimpses of the port of Paloukia. On the summit of this headland was a spectacular monument commemorating the Battle of Salamis.

It was an exquisite work of art which soared against the skyline. From its prominent position it had commanding views to the seaways: to the port with its shipping, and to shorelines where cargo boats lay at anchor together with gigantic cranes and dredgers.

The monument was a massive bronze prow of a ship with two Greek warriors standing one behind the other: the foremost with a foot braced against the prow, firing an arrow from his bow, while the one behind held a shield with a spear raised above his head aimed at the enemy. The bronze figures stood high on a white plinth and was a triumph of Greek art.

We climbed the slope to the monument and walked around it, admiring the power and strength of the warriors. Did their crested helmets represent Greek heroes from the Trojan War? Ajax himself, perhaps? I found it amazing that Ajax had been called upon during the Battle of Salamis to inspire the Greeks to overcome the superior

Persian fleet whose heavy ships far outnumbered those of the Athenian lighter vessels which were swifter and more manoeuvrable.

We gazed at the various headlands and bays with their modern shipping and shipyards, and their steel cranes rearing their heads skywards. It was strikingly beautiful in a stark, unyielding sense like the industrial paintings by L.S. Lowry.

We got back into the car and drove slowly away, heading next for the Archaeological Museum in Salamina town. I had been wanting to buy a local guide-book on Salamis, either from a bookshop or, at the very least, from the Archaeological Museum, but there were no bookshops in the town, and the museum sold nothing. "Why?" I asked those on duty at the museum. "Why does nobody on Salamis sell books, postcards or souvenirs? I am interested in your island and you have nothing to tell me about it!" I grumbled. They answered sadly that there was little tourism on the island. "But you should promote tourism here," I said. "If tourists don't come it's because you don't encourage them." They shrugged and look despondent.

There was a large chart on a wall in the museum showing the tactics taken by the Athenian fleet to outwit the Persians in the great battle. But I couldn't concentrate enough to make sense of the arrows showing how and where the Persian fleet had become trapped, and in their panic had collided with each other and sunk – tactics, apparently, ordered by the great Greek commander of the day named Themistocles, who alone had seen how best to lure the Persians to their deaths.

In the museum I saw pottery found in the Cave of Euripides and a mug bearing his name. An enthusiastic, bearded museum employee, who had been listening to my complaints regarding lack of books, information and even tavernas, apologized and said they were tied to bureaucracy. When he learned I was a writer, he was interested and wanted to help, and asked us to wait a moment. Soon he returned and handed me his one and only brochure on the island which he insisted I take. I thanked him profusely; it was in Greek and English and had useful information regarding the cave of Euripides, the temple of Ajax, as well as the bronze memorial to the Battle of Salamis; it also had at the back a map of the island.

We left the museum and had a salad lunch in Salamina town seated on the promenade beside the sea. From where we sat we watched shoals of small fish swimming where shafts of sunlight pierced the waters to the sea-bed. Ships lay at anchor across the bay.

It was the end of our stay on the island. The next day we were heading for the Peloponnese. I needed to visit Troezen, an ancient site, where the legendary Theseus had been conceived, and where his wife Phaedra had fallen passionately in love with her step-son Hippolytus. It was their story that had inspired Euripides to write his great tragedy *Hippolytus*.

CHAPTER 3

TROEZEN

We were told that to go by sea to Galatas on the east coast of the Peloponnese, we had to take the ferry from Salamis back to Perama, drive to the main port of Piraeus (no distance) and get a ferry to the island of Poros. From there a regular shuttle service took passengers and cars every half-hour to Galatas. Easy!

Fiona sat on the front seat with her SatNav on her lap. The reassuring voice built up confidence; but then Hilary took the wrong slip-road up from the coast, and we eventually found ourselves in a maze of streets somewhere above Piraeus. There the SatNav gave up. After blundering around looking for a street which would head down to the port, I did my usual: "Why not ask somebody. Look! that woman coming now!"

Hilary slowed down, and Fiona called to the woman: "Excuse me, can you tell us the way to – we want Piraeus and the ferry-boat for Aegina and Poros," she said.

The woman, who looked Asian, said instantly in good English, "Did you say for Aegina?"

"Yes. As you see, we're lost."

"I'm just about to go down there myself," she said. "I'm meeting a friend off the ferry from Aegina." She looked hopefully at the car, and needed no persuasion to be our guide.

I hoisted up the suitcase on the seat beside me, and the woman hopped nimbly in. She never stopped chatting while seated upright and calling out left, right, round here, round there, straight on, left again, now right, and so we came down to Piraeus and the arrivals gate from Aegina. There a beautiful young girl was already waiting. She looked like a hippy with long dark, unbrushed hair, and a baseball cap worn back-to-front, a nose-ring, and tatoos up her arms; emblems were stitched to her denim waistcoat.

Unfortunately, the ferry-boat departing for Poros via Aegina was from another gate about half a kilometre away. We had ten minutes in which to catch it. We were glad to have helped this woman (from whom we'd learned she'd lived in London ten years, but had then married a Greek), but we now had to help ourselves, and quickly.

Following her directions, we shot off along a busy one-way street looking for a turning which would bring us back into the other stream of traffic. We must have missed it, and eventually I shouted: "For God's sake just turn here! Never mind the 'no U-turn' sign! Go, go, go!" And Hilary, amidst much blaring of horns, U-turned into the oncoming traffic which grudgingly gave way for her.

"The police won't bother," I said. "Everybody breaks road regulations in Athens."

We caught the ferry with two minutes to spare.

"The gods were with us," I said, as we heard the grinding of the ramp being raised behind us. Maybe it was arrogance that made me feel I had a destiny to fulfil and the gods were helping me.

We sat on deck and watched the cheerful sparkle of the calm sea. Our boat put in briefly at Aegina to allow passengers to disembark, amongst them a Greek Orthodox priest walking erect in his billowing black cassock and tall black head-gear; if Aristophanes had witnessed such a figure in his day he, no doubt, would have made him a subject of amusement in one of his comedies. Aegina was an island I intended to visit before the end of this trip since Aristophanes spent his teenage years there.

Another hour or so later and we were approaching the island of Poros, passing flotillas of sailing-boats, their sails strikingly white against the gentian blue sea. Soon the terra-cotta-roofed houses in the port of Poros were visible, rising in tiers up the hillside and looking picturesque with low mountains towering either side.

We liked the cheerful atmosphere of Poros and, since we were there, Hilary suggested we go up into the surrounding hills and see something of the island before catching the shuttle-service on to Galatas .

By pure chance we saw a brown archaeological sign pointing to a temple of Poseidon. When we reached the site on the summit of a promontory, we found it was open to anyone who wanted to explore it. From the sanctuary I believed I was looking out towards the once important ancient city of Troezen on the mainland. Troezen was the setting for Euripides' tragedy *Hippolytus* in which Poseidon played a powerful role.

Returning to the port we had no problem catching the shuttle service; all we had to do was to board it – as though driving on to a bridge – and we were transported to Galatas about five minutes away.

We were soon relaxing in our out-of-town hotel with its sea views. There were several small offshore islands, and a strange, larger, ghostly island beyond them – ghostly in that it was the colour of a ghost. It was called Lion Island because it was shaped like a lion's head, though I thought it looked more like the Egyptian Sphinx.

That evening we picked our way along a seaside track to a taverna we'd been recommended. There was nobody else there until a yacht came silently around one of the small islands and dropped anchor in a cove there. A dinghy with an outboard motor brought the passengers four by four to our taverna where they sat at a long table. Considering they were all young, they were strangely silent and appeared totally oblivious of one another and their surroundings.

Hilary took out her map. "So where are we heading tomorrow?" she asked.

"Troezen," I said.

"Why Troezen? What's special about it?"

"It's a long story," I said. "Do you really want me to tell you?"

"Well, we've got all evening," she pointed out.

Fiona said: "Uh, uh, here we go!" and eyed me, her dark fringe swept sideways, her eyes sparkling. She rested an elbow on the table with her wine-glass held casually against her chin, an air of amused resignation on her face. I thought the clean-shaven waiter was rather taken with her. "Well," I said, "the story begins with Theseus' father King Aegeus, king of Athens." And I launched into the strange legend about Theseus' birth.

The story was that Aegeus had been married twice but remained childless. Anxious to have an heir, he enquired of the Delphic oracle how to remedy the problem. The answer came in the form of a conundrum advising him not to unfasten his wine-skin before reaching Athens. Not knowing what to make of it, Aegeus went on down the Peloponnese to ask the opinion of his friend King Pittheus of Troezen. King Pittheus had his own ideas, and that evening he encouraged Aegeus to get drunk, and saw to it that his daughter Aethra spent the night in his bed. In due course Aegeus was overjoyed to find Aethra had become pregnant by him.

To pass off his daughter's pregnancy, King Pittheus let it be rumoured that she had been loved by the god Poseidon, which is why tradition has it that Poseidon was also the father.

Before departing from Troezen, King Aegeus placed his sword and sandals under a great boulder, and told Aethra that if she gave birth to a son then, when he was old enough and strong enough, he was to lift the boulder and bring the sword and sandals to him in Athens. By recognizing his possessions, Aegeus would know he was his son and heir. In the fullness of time this is what happened and Theseus became king of Athens. When, later still, King Pittheus of Troezen died, Theseus inherited his kingdom too.

"The important thing to remember when we're at Troezen," I went on, "is that by that time Theseus had had a son of his own, born to an Amazon queen. The name of that son was Hippolytus. At some stage Theseus then married Phaedra, the daughter of the king of Crete, sister of Ariadne with whom he'd run away to Naxos after he'd killed the Minotaur," I added.

"Quite a colourful life," Fiona said. "Some people have all the fun!"

"Tomorrow all you really have to remember," I went on, "is that Phaedra became the chief character in Euripides' tragedy *Hippolytus*. So there you have it. That's why we're off to Troezen. It's where it all took place."

It was dusk when we left the taverna and picked our way back to our hotel in the warm semi-darkness along the track beside the calm, wine-dark sea (Homer's description); a half-moon hung in the heavens and the evening star shone brilliantly in the darkening sky.

★

We were on our way, and I was full of pleasurable anticipation hoping at the ruins to see the old palace, a monument to Phaedra which I'd read existed, as well as a Hippolytus shrine, a temple of Artemis and another of Aphrodite.

We drove parallel to the sea before turning left for Troezen at a roundabout, and across a flat plain towards formidable-looking mountains and ravines. Before stopping at Troezen, however, we drove past and up into the mountains to see a sixteenth century monastery dedicated to St. Demetrios, something Hilary was keen to do.

When we arrived we were told that the Mother Superior (some

monasteries in Greece have nuns but are still called monasteries) had gone down to Galatas to the dentist as she was suffering from toothache. Why was I surprised that nuns were human and could suffer like anybody else from such things? When driving through Galatas we had, in fact, seen a nun walking along the pavement; it must surely have been her?

Meanwhile, there at the monastery the church was locked and could not be visited till the Mother Superior returned. Wandering around the cloisters, we opened a door in the outer wall and found ourselves looking down on a narrow strip of vegetable garden cultivated with rows of runner beans. Beyond it the ground fell away and we had a bird's eye view looking down over the wide cultivated plain far below which stretched to the sea. To our right the road we'd come on twisted and turned up the mountainside. The island of Poros lay on the horizon. Was the ancient temple of Poseidon this side of it, I wondered?

It was along the seashore from Galatas that Hippolytus had met with a violent death in answer to Theseus' prayer to Poseidon for revenge, when he'd believed (wrongly) that his wife Phaedra had been raped by him.

We did not wait for the Mother Superior's return and went back to the car. Down in the plain we followed the signs to the Troezen archaeological site. When we arrived we discovered that the ruins were scattered over a wide area, and there were few notices to enlighten us; there was no perimeter fence, and the site was open to all who wished to visit it though, in fact, nobody else was there.

It was already hot and for a brief while we enjoyed the shade of a mulberry tree. From the lower branches we picked ripe white mulberries which were sweet and refreshing, before leaving its shade for the vast stony excavated site, looking at we weren't sure what. Eventually, however, we found a notice which said the ruins before us were those of the sanctuary of Hippolytus. But I had already mistakenly thought another rectangular ruin was his. Interestingly, one of them had slabs of angled marble laid along the outer edges of the site, presumably for drainage.

The only ruins I was certain of were several brick Byzantine archways where the remains of a basilica church once stood. A noticeboard told us that it was built on the site of an old sanctuary of Aphrodite – the goddess who featured so prominently in *Hippolytus*.

The sun was so hot we were none of us inclined to wander around without knowing positively which direction to take. I sat on a boulder in the shade of an old olive tree and stared towards the mountains whose lower reaches were clothed in olive-groves, above which craggy peaks reared up. Doves, symbol of Aphrodite, cooed gently and deep-throatedly close by in the branches of a tree.

It had to be somewhere here that the childless King Aegeus of Athens had come after consulting the Delphic oracle; here that his friend King Pittheus had his palace, and whose daughter had given birth to Theseus. It must also have been near here that Aegeus had concealed his sword and sandals under a great boulder. It was later that afternoon that we came across a huge boulder with a notice-board proclaiming it to be the actual hiding place. True or false, it was impossible to say. Theseus would have had to have been a giant to have lifted it. Fiona took a photo of me seated on it. THE rock! Well, well!

Meanwhile, there under the old olive tree with the doves cooing, I thought about Euripides' tragedy *Hippolytus*. The scene of the play is set outside the palace, and begins with the unfortunate Phaedra languishing from her unrequited passion for Hippolytus, her step-son. The drama was written by Euripides in 429 B.C. and won first prize at the City Dionysia in Athens.

In the play, on either side of the great entrance to the palace are two statues: one of Artemis, goddess of the hunt, the other of Aphrodite, goddess of love. The statue of Aphrodite represents Phaedra's all-consuming passion for her step-son, while that of Artemis receives every honour from Hippolytus, whose passion is the hunt.

During the course of the drama, Phaedra's Nurse manages to persuade Phaedra to tell her what is weighing so heavily on her mind that she neither eats nor sleeps. When Phaedra finally confesses that she is aflame with love for her step-son, the Nurse is at first shocked. But, recovering quickly, she speaks reassuring words: ...*Thou lovest. Is that so strange? Many there be beside thee!... (439-440)* And she consoles Phaedra by pointing out that many have suffered as a result of Aphrodite, and it's not as bad as Phaedra thinks. When all is said and done ...*all life lives from her* (Aphrodite). *Aye, this is she that sows Love's seed and brings Love's fruit to birth; and great Love's brethren are all we on earth!... (449-451.)*

What Phaedra needs is not scolding and punishment, but her help, she says. Why conceal her love, when she has only to confess it? Love is wonderful, not to be dreaded and kept under wraps. Let her love blossom! In her anxiety to help Phaedra the Nurse consoles and encourages. When Phaedra voices her fears that her honour is at stake, the Nurse bursts out: ...*Why prate so proud? 'Tis no words, brave nor base, thou cravest; 'tis a man's arms! Up and face the truth of what thou art, and name it straight!... (489-492.)*

To put it bluntly, there's no reason whatever to struggle against her sin, just go for it! ...*wilt but thou be brave!* are the words the Nurse uses.

Caught up with the thought that Hippolytus should be made aware of Phaedra's great passion, the Nurse turns confidently to the statue of Aphrodite, prays briefly for her help, and goes into the palace.

The road to hell is paved with good intentions – never was that saying more true than with the old Nurse's belief that Phaedra's love should be whispered into the ear of Hippolytus. Phaedra overhears her telling him in the strictest confidence and the result is mortifying. She hears Hippolytus' reaction on being told, and his outrage at the very thought. He bursts from the palace followed by the Nurse in great distress realizing her blunder. He rages against Phaedra, feeling he's now tainted with the knowledge, and put into an intolerable situation. Phaedra rounds on her old Nurse and is beside herself with shame. What is left to her but to die and bring an end to her wretched life? And Phaedra goes wildly off into the palace.

Soon an anguished cry is heard as the old Nurse finds the body of Phaedra who has hanged herself. At this point Theseus himself arrives. To cut a long drama short, he finds his wife dead and a note left by her accusing his son of rape.

And so disaster follows disaster. All those attending the first perfomance of this tragedy would have known the legend. But even knowing the story doesn't deflect from the dramatic intensity of a well-crafted plot. The spectators would have been drawn into the tragedy till it became their reality. Theseus' son has raped his wife ...*forgetting God's great eye? (886.)* How dare he! It is despicable!

In the play Hippolytus, hearing of his father's return, and knowing nothing yet of Phaedra's suicide, arrives eagerly to greet him. He stops on seeing the faces of those gathered round his father, then sees the dead body of Phaedra. What can have happened, he demands? What on earth has brought about her sudden death when he saw her not half an hour ago?

Theseus, believing his wife's note is the true cause of her suicide, cannot bear the sight of his son, supposing him to be feigning his innocence. He orders him to get out of his sight. He is banished, disinherited, an object of dishonour to be shunned by all, and no son of his!

Hippolytus is bewildered by his father's outburst. He cannot bear the looks of accusation from all present, and especially from his father. *...I swear...I never touched this woman that was thine! No words could win me to it, nor incline my heart to dream it. May God strike me down, nameless and fameless, without home or town, an outcast and a wanderer of the world; may my dead bones never rest, but be hurled from sea to land, from land to angry sea, if evil is my heart and false to thee!... (1026-1035.)*

That Hippolytus pretends innocence ignites ever greater fury in Theseus. He blazes with anger. His son must leave instantly!

And Hippolytus in his desperation says something which maybe he shouldn't have. He goes in to the attack, reminding his father how he, his son, was the consequence of Theseus' own violation of the Amazon queen, his mother.

Having this flung at him is dynamite, and Theseus storms off into the palace. Hippolytus prays before the statue of Artemis, then takes himself off, leaving the Chorus to pour out their grief for Hippolytus: *...Star among men, yea, a Star that in Hellas was bright, by a Father's wrath driven far to the wilds and the night... (1123-1126.)* Their singing marks a passage of time and is interrupted by a Messenger who comes hurrying on demanding to see Theseus, as he has terrible news concerning Hippolytus. Theseus comes out to him, at first unmoved and unyielding even when he learns his son has been in a fatal accident. The Messenger describes the horror he witnessed when Hippolytus was driving his chariot along the seashore: *...an angry sound, slow-swelling like God's thunder underground, broke on us, and we trembled. And the steeds pricked their ears skyward, and threw back their heads... And there, above the horizon, seemed to stand a wave unearthly, crested in the sky...And roar of gasping sea and spray flung far, and shoreward swept, where stood the Prince's car. Three lines of wave together raced, and, full in the white crest of them, a wild Sea-Bull flung to the shore... (1200-1216.)*

He describes how Hippolytus attempted to keep firm control of his horses but *...in front uprose that Thing and turned again the four great coursers, terror-mad... (1228-1229.)* The chariot overturned and Hippolytus was thrown out, yet held on to the reins. *...A dear head battering at the chariot side, sharp rocks and ripped flesh... (1238-1239.)* Whatever it was he'd been accused of, Hippolytus cried out his innocence as he was dragged along by the stampeding horses. And the Messenger goes on to say he is convinced the young man is not guilty of the crime he's been banished for. Theseus should see him while there is yet ...*some little vein of life still pulsing in him... (1247-1248.)* Before he dies, Hippolytus must learn that his father is aware that he has wrongly accused him. And the Messenger hurries off while the Chorus sing of the ruthless power of Aphrodite.

Then the voice of Artemis speaks from a cloud which wafts over the stage. She informs Theseus that, indeed, his son is innocent, and that Phaedra was the victim of passion cast over her by Aphrodite who ...*sent her fire to run in Phaedra's veins... (1302.)*

The goddess informs him that Phaedra fought against her passion but the Nurse had betrayed her to Hippolytus who had firmly rejected her. The voice of the goddess tells Theseus he is at fault for jumping to conclusions in supposing Hippolytus to be guilty, and for calling down on him Poseidon's wrath. She is come to tell Theseus that due to his son's innocence, he should be buried with due honours.

Theseus only slowly comprehends that he has been too swift to condemn. Hippolytus, torn, battered and dying, is brought before his father. Distraught, Theseus is faced with the dreadful fact that his wife is dead, that she'd lied and he'd believed her, and now his innocent son is dying because he supposed him guilty and had called on Poseidon to wreak divine vengeance on him.

In the final death scene words come from Artemis which are almost Christian in their intensity regarding Love, Forgiveness, and Purity.

Hippolytus asks as he is dying, why is it the guilt of his forebears have somehow landed on him, causing him to suffer as he does? ... *Me far away and innocent of sin? O words that cannot save! When will this breathing end in that last deep pain that is painlessness? 'Tis sleep I crave. When wilt thou bring me sleep, thou dark and midnight magic of the grave!... (1381-1388.)*

Artemis speaks with compassion: ... *Sore-stricken man, bethink thee in this stress, thou dost but die for thine own nobleness... (1389-1390.)*

Hippolytus is overwhelmed with love for the goddess: ... *Oh breath of heavenly fragrance! Though my pain burns, I can feel thee and find rest again. The Goddess Artemis is with me here... (1392-1394.)* To which Artemis responds: *He dies, but my love cleaves to him for ever. (1398.)*

And Hippolytus turns to his grieving father: *Father, where art thou?...Oh, thou sufferest sore! (1407.)*

With a heart-wrenching, prolonged death-scene between the grief- and guilt-stricken father and his son, Artemis – having brought the two of them back together – departs with the words: ...*Farewell! I may not watch man's fleeting breath, nor stain mine eyes with the effluence of death…that terror now is very near. (1437-1439)*

When Harry caught me wiping my eyes when I'd been reading it in bed one morning, he was kind enough not to tell me I was an old fool. He just said: "It's only a myth! The goddess floating overhead on a cloud? What nonsense!"

"Nonsense? Didn't God's voice come out of a cloud saying 'This is my beloved Son in whom I am well pleased?'" I'd retorted, blowing my nose. "They – or whoever wrote that in the New Testament might have got that idea from Euripides' play."

"A stupid idea, old thing!" had been Harry's firm pronouncement.

Was it? What was surely stupid – or astonishing may be a better word – was to be caught up in another person's tragedy. One that had occurred thousands of years ago if, in fact, it had ever happened at all? It seemed totally insane. But that was what drama did for you – whether you were reading it in bed, were seated at a theatre, or there at the legendary site where it was said to have once happened. That was what was extraordinary!

CHAPTER 4

EPIDAURUS

We left Troezen and Galatas and drove north to Epidaurus. As we sped along the coastal road, I was very aware we were following the route from Delphi which King Aegeus must have taken to consult his friend King Pittheus in Troezen about the oracle's response regarding his childlessness. The road we were on ran alongside a towering pinky-grey rocky escarpment on our left which had stretches of wide-meshed wire hammered to it to prevent boulders tumbling down onto the passing traffic. The sea glinted and sparkled a deep sapphire blue to our right. Could Hippolytus have been driving his chariot along the seashore here? Was it where the terrifying 'thing' had risen from the deep and startled his horses, causing them to bolt and overturn his chariot?

It would have been along here also that King Aegeus would have come when returning to Athens. He must have used the land route because he called in at Corinth where he'd come across Medea the sorceress and wife of Jason.

We planned to call in at Epidaurus first because neither Hilary nor Fiona had seen the theatre, a huge amphitheatre renowned for its acoustics. Epidaurus was where Apollo's son Asclepius, god of medicine and healing, worked miracles on the sick and infirm. It was a large site and included a stadium, gymnasium and theatre because it was believed that such things restored the sick to a state of well-being – the mind as well as the afflicted part needed healing.

"By the way," I said, leaning forward so the two in front could hear me. "Asclepius, god of healing at Epidaurus, brought Hippolytus back from the dead."

"That's amazing!" Hilary said.

"But Zeus was so angry that he dared reverse the laws of nature," I went on, "that he struck Asclepius dead with a thunderbolt."

"And then what happened?" Hilary asked, regarding me in her rear-view mirror.

"And then I've no idea," I replied and relapsed back on my seat.

The disembodied voice of the SatNav woman spoke: "At the next roundabout take the first turning left."

"Did you hear that?" Fiona turned her head to Hilary.

"Yes, left at the roundabout."

"I think there should be a lake somewhere along here on the right," I said. "That nice woman at the hotel, whatever her name was, said we'd see it from this road. Keep your eyes open."

"What about it?"

"They say Dionysos, when he was old enough, went down into the lake – where there's an entrance to Hades – and rescued his mother Semele who, if you remember, was reduced to a cinder when Hera persuaded her to ask Zeus to reveal himself to her in his full glory."

"Such a strange story!" Hilary remarked. "And even stranger, when you think of it, to be brought back to life when you're a cinder."

"I didn't think of that," I said.

The landscape now was of olive groves surrounded by mountains – we never saw the lake. We came to a ravine and found ourselves going down into it and across a bridge. The soil here was a rosy-red loam. This was an altogether different approach to Epidaurus for me. On earlier occasions with Harry we'd made the journey coming from the attractive small port of Nauflio; today we were approaching from another direction.

By the time we reached the great sanctuary site it was mid-morning and there were coachloads of tourists. We didn't intend to explore the whole site but to seat ourselves in this famous large fourth century B.C. theatre which curved round like an open fan.

We climbed one of the many aisles between the tiered seats and I sat high up leaving the others to reach the topmost ones. I watched the tour-guides demonstrate the acoustics to their groups: one struck a match and the sound rose clearly; a whispered word and it was audible.

Several years ago I'd come here with Harry after we'd visited Mycenae, the ancient kingdom where King Agamemnon had been monarch. Agamemnon had been commander-in-chief of the Greek army, and had fought heroically in the Trojan War to win back Helen, his brother Menelaus' faithless wife, who'd run off with Paris. After ten years of bitter struggle and the final destruction of Troy, Agamemnon had returned home to his wife and family only to be murdered by her. His story, and the tragedy that befell his son Orestes who was to avenge his father's murder, became the subject of Aeschylus' great trilogy, the *Oresteia*, the only surviving complete trilogy of those first dramatists.

The tragedy is still performed today, and in 1982 the London National Theatre staged it here at Epidaurus, with the cast wearing masks and dressed as they would have done in the first ever performance. How I would have liked to have seen it!

To understand the *Oresteia* it is probably helpful to know something about the curse cast over King Agamemnon's family. Agamemnon and his brother Menelaus were the sons of King Atreus of Mycenae. There was, however, bad blood in the family. It started with their great-grandfather Tantalus who killed his son, stewed up his shoulder, and served it to the gods to see if they could distinguish between human and animal flesh. They certainly could and, for this dastardly act, the gods condemned him for eternity to stand in water up to his neck, unable to quench his thirst because, whenever he leaned forward to drink, the water receded out of his reach.

Pelops, the son whom Tantalus had killed, was restored to life by the gods, and given a new shoulder made of ivory. He later became the father of Atreus and Thyestes, in whom the bad blood continued to manifest itself. Atreus became king of Mycenae and married Aerope who was seduced by Thyestes. On learning about it, Atreus took his revenge by serving up to Thyestes a casserole containing the boiled remains of his two young children. After the meal he told him what he had eaten and, out of sheer spite, showed him their hands and feet. As a result, Thyestes fled the kingdom and brought down a curse on the house of Atreus which was to run through the family for another three generations. Thyestes, with the bad blood in his veins, seduced his own daughter with whom King Atreus later fell in love and, not knowing she was his niece, brought her to the palace. She gave birth to a son, Aegisthus, who was brought up in the palace at Mycenae with Agamemnon and Menelaus.

These unsavoury details of the family's past are important to know as the curse resurfaces throughout the life of Agamemnon.

When Agamemnon grew up he married Clytemnestra, daughter of King Tyndareus of Sparta (sister of the beatiful Helen). They had three daughters and a son. The two daughters were Iphigenia and Electra; the former played an important but tragic rôle at the outset of the Trojan War (as described in Chapter 8), while Electra suffered the trauma of her mother's murder of her father on his return from the Trojan War. As for Orestes (the son), he was doomed to endure a trail of torments which followed on from these events.

When Harry and I had been at Mycenae a few years back, we'd stood before the massive Lion Gate, so-named for its great sculpted lions above the entrance-way, under which King Agamemnon would have passed when returning from the Trojan War. At the time I'd thought of his home-coming as portrayed by Aeschylus in his *Agamemnon*, the first of his *Oresteia* trilogy. In the tragedy he is accompanied by Cassandra, the daughter of King Priam of Troy who, after the fall of the city, has become his slave and concubine.

Legend has it that Apollo once loved Cassandra and, as part of his attempt to win her affection, had given her the gift of prophecy. But when she rejected him, he'd been so upset he'd added the proviso that, although her prophecies would be accurate, no one would believe them. It was why, at the end of the ten-year Trojan War when the Wooden Horse had been left by the Greek army in Beşik bay as a gift for the goddess Athena, its interior concealing the pick of the Greek warriors, Cassandra had cried out her warnings not to bring it into the city, but nobody had paid any attention. The result had been the catastrophic destruction of the city.

The drama *Agamemnon* starts evocatively with the Nightwatchman spotting the flare of a beacon, at last announcing the end of the Trojan War, victory to the Greeks and the imminent return of the king. In those days beacons were the fastest way of spreading news. The first would have been lit in Troy, from where successive beacons would have conveyed the information to Mycenae.

King Agamemnon arrives by chariot bringing with him Princess Cassandra. He has no knowledge of the fact that during those ten long years of war his wife Clytemnestra and his cousin Aegisthus, (who he'd entrusted to rule Mycenae in his absence), have become lovers. Nor does he realize that Clytemnestra has never forgiven him for sacrificing their daughter Iphigenia to appease the goddess Artemis, who only then released the winds to allow the Greek fleet to set sail for Troy.

So Agamemnon returns to his palace unaware of the festering thoughts that have been eating away at the mind of Clytemnestra. He arrives full of joyful anticipation at being reunited with his family. The very sight of his walled city and gateway must have filled him with happiness.

Clytemnestra comes to meet him at this massive entrance-way and puts on a good act of the faithful, loving wife. In the tragedy a Chorus of elders remind the audience of past events and of the present moment, preparing everyone for what is to come. The queen speaks of the years of grief she's suffered during his long absence: ...*on my bed mine eyes were worn with watching, early and late, grieving because the fires of thy return were still unkindled. And midst my dreams the gnat's small peremptory tones would wake me, while seeing more dangers than the time could hold assailing thee... (888-903.)*

She's not blind and sees that her husband is accompanied by the beautiful Cassandra. Nevertheless she continues to play the overjoyed wife, while concealing the seething dark thoughts that obsess her. Here at last is her chance to take her long-awaited revenge on the man she loathes who's dared return alive from the war; the man who offered up their daughter as a sacrifice, and slit the young girl's throat. Back again! Back home to come between her and her lover Aegisthus. Nothing less than his death will be good enough! And it will leave her free to marry Aegisthus so together they can rule Mycenae. Soon, very soon, she will carry out her plan!

Female attendants begin to lay down a red carpet for Agamemnon, who says: ...*To the gods alone such tribute should be paid. For mortal man to trample on rich webs of varied hue to me is a thing by no means void of fear. I seek for human honours, not divine. Fame needs no carpets nor embroidered wefts beneath her feet, to sound her note of praise and modesty is Heaven's best gift. When one shall end a happy life in peace and joy, then celebrate his glory! By this rule we still may live and prosper, safe from harm. (923-933.)*

He and his wife exchange light banter as might any cheerful married couple. Agamemnon is asked by his wife to remove his shoes before walking on the carpet, to which he says: ...*Is this a battle in which you care to win?* To which Clytemnestra replies. *Come, let me triumph on the taker of Troy! (942.)*

At this point he draws attention to Cassandra: ...*receive, I pray thee, this stranger-woman kindly. Heaven still smiles when power is used with gentleness. No mortal is willingly a captive, but this maid, of countless spoils the flower and crown, was given to me by the army, and attends me home... (950-956.)* With these words he departs into the palace with his wife while the Chorus sing of impending doom.

When Clytemnestra returns, she impatiently orders Cassandra

to descend from the chariot, and the Chorus implore her to do so. But Cassandra is filled with foreboding. She refuses to obey, and Clytemnestra loses patience: *Sure she is mad, and follows crazy thoughts…I'll not demean myself by throwing more words away. (1064-1070.)* And she returns into the palace.

The Chorus speak of their compassion for Cassandra but begin to fear her as she calls on Apollo – Apollo who granted her the gift of prophecy; Apollo, the builder of the walls of Troy but who allowed them to be destroyed! Apollo, who granted her prophetic powers only for them to be disbelieved! *Oh my Apollo! Builder! Destroyer!… Destroyer of me!… (1079-1081.)*

The Chorus become ever more alarmed as she stands in the chariot crying out all that she sees. *…Guilt-stained with strangled lives, with kinsmen's blood; a place of sprinkled gore, of clotted horror!… (1086-1088.)*

Cassandra is *…like a hound she snuffs for blood…* the Chorus think; but she is unstoppable: *Yea! There, there, there!…I see, I hear them! Little children whose throats are cut, still wailing of their murder, and the roast flesh, a father tasted – swallowed! (1095-1098.)*

The Chorus implore her to cease her terrible pronouncements yet she is in full flow: *Wretch! Wilt thou do it? Ah me! The lord of thine embrace…How shall I tell? 'Twill come! 'Tis here! She lifts her hand; she launches at him blow following blow… (1107-1111.)*

What is it she fears the Chorus ask? But Cassandra is deaf to them and continues with her warnings; there is treachery and blood everywhere: *…Oh, the pain! What is it? Some net of Death and Hell?… Howl, 'Out upon the butchery! Stone her! Stone her!' (1114-1117)* and she lists the terrible disasters that have befallen the royal family in Troy, and the horrors that she knows are yet to come here in Mycenae.

The Chorus are filled with dread. If Cassandra knows the doom she faces, how is it she can *…walk boldly toward the altar of thy death? (1298.)* And, as Cassandra enters the palace, she cries: *These halls exhale with murder! Drip with death! (1309.)*

Soon screams are heard from within. The sound is bloodcurdling, and Clytemnestra is revealed standing triumphantly over the body of her dead husband: *…I smote him, twice: and with the second groan he sank: and when he had fallen, I gave a third last stroke, to crown the sacrifice…his soul on wing for Hades, his keen breath smote me with drops of slaughter, whose dark dew refreshed my spirit, even as the bladed corn that swells to the ear, delighteth in heaven's rain… (1382-1389.)*

Dike (justice) has been done for Agamemnon's sacrifice of their daughter Iphigenia. But the gods look down and see it as a crime: every evil prompts another resulting in revenge and further deaths.

When the Chorus condemn Clytemnestra's murder of her husband, she retorts: ...*Should he not have been banished by your voice to purge the state? Yet, hearing of my deed, ye are swift and harsh in judgement. (1422-1424.)*

The Chorus are not convinced: *Haughty thy spirit, and proud thy vaunting...while lurid light is in thine eye, intoxicate with impious butchery... (1425-1429.)*

But Clytemnestra has no regrets. What is more, she can claim with pride that Cassandra has also been slain by her: ...*she too now lies in death, they have full recompense...she tuned her lay most swanlike for her end, wailing their doom. So died the damsel this man brought to lend new savour to the softness of my bed. (1443-1448.)*

Accusations and defiance are exchanged. Clytemnestra feels only triumph. Her lover Aegisthus joins her in celebration: *Sweet day of recompense, I hail thy light! Now, lords of yon wide heaven, I recognize your jurisdiction o'er the griefs of men, when I behold this man, to my great joy, laid in yon shroud... (1577-1581.)* And so the warnings of Cassandra have been fulfilled.

It is possible from the great throne-room at Mycenae to look out across the Argolid plain to the distant mountains, and a strip of sea where, perhaps, King Agamemnon had first set foot back on his home soil. What indignity, after enduring those ten long years of deadly battles, to return home victorious only to be murdered by your supposedly loving wife! What worse fate than that can anyone imagine?

After the murders of Agamemnon and Cassandra, Clytemnestra sends her young son Orestes (now the rightful heir to the throne) to Phocis where he is brought up at Delphi by the king. For a while the queen lives happily with Aegisthus and they rule Mycenae with a rod of iron. On reaching manhood, however, Orestes consults the Delphic oracle and is told it is his duty to avenge his father's murder. He must return to Mycenae to do this. His story is told in Aeschylus' *Libation Bearers*, the second drama of his *Oresteia* trilogy.

★

The setting for *Libation Bearers* is outside the tomb of Agamemnon. It is an impressive bee-hive tomb, discovered by the self-styled German archaeologist Heinrich Schliemann in the nineteenth century. It is situated a hundred or so metres outside the fortified city of Mycenae, and its construction is fabulous. The tomb is cut deep into a hillside with its approach flanked by massive blocks of stone to an eighteen foot high doorway with a great lintel above. The stone-built interior at its highest point is forty-four feet.

In the drama, Orestes has returned from Delphi to avenge his father's death. He is now a young man disguised as a messenger, and is accompanied by his childhood friend Pylades. He stands beside the tomb and prays to his father's 'shade' to help him accomplish what Apollo has instructed: to slay his mother. He cuts two locks of his hair and lays them on the tomb: one symbolic of life, the other of death.

His sister Electra appears with a Chorus of Trojan slave-women. She has been sent by Clytemnestra to pour a libation at the tomb because that night she had a nightmare in which she'd given birth to a serpent, and she fears the ghost of Agamemnon.

At the tomb Electra comes across Orestes and Pylades. Despite his attempt to go unrecognized, Electra gradually notices certain features of her brother although she hasn't seen him since he was a small boy. She brings him to Clytemnestra pretending he is a messenger from Delphi bearing the sad news of Orestes' death. Clytemnestra, on hearing the news, acts the part of the grieving mother: *Ah me! what ruin clamours in this news! Oh, ill-averted curse upon this house... Orestes, whom we thought withdrawn from ill, with free foot rescued from the slippery slime, dies, and bereaves me in my wretchedness!... (693-700.)*

Oh, the curse of the House of Atreus! Cause and effect! It was what Aeschylus was fully conscious of: an evil act did not end with the perpetrator but had far-reaching consequences down the generations.

Orestes' old Nurse appears, and when she hears the news her grief is genuine: *How can that be? Orestes was our hope, and he is gone! (778-779.)*

The Nurse goes to fetch Aegisthus who should be informed at once of the tragic news. He hurries in, feigning shock and dismay: ... *Orestes dead! Again, this house, long gangrened with a rankling wound, must be new-burdened with blood-dripping death... (837-842.)*

Aegisthus departs and soon his screams are heard as Orestes first takes his revenge on him, his mother's lover. Clytemnestra returns having heard the screams. She now confronts Orestes who reveals his true identity. Yes, he is there to avenge his father's murder. *Oh, wilt thou kill thy mother? Oh, my son! (920)* she cries.

But Orestes answers her firmly: *I kill thee not. Thy sin destroyeth thee. (921.)*

The death of both Clytemnestra and Aegisthus, however, does not bring Orestes peace; rather does it exacerbate his troubles. With matricide comes the awakening of the Furies, dreaded creatures who rise from their slumber and swoop in to the attack of anyone guilty of such a crime. Orestes is now driven demented by them; unable to sleep, unable to escape, they torment him continually till he is compelled to return to Delphi to consult the oracle of Apollo yet again.

And so the second play ends and the third of the trilogy the *Eumenides* begins.

★

The towering crags of the twin Phaedriades rocks, the great Parnassus mountains with their chasms and ravines, make a dramatic backdrop to Apollo's ancient oracle site at Delphi.

Today only a few Doric columns remain of his former temple. Here and there groups of cypress trees stand erect like sentinels in the landscape.

The first thing Apollo did was to kill the monstrous serpent which inhabited the area and guarded the original oracle of Gaia (mother earth). To atone for this killing, he established the Pythian Games and the priestess of Apollo was endowed with the title Pythia.

The *adyton* or cella, the most sacred part of Apollo's temple, was at the western end of his temple. It was believed to have had a few steps leading down to a chasm over which the Pythia would sit on her tripod. Some said that the bones and teeth of the Python were kept in the bowl of the tripod. Whilst seated, the Pythia would chew on laurel leaves which were sacred to Apollo. Whether from the leaves, or from inhaling vapours said to rise from the chasm, she would fall into a trance before uttering the words of the god in answer to the questions put to her.

Sometimes the questions asked were complex political ones and were answered in riddles and had then to be interpreted by the temple priests; sometimes they were simple ones such as whether to marry or not, in which case the answer came with a plain 'yes' or 'no'.

In the *Eumenides*, this third drama of the *Oresteia*, Orestes is back in Delphi pursued by the dreaded Furies ...*dark of hue and altogether hideous, breathing out their snorting breath in gusts not to be borne, distilling from their eyelids drops of hate... (50-53.)*

There at Delphi, with these Furies harassing him relentlessly, Orestes clings to the Omphalos, a large, off-white oval stone, said to have been kept in the temple, marking the navel of the world. When Zeus one day had wanted to know where the centre of his earth was, he'd let loose two eagles from the opposite extremities of the globe and, where they'd collided, he'd pronounced that to be the centre.

Clinging to this Omphalos, Orestes implores Apollo to free him from these terrifying Furies. Apollo's response is that Orestes must go to Athens to seek the wisdom of Athena and there face judgement.

Gazing around the ruins from the temple was amazing. On the lower slopes, where the Sacred Way wound its way up the ancient terraced sanctuary, the remnants of numerous marble monuments and marble statues were to be seen, each one presented to the site by a city-state, an island, or an individual in gratitude for some divine favour. Amongst them was the Treasury of Athens in the form of a miniature temple.

Pilgrims arriving in antiquity would have started their ascent from the Castalian spring down beside the Athens-Delphi highway. Water trickled down a cleft between the Phaedriades crags into a paved area overshadowed by plane trees. Those coming to enquire of the oracle would have first purified themselves there before entering the sanctuary.

There are very many stories attached to Delphi: for instance, the coming of Oedipus who was told by the oracle that he would murder his father and marry his mother (see chapter 9); or King Aegeus of Athens who came to enquire how to cure himself of being childless, as described in Chapter 3; or the envoys sent by Athens to consult Apollo on how to defend themselves against the Persians – and the list goes on.

It is now to Athens we must go for the final scene of Aeschylus' *Eumenides*.

★

On the Acropolis, Orestes is supplicating Athena; he is on his knees, his arms around the ancient olive-wood image of the goddess (said to have fallen from heaven in deep antiquity), and kept within her ancient temple on the north side of the Acropolis where now the Erechtheum stands. The Erechtheum, as it is seen today, is recognizable by its six Caryatid maidens supporting the upper structure of the building.

The Chorus of Furies press around Orestes as he prays. In her wisdom, Athena calls for a tribunal to be set up on the Areópagus, a low rocky elevation a hundred metres or so to the north-west of the Acropolis. Harry and I had once climbed up it. It is now easy to do as a metal stairway like a fire-escape has been clamped to it, and a gridded metal walkway encircles its summit. But those many years ago, on our first ever trip to Athens, it had been a slippery and uneven rock to clamber up and walk on – an easy place to slip and break a leg.

In the *Eumenides* the Chorus of Furies have arrived in pursuit of Orestes: *So! 'tis his trail beyond a doubt. Pursue the voiceless guide's direction. Like a hound tracking the blood-marks of a wounded fawn, I quest and follow where the gore-drops lie… (245-248.)*

Apollo arrives to defend Orestes: *I am here in evidence, to prove this man a lawful suppliant who approached my shrine and there by me was purged from guilt of blood; also to plead, myself, in part; for I am charged with Clytemnestra's death – Athena, open the cause, in due form, thine own way. (577-582.)*

And so the trial commences. The Furies are shrill in their condemnation of matricide; they will never stop their harrassment of Orestes; no amount of ritual cleansing can wipe away the deed. Orestes pleads guilty, and Apollo tells the court that in his oracles he only voices the will of his father Zeus: *I never spake from my prophetic seat concerning man or woman, people or state, save what the father of all gods had bidden… (619-621.)*

Lots are cast by the citizens of Athens and the resulting verdict is divided equally. Athena casts the deciding vote and Orestes is acquitted. The Furies are appalled. They are deities even more ancient than the Olympian gods, and they cry out against these younger gods: *Ah! Ah! Young gods, ye have ridden down mine ancient right; Ye have torn from out my hand the meed of honour…A cankerous growth shall cover all the land; no blade shall spring, no child; but feuds unreconciled stamp the hard soil with life-destroying brand. (778-792.)*

Athena placates them, assuring them of the importance of their role in a civilized society; it is men's fear of them that keeps them from offending, she tells them: *…Thou wilt yield to kind persuasion, and not launch the curse of barrenness on all fruit-bearing things. Lull the dark billows of thy bitter mood to share mine honours and my dwelling place; and thou shalt find, as thy first-fruits come in from the wide region, both* *of marriage dues and child-birth offerings, good cause to bless eternally this utterance of my tongue. (829-837.)*

But, oh, how the Furies rant and rave: ... *Unhonoured and abhorred! I pant with fury, breathing nought but hate... (840-841.)*

Athena is superb in her quiet determination to calm their objections and threats. She assures them they have in no way been insulted as older gods, but will be greatly honoured from now on, and she offers them a place on her Acropolis, a cave on the north side on the lower slopes below her ancient temple; there they will be honoured and respected by all Athenians. From then on, she tells them, they are to be known as the Eumenides (the kindly ones).

I, of course, find it interesting that Aeschylus worked into his drama the idea that a soft word turns away wrath. The same wisdom is to be found in Proverbs in the Old Testament: *A soft answer turns away wrath, but a harsh word stirs up anger...* Which, I wonder, came first?

★

"Sorry to interrupt – " It was Hilary, her flowing cotton skirt billowing in the breeze as she came down and sat on the stone seat across the narrow aisle from me. "We think we should get on if we're to stop at Corinth."

I glanced at my watch. "Yes, we should."

Wistfully, I looked down at a tour-guide reciting a line from Shakespeare to a group seated on the tiered stone seats: *To be or not to be, that is the question...*

Several years back, after visiting Mycenae, Harry and I had come here late one evening when only a few visitors had been present. A few brave souls had taken their stand on the altar of Dionysos, the round marble slab at the centre of the *orchestra*, and had sung or recited. I, and a Spanish girl seated close by, discovered that we both longed to go down and perform also. I didn't know the girl, but she was young and beautiful. We decided on a Frank Sinatra song 'I Did it My Way', using 'la, la, la' for the numerous lines we didn't know. Harry totally disowned me, then joked afterwards that I'd sounded like Cassandra wailing her forebodings.

Never mind how I'd sounded! I'd found it an extraordinary privilege to have stood there and done anything at all. As the Spanish girl had said, it was one of those magical moments in life – standing centre-stage at Epidaurus and performing – one you will never forget.

CHAPTER 5

CORINTH

Anyone who speeds along the motorway on the east side of the Peloponnese on their way to Corinth cannot help but notice the gargantuan hump that rises from the plain. This is Acrocorinth, an imposing rocky elevation which in antiquity had on its summit (over five hundred metres at its highest point) a large and important temple of Aphrodite, goddess of love.

Corinth, of course, is famous for St. Paul's Epistle to the Corinthians about love. He had lived on and off in Corinth for two years c.50 A.D. and oh, how he must have frowned and pursed his lips in disapproval at Aphrodite's temple with her many hundreds of *hetairai* who served her. *Hetairai* were prostitutes (courtesan might be a more respectable word). They were there to give pleasure to the many seafarers and merchants who put in at the local ports around Corinth.

To St. Paul the erotic and sensual love of Aphrodite would have been anathema. Only chastity, or the far more difficult-to-achieve faithful love within marriage, was to be encouraged. St. Paul's famous First Epistle to the Corinthians had been written when he had been in Ephesus. There he'd heard reports that his converts at Corinth had broken into factions and, far from loving each other (platonic love, of course), they were quarrelling fiercely amongst themselves. He was aghast at the news he was getting, and was particularly shocked to hear that one of his converts had been having a fling with his stepmother. 'Shall I come to you with a rod, or with love in a spirit of gentleness?' he wrote. Would he have known the story of Phaedra, and heard of Euripides' *Hippolytus*? It was against even pagan standards that a man should have it off with his father's wife, so for a Christian! They should be setting examples of Christian chastity and virtue!

We were not, however, visiting Acrocorinth on this occasion but making our way to Corinth itself. We reached the rather dreary town of Corinth and, after following an obliging young man who led the way in his car as Fiona's SatNav had given up on her, we eventually arrived.

★

"So come on, tell us why we're here? You must have a reason." It was Fiona speaking. We were fortifying ourselves with food before tackling the archaeological site.

I didn't need much prompting, and told them briefly the story of Medea. It was to Medea's home in Colchis that Jason and his Argonauts had sailed in search of the Golden Fleece, and there that he'd met Medea, the king's daughter, who fell passionately in love with him. By using sorcery and witchcraft (in which she was adept), Medea helped Jason steal the Golden Fleece from under the watchful eye of the ever-wakeful dragon, and the Argonauts then set sail for home again taking Medea along with them.

After escaping many hazards, the Argonauts eventually returned to Jason's home at Iolchos in the Mt. Pelion region of Thessaly. There, they'd handed over the Golden Fleece to King Pelias, usurper of Jason's father's throne. It had been agreed he'd step down in Jason's favour if he succeeded in bringing back the Golden Fleece. He never expected to see Jason again, and promptly went back on his word when he returned. Such treachery on the king's part put Medea in a towering rage. Medea was a woman of violent passions who, when aroused to anger, was deadly. She soon resorted to witchcraft. She suggested to the daughters of King Pelias that they might like to rejuvenate their father as she had just done with Jason's father. However, she deliberately withheld her magic and the king died a painful death; the result was that she and Jason, and their two young sons, had to flee to Corinth.

"All right, they've come to Corinth – so?" It was Fiona speaking.

"Yes, what happened when they came here?" Hilary asked.

I explained how Jason unfortunately fell in love with the king's daughter. Jason, at any rate, tried to convince Medea that he wasn't in love with Glauke but, if he married her, they would be better off financially, and he would see to it that she and their two sons would be well provided for. Medea had very naturally been furious, but had then pretended to go along with the plan, and had woven a beautiful garment for Glauke as a wedding-gift. When the poor girl had tried it on the garment (which Medea had impregnated with lethal substance) caught fire, and in agony Glauke had leapt into a fountain and died. Glauke's Fountain is still to be seen here in the archaeological site and, although I'd seen it before, I really wanted to check it out again since I was writing about her.

When we got to the kiosk where tickets were being sold, I asked the friendly man on duty if it was possible to enter without paying as we had a long drive and needed to move on immediately – I just wanted to see Glauke's Fountain, I said. But, friendly as he was, he said firmly that tickets had to be bought before he could let us in. I could hear Harry whispering in my ear 'wicked waste of money, you've seen it!'

Another man on duty led us to the railings and pointed out the remaining Doric columns marking the temple of Apollo to the far right and, in answer to my question regarding Glauke's Fountain, said it was in front of us, though it was out of sight from where I stood. However, I knew it to be a monolithic rock with two small cave-like apertures with water still flowing from them into a channel.

"Well, if we're not going in I'd quite like to look at the shops here. I need to buy some presents," Fiona said.

Since I could see the site I stayed where I was while they went on their spending spree. I was content just to sit in the shade of a pine-tree with the ancient sanctuary site before me. I took out my *Medea* and scanned the marked passages.

Medea had an interesting ancestry. Her paternal grandfather was Helios (the Sun) and her father was King Aeetes of Colchis (today's Georgia on the Black Sea). One of her aunts was Circe, the enchantress who'd entertained Odysseus for a year and turned his companions into swine; another was Pasiphae, the wife of King Minos of Crete, whose unnatural passion for a bull resulted in the birth of the Minotaur, half-man, half-bull, which the family kept hidden away in a labyrinth till it was killed by Theseus.

Medea's story is the stuff of tragedies, and Euripides, in his drama *Medea*, made the most of it. The play begins with Medea's faithful Nurse agonizing over Medea's distraught state of mind having been told by Jason he is about to leave her. ...*All fasting now and cold, her body yielded up to pain, her days a waste of weeping... since first she knew that he was false... (28-30.)*

How understandable when your trust and confidence have been

blown up in your face. Yet we, the audience/readers know that Medea is malicious and evil – she is as legendary today as she was when the Athenian audience sat and watched the first performance of the play. The depth of her despair, anguish and rejection quickly turn to hatred of Jason, and then to revenge – what else after such betrayal?

In the tragedy, an Attendant makes his entry accompanied by Jason and Medea's two young sons who are unaware of their mother's desolation. They bring with their presence a brief interlude of innocence, childish love and trust after the grief and passion in the drama. But the undercurrents of disaster are still there, and we know their young lives are doomed.

I think how it must be somewhere around here (where I am now seated) that the young boys would have played; here that Medea's nurse would have had her forebodings; and somewhere here that King Creon of Corinth had come to confront and inform Medea that she and her sons were to leave his kingdom. It was for the best, the king assured her.

Banished? To where? What was to become of her? She had given her all for Jason, the one man she loved! She'd risked everything, and had left the protection of her father and home! Where could she go now, alone with two young sons and no support? Surely death would be better?

She throws herself at the feet of the king in supplication, and pleads for a day at least to prepare herself before being sent into exile. And the king concedes.

With the king gone, Medea holds forth in a soliloquy. Dark thoughts take over and she sees death as an escape from all her looming troubles; to kill her family seems to her the best solution as then her boys will be released from this bitter life, and their death will deprive Jason of them too which will haunt him for ever. Yes, that is what she can and will do in revenge for what he has done to her.

Jason arrives on the scene and points out that their dilemma is Medea's fault. It was Medea's murder of his uncle that had forced them to flee. Let her rail on regarding her lot, but hasn't she brought it on herself? Seeing her distress, he then tries to reason more gently with her by saying he has come to her not as an enemy but to try to do what is most beneficial for them all. To marry Glauke will solve all their problems: since Glauke is a princess, their two sons will be well provided for and he himself will see to it that she, Medea, has everything she needs – she has nothing to fear.

I can imagine my feelings had Harry come up with that solution during our early years of farming when we were on the bread-line – let him divorce me and marry a beef-baron's daughter! He would then be able to keep me in comfort! Marry a beef-baron's daughter to improve MY lot? Huh! ...*Evil, most evil* (Medea's words). She turns to the Chorus and says: *'Tis but of all man's inward sicknesses the vilest, that he knoweth not of shame nor pity!... (476-478.)*

To abandon her for a royal bride taking the two children with him? – Jason, the great hero of the Greek world! Her lover! To ditch her after all she has done for him? What can he do for her if she is banished? No, no, no!

Jason retaliates. Hasn't she willingly done all she has because she herself was eager to escape from her barbaric country to Greece, a far more civilized nation in comparison?

And so the defunct marriage with the customary ding-dong squabbling of two resentful and aggrieved people ends in bitterness, with Jason swearing by God that he is marrying the king's daughter to get out of the curse of poverty – it will be far better for her and for their two sons, he insists.

Medea remains on stage totally shattered. It could be that the ruins I am looking at beyond the railings are all that are left of the former palace where Glauke was born and grew up.

It is while Medea is grieving over her fate, that King Aegeus of Athens passes on his way back to Athens from his visit to Troezen. Faced with the distraught Medea, he asks her why she looks so distressed? He is tactlessly blunt: *Thy frame is wasted, and the fire dead in thine eyes... (686-687.)* Most women would flinch at such a crushing remark. Not so Medea. She sees this king of Athens as an escape route for her. She tells him the problems she is facing and the threat of exile; she makes Jason out to be a complete rat. She pleads with Aegeus to take her to Athens, and falls to her knees before him, supplicating him in this her hour of need. She will bear him children, she says. Will she just!

On the spur of the moment King Aegeus sees this as a rather good idea. He tells her, however, that as she is being banished by the king of Corinth he, as king of Athens, must not be seen offering her sanctuary; but, if she comes of her own free will to Athens, then he will certainly welcome her.

With that settled, the king continues on his way, and the dark, malicious streak in Medea's character now takes full possession of her.

If she cannot have Jason for herself, certainly no other woman is going to have him!

She realizes she must first pretend to accept Jason's plans. She will tell him that she at last sees the benefits to be gained from what he has suggested, and she will even befriend his intended bride. Yes, that's what she'll do. Her spirits rise at the thought. Secretly, however, she intends to weave the girl a poisoned robe which, when put on, will kill her. A woman scorned... hell hath no fury... And so she pretends to him she now sees reason: ...*See, I surrender: and confess that then I had bad thoughts, but now have turned again and found my wiser mind... (893-895.)*

Medea calls the children to her, and tells them to greet their father. As they go to him emotion sweeps over her, and tears flow; the children run to comfort her. The audience is caught up in the poignancy of her mixed emotions as she says: ...*I sought to smooth away the long strife with your father, and, lo, now I have all drowned with tears this little brow! (903-905.)*

Jason feels only relief that at last Medea has come round. Having his sons with him at the palace will give them a good start in life, and they will grow up as princes and be respected – Medea need have no anxiety whatever regarding them. But why is she weeping?

Medea excuses her emotional state, but parting with her children and going into exile – yes, she can see it is best all round, but it is difficult for her. With great courage, and concealing her evil intentions, she quickly kisses her children goodbye, and they depart with their father as Medea enters the palace.

The Chorus now take up the story as it gradually unfolds until Medea returns, and a Messenger arrives with shocking news. Glauke is dead! He describes how the two small boys brought the wedding-gift from Medea and presented it to Glauke as a token of her good wishes for her marriage to their father.

The Messenger goes on to explain how Glauke had been reassured by this apparently thoughtful gesture from Medea. Jason had then left Glauke alone to try on the garment, taking his two sons with him. With nobody around her, Glauke eagerly tried on the gold embroidered robe (some say it was a coat). She'd ...*bound the golden crown through her long curls, and in a mirror fair arranged their separate clusters, smiling... So passing joyful in those gifts was she!... (1164-1171.)*

And the Messenger goes on to describe how the young princess had turned this way and that before a mirror admiring the long folds of her garment, until suddenly she'd grown pale and, stumbling, she found a seat and sat in sudden speechless agony. One of her attendants raised the alarm as ...*through her lips was seen a white foam crawling, and her eyeballs back twisted, and all her face dead pale for lack of life...* *(1174-1177.)*

The Messenger continues with his story: how Glauke's father had been quickly summoned and, on seeing his daughter dying before his eyes, had gathered her up in horror, embracing her already dead body till he himself had been contaminated by the lethal poisonous burning garment, and writhed in agony till he too was dead.

The story as told by Euripides in his tragedy doesn't, in fact, fit with the legend that is generally accepted: that the unfortunate bride-to-be, when she put on the garment, found that her flesh began to burn, and in agony jumped into the fountain to get relief but died. Often playwrights in those days, for whatever reason, wrote their own version of a story.

We know Medea intends to kill her sons to spite Jason. In her deranged state she has the two little boys locked up in the house with her. She bolts the doors and soon the cries of the children are heard. The Chorus of women beat at the door and try to get in, but without success. Jason arrives urgently because he has heard that his beautiful Glauke and her father have been murdered by Medea. He is terrified that she is about to kill their two boys also. Their cries have ceased, and now Medea appears on the roof-top of her house in a chariot pulled by winged dragons. She exults in her success at causing Jason such horror and dismay. There are no words that can adequately describe his feelings as he screams at her: *Thou incarnate curse... a bride of hate to me and death – tigress, not woman, beast of wilder breath than Scylla...* *(1341-1343.)*

But Medea is triumphant and cries out: *My claws have gripped thine heart, and all things shine.* She says: *I love the pain, so thou shalt laugh no more. (1359-1362.)*

Medea's last words to Jason foretell his doom: ...*For thee, behold, death draweth on, evil and lonely, like thine heart: the hands of thine old Argo, rotting where she stands, shall smite thy head in twain, and bitter be to the last end thy memories of me. (1385-1389.)* And her chariot rises bearing her off to Athens, leaving Jason bereft of all his hopes for the future – no bride, no kindly king for a father-in-law, no children, no prospects.

Medea's prophecy that Jason will meet his death as the result of his ship *Argo* came true. He went back to live where it had been drawn up on shore and, while sheltering in her shadow one day, some rotting planks of wood fell from her hull and cracked his skull killing him instantly.

A tragic ending to a legendary hero who took full advantage of a woman's love while it suited him, but wanted also the love of another because that suited him also. Or was his love for Glauke genuine? Love! Passion!

So what happened to Medea in the end? Well, she married King Aegeus and, when Theseus as a young man arrived with his father's sword and sandals which he'd successfully retrieved from under the rock where they'd been hidden, Medea wasn't best pleased to see this elder son of Aegeus, the rightful heir to the throne. By then she herself had had a son by Aegeus named Medus. Using all her wiles she attempted to murder Theseus but her evil intentions were found out and she and her son had to flee Athens. It is said she returned to her father in Colchis.

The man on duty here pointed out the bema to me. It was to my far left – a rectangular stone platform near the Roman agora – from which St. Paul had addressed the Corinthians.

Could St. Paul have known the story of Medea? Well, why not? There's every reason to suppose he did – he may even have seen a performance of the tragedy. St. Paul, who lived several years in Corinth, was surely not cut off from the people around him? The Jewish Christians must have mingled with the inhabitants in order to preach about Christ's Resurrection? Did they never take time off to relax? Did they not go to the theatre? There was one at Corinth so presumably dramas were put on.

I closed my *Medea* and sat waiting for the others to return. It was pleasantly cool seated there in the shade of the tree, with a gentle breeze fanning my face. I took out my note-book and checked on the back page for anything else I'd noted down that I should be remembering while here at the ancient city of Corinth.

Yes, there was! How could I forget it! It was here that the legendary King Oedipus grew up. For reasons which I will give later, Oedipus, when newly born, was left exposed on a mountainside outside Thebes. But the herdsman who'd been ordered to leave the baby found him still alive after several days, and handed him over to a shepherd who'd come up from Corinth. The Corinthian shepherd had brought the new-born back here to the childless king and queen who'd lovingly brought him up. His story became the subject of many dramas in the fifth century B.C.

A hand on my shoulder brought me out of my reverie. "Well, that's been a worthwhile day's shopping!"

I looked up and saw Fiona in cheerful mood with several parcels poking out of her shoulder-bag. "We've had a great shopping spree. Aren't you going to get anything for Harry and the family?"

"No," I said. "Harry told me not to – a wicked waste of money, is how he sees it."

"It probably is, but I like to get things all the same." Fiona was glowing; we'd all in our different ways had a successful afternoon at Corinth.

"Come on, you two, we'd better get going. We have to find our way out of Corinth and we've a long drive still."

We reached our next hotel at Megara by early evening, passing on the way oil-refineries and a glimpse of Salamis across the narrow straits with its oil tankers, similar to the ones we'd seen from Euripides' cave. It seemed that on this trip we'd come full circle.

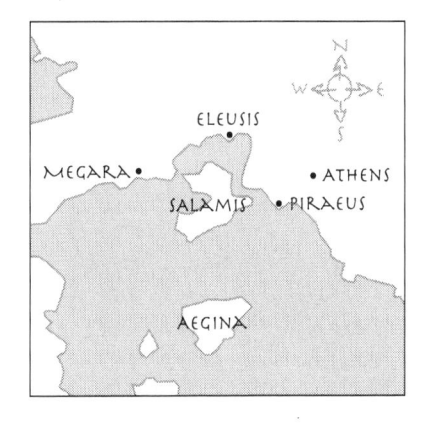

CHAPTER 6

ELEUSIS

We are in the great sanctuary of Demeter, goddess of corn and agriculture, and her daughter Persephone (also known as Kore). It is a sad reality that her sanctuary, once surrounded by fields of standing corn, is now swallowed up by the industrial suburbs of Athens. I am mainly here, however, because Eleusis was home to Aeschylus, first of the three great tragic playwrights.

From where I stand I look across over the flat rooftops of houses and the eyesores of heavy industry, to the sea and the island of Salamis. The Cave of Euripides which we visited would be at the further end of the island.

At the time of Aeschylus, this sanctuary of Demeter at Eleusis was of great importance. According to Homer's *Hymn to Demeter*, it was here that Demeter came searching for Persephone, her lovely young daughter. The story goes that one day Hades, seeing Persephone picking wild flowers in a meadow, snatched and dragged her screaming to his subterranean kingdom in the underworld. Demeter, unaware of what had happened, and anguished by the disappearance of her daughter, searched the world for her. In due course she learned from the Sun that Zeus had given her in marriage to his brother Hades.

Distraught, Demeter came by chance to Eleusis where, disguised as an old crone, she sat beside the ancient Kallichoron well and wept. She was discovered there by the daughters of the then king who, seeing the woman in distress, invited her back to the palace. There she was welcomed by the queen who appointed her nurse to her baby son. Demeter fed the child on ambrosia, the food of the gods, and by night attempted to immortalize him by holding him over the flames in the hearth. One night the queen caught her doing this and was horrified.

At this point Demeter threw off her disguise and showed herself as the great goddess she was. She then told the king about her secret rites which were only to be revealed to those who were initiated into her cult. From then on the Eleusian Mysteries were to be celebrated annually; and so a temple (known as the Telesterion) was built here in her honour close to the Kallichoron well, though on a higher level from it.

While she still mourned the loss of her daughter, however, the great goddess Demeter neglected her agricultural duties so nothing grew and humans starved. Even the gods suffered because men stopped sacrificing to them as there was nothing to sacrifice. Something had to be done because the gods realized that without men to honour them there was no point in being gods. As a consequence Zeus ordered his brother Hades to release Persephone to the upper world. It was finally agreed that Hades could have her for one third of the year (the four winter months) but she must be above ground with her mother for the other eight.

Most Greek sanctuaries were open to all to honour a god or goddess, but Demeter's was an exception. Before anyone could take part, he or she had to be initiated into her Eleusian Mysteries. It was imperative that the candidate was of good character. If those wanting initiation were acceptable – and all men, women and children, as well as slaves were eligible on condition they were of good repute and spoke Greek – then they were initiated at the Lesser Mysteries, a ceremony held in the early spring on the banks of the Ilissos river, east of the Acropolis. Their belief was that there was nothing to fear in death because there was life again, a sort of immortality of the soul – a resurrection of a sort.

The Greater Mysteries were celebrated in the autumn, a festival which lasted nine days. It began here when her 'secret things' were carried in procession to Athens (a distance of some fifteen miles). They were deposited on the Acropolis, and her arrival was announced to the goddess Athena's priestess. On the fifth day these 'secret things' were carried in a spectacular procession and brought back to Eleusis. That is all that need be known for the purpose of this book.

When Aeschylus was born in Eleusis in 525 B.C. there'd already been a temple standing at Eleusis for over a thousand years. By his day Eleusis, because of its strategic position on the route from Athens to the Peloponnese, had changed from being an independent city-state to being a deme, in other words a part of Athens.

ELEUSIS 61

Aeschylus' father had been a wealthy, well-respected citizen of noble family who made sure his son received a good education. As a young man Aeschylus is said to have worked in a vineyard till one day (so legend has it) Dionysos visited him in a dream and ordered him to write tragedies. Obedient to the divine command, Aeschylus wrote his first drama (now lost).

Aeschylus was initiated into the Eleusinian Mysteries so, undoubtedly, took the required oath never to reveal the secret rites on penalty of death. Apparently some indiscretions were noticed in his dramas for which he was prosecuted. However, he pleaded his innocence and was fortunately acquitted. It is thought he might well have been dealt with leniently because of his distinguished military service – all men of a certain age were expected to fight when called upon. He'd fought first at Marathon against the Persians, during which battle his brother had been killed which at the time had had a profound effect on him. Ten years later he was in the Battle of Salamis – both occasions against the Persians.

It was his experience of war that prompted him in 472 B.C. to write *Persians*. It is his earliest surviving tragedy and it won him first prize at the City Dionysia.

Persians is the only play by Aeschylus on a topical subject; the plots of all his other dramas being about legendary stories. Rather surprisingly it is written from the Persian perspective. It begins with a Chorus of Persian elders at the court of Xerxes (son of the deceased Darius and now king of Persia). In the drama the Chorus wonder how the army is faring under this impetuous young king.

Xerxes' mother Atossa joins the elders, and tells them that she has been having recurring and disturbing dreams which fill her with foreboding. She asks them what is so special about Athens that Xerxes wants to subdue its citizens. The elders reply: *They call no man lord or master, buckle under no man's word. (245-246.)* Aeschylus was living when democracy was in its fledgling state, and a golden age of cultural excellence was just dawning.

A Messenger arrives at the palace with news of the calamitous loss of the Persian fleet at Salamis. He describes the *crashing of prows and the bodies of warriors miserably slain which choke her bays... (274-275.)* The Messenger hates to be the deliverer of such disastrous news but says ...*Some power unearthly swayed the balance there... The gods themselves protect Athena's town. (345-347.)*

Certainly there were reports of divine interventions. It was said that during the Battle of Salamis, two men had seen a swirl of dust rising from Eleusis as if made by some thirty thousand men. At the same time they'd heard the cry of multiple voices. One of the men knew it was the sound of the mystical 'Iacchos' (a seldom heard of deity identified with Dionysos, and involved in the Greater Mysteries). He explained to his companion, who was a stranger to the rites, that the unearthly cry must be a form of divine intervention designed to strike terror in the enemy. The historian Herodotus also wrote about the intervention of the gods at Delphi when Xerxes and his army were marching on Apollo's sanctuary, intent on looting the treasures from it. Without anybody lifting a finger, weapons had moved of their own accord and placed themselves before the shrine. Also, as the Persians closed in (according to Herodotus), lightning struck Mt. Parnassus causing two peaks to break away and bear down on the Persians who were crushed or fled.

In Aeschylus' *Persians* the Messenger gives his eye-witness account (no doubt Aeschylus' own) of the Battle of Salamis: ... *The Persian fleet, in a perpetual stream, at first appeared invincible; but when their numbers in the narrows packed and hemmed grew dense, they cracked their oarage in the crowd, and smote each other with their beaks of brass, and none might help his fellow. Aware of this, the Grecian shipmasters with cunning skill jostled us round and round, – till hulls capsized, and all the sea was hidden from our sight with wrecks and human carnage covered o'er... (411-420.)*

The palace Elders and Atossa resort to prayer. Atossa pours libations and prays to her deceased husband, and the ghost of Darius appears asking what problems have arisen that he has been summoned: ...*What grief afflicts the state? Why groans the plain with shuddering tramp of crowds in agony?... (680-681.)*

When he hears of his son's determination to add ever more wealth and territory to exceed what even Darius himself had achieved, and the calamitous loss of the Persian fleet at Salamis, he despairs: ... *mad the boldness of his thought! (725-726.)* He warns that the gods will take their vengeance for the sacrilege of plundering the shrines: ... *altars laid in dust, statues uprooted from their pedestals, all things divine o'erturned, attest their guilt... (811-813.)* And he voices what are surely the views of Aeschylus himself: ... *Three generations hence those heaps of slain voiceless shall blazon to posterity loud warnings against human pride. That flower soon falls, and yields calamity for fruit, unlooked-for harvest of dire misery. Mark well the wages of their sin, and bear Hellas and Athens ever in mind. Let none, raising his heart above the things he hath in passionate love for plans unrealized, make shipwreck of great fortune. Zeus brings on his inquisition at the destined hour... (819-829.)*

Darius' last words to Atossa before he vanishes back down to Hades, are that when Xerxes returns after his devastating losses she should *...Soothe him to mildness with consoling words... (837.)* And to the Persian elders: *...Agèd friends, though in affliction, give your hearts to joy, and cheer your souls with comforts day by day, since wealth avails not to the world of death. (839-842.)*

The play ends with the hapless Xerxes arriving to face up to the consequences of his greed that has brought nothing but death and loss. He has to endure the expressions of blank dismay from the Persian elders and of his disconsolate mother. Such humiliation! He cries: ... *Woe is me! How shall I face my destiny? When I behold yon reverend train, strength fails my limbs...(910-913.)* And the Chorus are no comfort whatever, responding: *...Our country groans for the young life she reared in vain...Alas the heavy hour!... (920-921,928.)*

When the play was first performed in 472 B.C. at the City Dionysia, it would surely have been received with prolonged cheers, since the audience would have consisted of representatives from the colonies and islands who'd been overrun by the Persians. Had Persia been victorious over Athens she would undoubtedly have become more greedy till all of Europe had been conquered, and the course of European history would have been altogether different.

From where I am standing I have Demeter's Kallichoron well on a lower slope before me; it is called Kallichoron because it is around that well that Demeter's initiates danced – *kállos* meaning 'beautiful', and *chorós* 'dance'. If I turn my back on it, Demeter's sacred building, the Telesterion, is on a higher level to my right, and to my left is the dark mouth of the cave known as the Ploutonion; it was from there that Persephone returned annually from Hades. Peisistratus, who founded the drama festival in Athens, built a sanctuary here in honour of Hades who was otherwise known as Pluto, hence Ploutonion – Pluto meaning 'rich one'. The last extant comedy of Aristophanes was entitled *Plutus*.

In mythology Plutus was a god and son of Demeter by a certain Iasion, and the name Plutus was symbolic of abundant wealth and good harvests. In Aristophanes' comedy, the personified Plutus has become blind and mistakenly bestows his wealth on crooks and criminals, not on those who deserve it. It is arranged for Plutus to have his sight restored by Asclepius, god of healing, so that he can again distribute his money to the most deserving. Poverty (personified) appears as an old crone. She is greatly disliked by everyone, but is well able to stand up for herself. Without her, she says, who on earth would want to plough or gather in the harvest of Demeter. The unfairness of life is held up in a light-hearted manner, leaving the audience or reader aware of Aristophanes' many truths spoken in jest.

Aristophanes, ever ready with his perceptive eye and lively mind, also saw a farcical plot in one of the goddess Demeter's festivals, the Thesmophoria. In it women only took part; it was an annual three-day event and took place at the time of the winter sowing in autumn towards the end of October. Its purpose was to promote fertility, both agricultural and human.

Such a festival was just up the comic playwright's street and in 411 B.C. he threw himself with gusto into writing *Women at the Thesmophoria*. I place it here now because it is concerned with the honouring of Demeter, and there's nothing like a little comedy to lighten the seriousness of Demeter's secret rites and festival.

Much of the dialogue is of a wildly explicit sexual bawdiness – crude and uninhibited and boisterous. As ever, Aristophanes can't resist poking fun at Euripides. The comedy begins with Euripides who has heard that women plan his death because they don't like the way he portrays them in his tragedies – Phaedra in his *Hippolytus*, for example, and the deranged Medea in the play by that name, and others.

With a great deal of slapstick and coarse vulgarity, Euripides persuades Mnesilochus, his elderly father-in-law, to dress as a woman and merge with them at their festival to find out what exactly they are plotting against him. Mnesilochus becomes a Widow Twanky pantomime figure, and only consents after Euripides has sworn to come to his assistance if things get out of hand.

The action takes place on the Pnyx in Athens where the assemblies were held. A woman named Mica takes to the rostrum and voices her grievances against Euripides: how they have all been besmirched by the playwright, this son of a 'cabbage seller'. Mica objects strongly that at every opportunity Euripides has made women out to be deceitful and the greatest curse to men, so naturally ...*men all come home after the play and give us that nasty suspicious look, and start hunting in all the cupboards for concealed lovers... (399-401.)* Men, Mica complains, regard everything women do with the deepest suspicion as though they are secretly planning to escape to their lovers. It is why men make sure their rooms are secured with locks and bolts and guard dogs. The Chorus respond to Mica's address with hearty approval.

A wreath-seller is next on the rostrum with the complaint that Euripides keeps hinting that the gods don't exist and, therefore, her sales have halved.

With courage, Euripides' disguised relative takes to the rostrum next and addresses the women. He/she can see that Euripides has upset them all, but as women they should be honest with themselves, and he/she points out that Euripides could treat them far worse; he's only homed in on a few of their crimes, but they all know there are many more secret misdemeanours they've been guilty of.

Up springs Mica, the first speaker. How can anyone try to defend Euripides when he does nothing but drag the reputation of women in the dust! He has never, for example, written about the good and loyal Penelope, wife of Odysseus, who for twenty years waited patiently for his return.

The banter is interrupted by Cleisthenes (an informer) who comes to warn the women that a relative of Euripides is there amongst them in disguise. The comedy gathers pace as Mnesilochus is discovered (or rather uncovered) and found to be male. They stand guard over him, and in desperation he snatches a baby from its mother and threatens to sacrifice it to the gods if he's not set free. He proceeds to undress the infant only to discover it's a full wineskin. He punctures it and the women rush to catch the wine in a bowl – such nectar must not go to waste!

The women eventually sing their own praises; compared to men women are blameless, they claim. Look at the political scoundrels, look at the men who are robbers, muggers, pullers of strings and other such disgraceful conduct. Whereas women just sit at home with their looms, and baskets of wool.

Mnesilochus is in a state of desperation. Why hasn't Euripides rescued him as he vowed he would? He sees Euripides approaching and suddenly decides to entertain the women by playing the part of Helen in Euripides' brand new drama by that name (see Chapter 11). In it Helen is not in Troy, as maintained by Homer, but has spent the ten years of the Trojan War in Egypt. Mnesilochus (acting Helen) strikes an alluring pose. Seeing his father-in-law acting Helen, Euripides is quick to take his cue by entering disguised as her cuckolded husband come to take her home.

At this point in Aristophanes' comedy a Magistrate, together with a Scythian policeman enter to arrest Mnesilochus for impersonating a female and intruding on a private festival. And Aristophanes' farce continues till, to confuse matters further, Echo enters. Echo has an unfortunate affliction brought about by Hera in a fit of rage because Zeus had seduced her: she is unable to speak complete sentences but can only repeat the last few words of what another person has said. Aristophanes makes the most of this unfortunate short-coming, and the comedy ends in a riot of nonsense with the Scythian policeman falling asleep, and Euripides leaving only to return disguised as a procuress with a beautiful dancing-girl. When the Policeman wakes, he is entranced by the girl and goes after her. Euripides calls a truce with the women, promising never to write a bad word about them in the future. He and his long-suffering relative escape before the Policeman returns to find his prisoner gone. The women point them out and he races after them, but in the wrong direction.

I join the others at Demeter's ancient Telesterion. The building is said to be unlike any other. It once had a roof with a hole in it, or a sort of chimney, from which during the Greater Mysteries a holy fire would erupt. Plans for it had been drawn up by Ictinus, the architect responsible for the Parthenon no less. Very little is known about what actually happened here since the initiates were sworn to secrecy; what has been gleaned has come from inscriptions, archaeological discoveries, and literary sources. It is known that on one of the days there had been a sacred pageant which told the story of the abduction of Persephone, the search for her by Demeter, and the final joy of their reunion. The pageant was held at night. During the course of its enactment, the darkness was pierced by bright flashing illuminations with shadowed tableaux, while the high priest intoned the story of Persephone's descent to the dark and fearful halls of Hades.

From where we stand, the mouth of the cave of Hades is visible. "When the return of Persephone was proclaimed," I tell the others, "they sounded an enormous gong, while fire erupted from the hole in the roof, and Demeter's most secret things were revealed by the high priest."

"And what were they, these 'secret things'?" Fiona asks.

"Ah. That is what remains secret," I say mysteriously. "I can only tell you that one of the early Christian Fathers said they were so lewd he blushed even to think of them."

While we walk back to our car, I tell them how at the beginning of the nineteenth century an English professor E.D. Clarke thought he'd discovered the cult statue of Demeter here at Eleusis. It was seen protruding from a dung heap beside the Lesser Propylaea (entrance gates). Interestingly, by that time the locals were addressing her as Agia Demetria (Saint Demetria). "They invoked her in her new Christian role to send them plentiful harvests," I tell them. "Don't you think that fascinating? Clarke managed to persuade the authorities to get the great statue back to England where it's now on show in the Fitzwilliam Museum, Cambridge. I've actually seen it there."

"Saint Demetria, how curious!" Hilary remarks.

"But – and this is a big BUT – what Clarke thought was the cult statue was later identified by archaeologists as one of several caryatid figures in the Lesser Propylae. So the Christians were endowing an unimportant statue with sainthood. And even more curious," I add, "Eleusis, as you see it now, is something of an eyesore, while all around Cambridge are fields of standing corn. Don't you think that interesting?"

"So much that's unexplainable!" Hilary agrees.

As we drive away I say a silent farewell to Eleusis, home to the great goddess Demeter and her daughter Persephone – not forgetting that it was home also to the great tragedian Aeschylus.

★

Later that evening we relaxed with our wine seated on our hotel terrace. The sea was an inky blue and, as the warm evening became cooler and it grew dark, we could make out the landmass of the Peloponnese with its cluster of twinkling lights. We reckoned we must be looking south of Corinth, perhaps to the port of Palea Epidaurus. Due south from us was another galaxy of lights scattered along the coast on the looming mass of Salamis, and further south still was the dark outline of Aegina. Two islands with links to the early dramatists – the one to Euripides and his tragedies, and the other to Aristophanes and his comedies. The one who could never resist poking fun at the other. What was the reason? Well, I supposed that for somebody who could only see the funny side of things, it was a great temptation to fire humorous barbs at the continuous outflow of woes from the other. In all events, Aristophanes chose laughter rather than tears, and tomorrow we planned to spend the day (our last on this trip) on Aegina.

CHAPTER 7

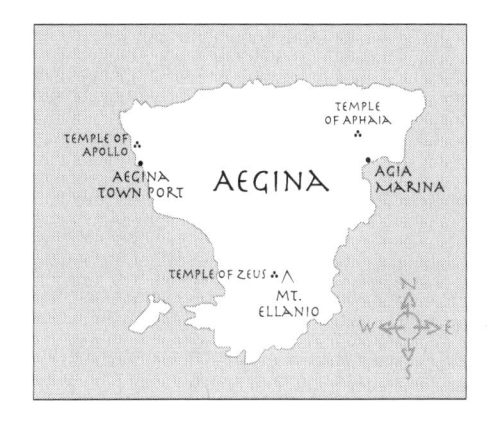

AEGINA

We are on our way to Aegina on a Flying Dolphin which skims the waves rather than ploughs through them. The mid-morning sun is glinting and the sea sparkles, and the sky is a cloudless blue. The port of Piraeus rapidly recedes and we can see the long coastline stretching out to the east to Sounion with its great temple of Poseidon. We are travelling the seaways as Aristophanes would have done from mainland Greece to the nearby island of Aegina where his teenage years were spent.

I am glad to get away from Piraeus where we'd had to wait half an hour before departure. Seated in the waiting area, a woman on a bench in front of us had turned her weather-beaten face around and mimed sleep by placing both hands under her head and closing her eyes, and food by putting her hand to her mouth before holding it out towards us. Hilary and Fiona had said to ignore her, but I'd felt, since I was being wildly extravagant taking taxis and staying comfortably in a hotel, it was my duty to give her all my spare cash – and oh, how uncharitable that was! She'd snatched the money and continued miming, her eyes fixed in vain on the other two.

A young woman in a headscarf with a toddler in a pushchair had then stopped and held out her hand with pleading eyes saying such words as 'no food – baby'. Having given away my small change, I didn't want to offload what I knew was needed for taxis, and shook my head.

Hilary murmured: "There's somebody asleep behind our seat." I glanced back at a stretched out bundle of rags on the ground, then forwards where the girl was standing with her hand out. "Baby – no food – " The weather-beaten woman was also still miming sleep and food, while I noticed a man in ill-fitting trousers scavenging in a litter-bin –

The Flying Dolphin arrived, and we were able to leave the area where destitutes begged, to travel amongst those who did not. How blind Plutus had been there in Piraeus! Had it always been so, prompting Aristophanes to write his play?

Aristophanes knew very well the tragedies caused by war and the consequences brought about by corrupt politicians. He was born 448 B.C. and, at the start of the Peloponnesian War in 438 B.C., although Aegina was an ally of Athens, there'd been signs that she secretly supported Sparta, so Athens had expelled all the island's inhabitants and replaced them with Athenian citizens. Amongst those who'd been given estates was Aristophanes' father which was why Aristophanes had passed his teenage years on the island.

★

We are coming in to the town Aegina, the main port of the island. Our Flying Dolphin draws alongside the quay, ropes are thrown out to secure its mooring, the gangplank lowered, and we disembark for our day's outing to the island. There are certain landmarks here I've come to see – landmarks Aristophanes would have known which would have stamped themselves on his adolescent mind.

We begin to walk. I've already briefed the others on the main reasons for this visit. The road runs parallel with the sea, and horse-drawn carriages wait hopefully to take tourists on a trip around Aegina town. I lead the way along the sea-front towards what was once the original old port where blocks of submerged stones, and the remains of semi-submerged piers are still to be seen.

The road leaves the picturesque port of pastel coloured houses dominated by its large church with its backcloth of mountains, and follows the contours of a low hill to where a single tall Doric column rises up against the skyline. As we draw near, we see it is enclosed within a high wire-mesh fence. The single column stands proudly; it is all that remains of what must at one time have been a magnificent temple of Apollo. Somewhere near here, but further inland, was also a small temple of Dionysos together with a large ancient theatre, both long since destroyed by earthquake.

According to myth, the name of Aegina for the island came from a river-nymph named Aegina whom Zeus brought to the island and seduced. She gave birth to a son named Aeacus, and it was he who in his turn became the father of two sons: Telamon (father of Ajax) later to become king of Salamis, and Peleus (father of Achilles) who became king of the Myrmidons in Thessaly.

Where the gods were concerned, Aristophanes accepted traditional beliefs, though in his comedies he treated them with friendly humour. No doubt, here on Aegina religious festivals would have been observed and taken seriously as communal events.

We return from the temple of Apollo to a taxi-rank near the port; we can't come to Aegina without visiting the great temple of Aphaia some thirteen kilometres away. I sit in front beside the driver ready for Greek conversation, but soon discover from the driver's curt, staccato replies that he's in a foul mood. He gets on his mobile and shouts orders to some unfortunate and, as soon as one call ends, he begins another; his voice is loud and domineering. The words *grígora* (fast) and *graphéio* (office) are repeated over and over again, till eventually just to annoy, I say: '*Oxi tosso grígora, parakaló*' (not so fast, please) – he is accelerating downhill towards a warning sign showing a sharp bend. Instead, he goes more *grígora*. He wants to annoy me also.

The road is taking us through the centre of the island and we are now surrounded by high hills and mountains; occasionally I glimpse sparkling blue sea between two mountain slopes. While his voice continues to rasp angrily into his mobile, the road gradually climbs and, after about twenty minutes, we at last arrive at the temple of Aphaia standing alone and supreme on a high elevation.

Before we'd set out, I'd said to our driver we would like him to wait ten minutes while we take a quick look at the temple, and then bring us back; but by now I've taken such a dislike to him, and the location is so awe-inspiring, it would be criminal to rush away.

I put my head through the passenger window and tell him to go. I can't resist adding that it wouldn't hurt him to smile a little – nothing like a smile, I say. He looks startled but says nothing.

So here I am at last, wandering about this great temple of Aphaia. The others are exploring the site together and leaving me alone, which they know is how I like it. There are various legends regarding the goddess Aphaia, but the one I prefer is as follows: Aphaia was a Cretan goddess known as Britomartis. Her father was Zeus (of course!) and she liked hunting which endeared her to the goddess Artemis. King Minos of Crete became enamoured of her and, in order to escape his advances, she dived into the sea where she became entangled in fishermen's nets and was rescued by Artemis who brought her to

Aegina. King Minos pursued her but Artemis hid her in a sacred grove on the island – possibly where I am now within this temple precinct. Then, because she was nowhere to be seen, this temple was built in her honour by the people of Aegina who worshipped her as Aphaia ('aphaia' meaning 'invisible').

This present temple is amazing! It stands with its many Doric columns supporting the architrave and pediments rising up against the vivid blue sky. It was built in the early fifth century B.C. replacing an earlier temple built over a century before which had been destroyed by fire. From here I have a three hundred and sixty degree panoramic view around the entire island. To the east, down a gentle slope by the sea, is the resort of Agia Marina which nestles in a bay with many small colourful boats moored up; to the south rises the tall and highest mountain on which is perched a temple of Zeus. At the time of Aristophanes, the temple would, no doubt, have been a landmark to which the inhabitants would have climbed for festive occasions. It is said that the first temple had been built by Aeacus. When the Delphic oracle was questioned as to how to bring an end to a prolonged drought on the island, Aeacus was advised to pray to his father Zeus for rain. When rain was granted, Aeacus built the temple on the highest mountain peak on the island in gratitude to his father.

I sit and make notes while the occasional visitor walks by. A young woman in a baseball cap, who has just blown a whistle and waved an arm at a young man who has jumped onto a ruined wall, approaches. Seeing me sitting with my notebook, she stops. I ask her if the tall mountain I see is the mountain where Aeacus built the temple of Zeus. She confirms that it is, then points to the Greek mainland on the horizon, and says: "You see the houses there? That is Athens. On that higher rise above the houses, that is the Acropolis. You can see the Parthenon."

"What? You can see the Parthenon from here?"

She is delighted she has surprised me. I feel sure there has to be something significant in it. This present temple of Aphaia here, she tells me, is also known as the temple of Athena Aphaia creating a link between the two. Although I cannot see it from here, the temple of Poseidon on the headland at Sounion, together with the Parthenon and this temple, make an equilateral triangle. Without any warning the woman gives another shrill blast on her whistle. "You must excuse me," she says, and goes to have a word with another culprit breaking regulations.

I begin to wander. The light all around is clear, and there is a magnetism about the whole site. Aristophanes would have come here to pay his respects to Athena Aphaia. The tranquillity of the island must have influenced him compared to life in Athens with its orators, law-suits, war-mongering politicians, and things that made life unbearably uncertain. Why did politicians bring about war? He knew how people could enjoy the finer things of life peacefully, but oh, the folly of mankind! Or oh, the folly of the gods who let men have their heads (or maybe lose them) to fight wars and kill one another!

Over the course of his lifetime (he died 385 B.C.) Aristophanes saw Athens blossom in what became known as the Age of Pericles, when the Parthenon was built in all its glory on the Acropolis, and the city grew rich and ever more powerful. When, however, her allies realized Athens was, in fact, enriching herself at their expense by imposing tribute money, they rebelled and allied themselves to Sparta – hence the Peloponnesian War. How right Aeschylus was to warn against excess and greed in his drama *Persians*. The Peloponnesian War brought with it devastation and food shortages. It was starvation that eventually forced Athens to surrender to Sparta in 404 B.C.

But Aristophanes, instead of being inspired to write tragedies like his near contemporaries Euripides and Sophocles, threw himself into comedy, preferring by boisterous clowning, to highlight the reasons for the wrongs, and make the tragedy of reality appear ridiculous. It was his light-hearted way of drawing attention to the follies of mankind that appealed to his audiences.

The plague which followed the first year of the Peloponnesian War claimed Pericles as a victim, after which the bullying demagogue Cleon came to power, a politician Aristophanes loathed and lampooned to such a degree that in 426 B.C. he was prosecuted for libel though, apparently, nothing came of it. In fact, the experience only added fuel to Aristophanes' fire-power and he wrote two comedies which were highly inflammatory: *Knights* which won first prize at the Lenaia in 424 B.C., and *Wasps* which came second in 422 B.C. – both these comedies held Cleon up to ridicule.

The main characters in *Wasps* are a father named Procleon, and his son Anticleon. Times are hard after nearly a decade of war with Sparta, and Procleon (the old father) scrapes a living by earning three obols a day by rising at dawn and doing jury service. This gives him a feeling of importance. His son, however, sees it as a mania and thinks Procleon is being duped earning a measly three obols while the politicians are lining their pockets with bribes, taxes and suchlike.

The play begins as a farce: Anticleon has thrown a net over the house in an attempt to stop his father escaping for his dawn attendance at the law courts. But Procleon is not to be beaten, and is seen trying to escape through a window; then his head appears from the chimney; next from a hole he makes in the roof by removing some tiles; he tries to gnaw through the netting, but on each attempt he is frustrated.

Procleon pleads his case and lists the advantages of doing jury service – he is desperate not to be late: *...Can you think of any living creature that is happier, more fortunate, more pampered, or more feared than a juror? No sooner have I crawled out of bed in the morning than I find great hulking fellows waiting for me at the bar of the court... (550-553.)* And he tells his son how they all try to plead their innocence and ask if he hasn't broken the law himself sometimes. At any rate, it makes him feel important and gives him a purpose in life: *Then, after they've all crawled to me and tried to soften me up, I go behind the bar and take my seat, and forget all about any promises I may have made. I just listen to what they say – and there's nothing they won't say to flatter the jury in their efforts to get acquitted. Some of them bewail their poverty and pile on the agony... And if he can't win me over that way, he drags his children out in front – all his little girls and boys: and I just sit and listen while they all grovel in a heap, bleating, and their father stands over them and pleads with me to ratify his accounts, for all the world as if I were a god... (564-575.)*

Anticleon, however, forces his father to look at reality: *...reckon up, roughly – on your fingers will do – how much tribute we get altogether from the subject cities. Add to that the revenue from taxes, percentages, deposits, the mines, market and harbour dues, rents, and confiscations. Add these up and we get a total of nearly twelve million drachmas a year. Well, now work out how much of this annual sum goes to the jurors... (654-660.)* Anticleon says he's only trying to take care of his dear father by pointing out the facts.

After thinking about it for a while Procleon sees how he's been conned all this time and lets out a wail of misery. He tries to kill himself with a sword, crying: *Speed, speed, my soul!* But the sword gets tangled in his beard.

The farce continues with the son attempting to curb his father's passion for jury service by ridiculing it. He sets up a court in their own house where Procleon's dog accuses Labes (Anticleon's dog) of stealing a Sicilian cheese.

The First Dog takes his place on the prosecutor's stand and says: *Gentlemen of the jury, you have heard the terms of the indictment filed by me against the defendant. He has committed the most atrocious offences, not only against me, but against every single rating in the fleet – to wit and namely: ran away into a corner and sicillated a large quantity of cheese and stuffed himself with it in the dark. (922-928.)* The case seems to be proved against Labes, but he takes the stand to defend himself and Anticleon speaks up in his defence, telling the jurors that he is really a very good dog: *...the finest dog alive. Capable of guarding any number of sheep... guards the house. And he's a noble dog in every way. (964-968.)* He *...slaves away untiringly, eating up the gristle, devouring the fishbones, always on active service... (981-982.)*

Procleon begins to feel sympathy for poor Labes, and his son calls for Labes' puppies to be brought in to court. A slave brings them in and they huddle around the feet of Anticleon whimpering miserably until everyone is reduced to tears. It is time for the jurors to cast their votes to pronounce him guilty or not guilty – this was done by putting a pebble into one or other of two urns – and Anticleon manages to steer his father to the urn that acquits Labes. When he realizes that he's let Labes go free he passes out in a dead faint. His son brings him round by splashing cold water in his face, and tries to cheer him up by telling him that from now on he'll take him out to *...dinners and drinking parties and shows, and you'll be able to have a really good time... (1010-1011.)* And Procleon finds himself obeying his son who leads him back indoors.

The Chorus are all dressed up as wasps with stings protruding from their backsides, and the Leader now addresses the audience directly speaking on behalf of Aristophanes.

It should just be said here that at the production of Aristophanes' earlier second comedy *Babylonians* (now lost) which he presented under another name, he'd compared the allies of Athens to Babylonian slaves who were completely under her power, while she (Athens) was growing exceedingly rich at their expense. The demagogue Cleon had been enraged by this, especially as *Babylonians* was staged at the Great Dionysia where representatives from those so-called enslaved islands and colonies would have been attending this popular spring festival. The last thing Cleon wanted was to be ridiculed in front of such visitors. When it was discovered that the real identity of the playwright was Aristophanes, he'd been promptly prosecuted and fined. He was, in fact, lucky to get away with his life and not executed.

Aristophanes, however, was not to be reined in, and he continued annually to attack Cleon. So now in his comedy *Wasps*, addressing the audience directly, the Leader of the Chorus says: *Now once again, spectators, if you love to hear plain speaking, pay attention, please! The author has a bone to pick with you for treating him unfairly, when, he says, you've had so many splendid things from him. Not always openly – in earlier days full many a joke of his came from the lips of other poets, while he lurked unseen* (because his first comedies were under another's name) *and spoke through them, with ventriloquial art… he made assault on all those plagues and fevers, nightmare shapes that came and hovered by your beds at night, smothering fathers, choking grandfathers and passing lawsuits, summonses, and writs on harmless, peaceful folk, till many leapt in terror from their beds… So once again your Champion fought for you and sought to purge the land of grievous ills… (1009-1019, 1044-1053.)*

Back to the comedy. Procleon is still not cured of his passion for jury service and once again dons the brown cloak of a juror. By now he is very much under his son's control who attempts to teach his 'dear old' father how to converse when in the company of polite society; in other words how to outsmart anything said by high flyers such as Cleon and his fellow bigwigs. He must speak of such subjects as boar hunting or torch racing and other similar pursuits. Satisfied that his father won't let him down, he takes him out to a party as promised, on condition he gives up jury service.

Unfortunately Procleon gets uproariously drunk and abducts the Flute-girl at the party, and staggers home wearing a garland with the Flute-girl on his arm. Angry Citizens, whom he's abused and assaulted, follow him, but he keeps them at bay with a flaming torch. Because of his wild, drunken behaviour they intend to prosecute. He, however, after his son's training, knows how to outwit the cleverest of them with repartee. When a Citizen declares he is going to bring an action against him for assault, Procleon is able to tell a way-off-the-point story which leaves the Citizen baffled. Procleon points out that, if he's suffering pain from the assault, why come to him about it since he's not a doctor; much better get himself to the hospital. After much drunken nonsense, the Citizen and his friends depart, and Anticleon throws his father over his shoulder and carries him indoors.

The comedy ends with Procleon flinging open the doors of his house dressed ludicrously in dancing tights. In his inebriated state he is a total embarassment to his son, as he cries out: *What ho!… Fling wide the portals, ho!… let the dance begin! Tensed up to spring the dancer stands, with ribs stretched taut like metal bands... with nostrils flared he snorts amain, his backbone creaks beneath the strain; look out, he's going to leap again... With soaring leg I touch the sky! Can modern dancers kick so high?... And as the dancer leaps and whirls each joint within its socket twirls... (1482, 1484-1488, 1490, 1492, 1496-1501.)*

And on this note of high comedy and carefree exuberance, this political farce closes.

Maybe it was just as well for Aristophanes that Cleon died the following year. He was killed at Amphipolis trying to regain the island of Thassos for Athens from Sparta.

After the death of his most hated political figure, Aristophanes began writing anti-war comedies. He produced his extraordinarily imaginative *Peace* at the Great Dionysia in 421 B.C. where it won second prize, and *Birds* in 414 B.C. which also won second prize. His *Lysistrata*, about women who decide to go on a sex-strike till men stop fighting, came later still in 411 B.C.

I meet the woman with her whistle again and ask her about the sculptures on this temple. She tells me that the pediments portray the battles fought in the two Trojan wars, but that they are now in the Glyptothek Museum in Munich.

Two Trojan wars? I thought there was only one, and I tell her so. No, she replies, there was an earlier war before the famous Trojan one. The first was led by Heracles against King Laomedon of Troy (the grandfather of Paris who ran off with Helen). And, seeing that I'm interested, she tells me that the eastern pediment of this temple featured at its centre the goddess Athena, and showed Telamon (Ajax's father) doing battle against King Laomedon. The Western pediment also had Athena at its centre, but had Telamon's son Ajax with shield and spear amongst fallen Trojan warriors.

I catch sight of Hilary and Fiona on the far side of the temple waving and signalling that they are about to go down to the tourist shop and café. I wave back and make my excuses to this informative young woman, but not before I tell her that I write books, and that the last one was about my travels with Harry to Troy and the palaces of the kings who fought alongside King Agamemnon. She makes a note of the title, and we part company.

I tear myself away from this architectural gem, this sparkling solitaire, built in harmony with the landsacape, and join the others. We descend to the tourist shop behind which is a terrace with chunky stone slabs on chunky stone pedestals which act as tables. From here there is a panoramic view over a forest of emerald green trees descending to a brilliantly gleaming bay. The sky is the colour of a forget-me-not, and swallows swoop and skim the trees below us.

We relax with glasses of freshly squeezed orange juice and toasted cheese sandwiches.

"So what is this about?" Hilary asks, picking up my copy of comedies by Aristophanes which I've put face down on the table. "*Birds*," she reads. "One of his crazy fantasies?"

I drink some of my orange juice through a straw, then say: "He was fed up with endless war, and has two characters who decide they want to join the birds and build a city in the sky away from men."

"Crazy idea!"

"They call their new city Cloudcuckooland," I add.

"Is that where we get Cloudcuckooland from!" Fiona comments.

"Yes, as a matter of fact."

"How amazing. I never knew that!" Hilary's astonishment is genuine. Then she says: "So what happens with their city in the sky? How do they set about it?"

As we eat our toasted cheese sandwiches, I glance at my copy of *Birds* with its highlighted passages and numerous scribbled notes, and briefly tell them the storyline. Two middle-aged disgruntled Athenians decide they want to escape from the world of men, and so they get a Crow and a Jackdaw to lead them to Tereus; he is a former king of Thrace who, due to his wicked rape of his sister-in-law, the gods turned into a hoopoe. Peisetairus, one of the Athenians, feels sure Tereus, with his experience first of being human, and now of being a bird, can give him worthwhile advice about building his new bird city. They meet and are told by Tereus that being a hoopoe is actually quite nice as there's no need of a purse: *We feed pretty well too in the gardens: sesame, myrtle berries, poppy seeds, mint… (193-194.)*

So how, asks Peisetairus, can he and his companion build their new city? Tereus says it shouldn't be difficult; since becoming a hoopoe he has taught his fellow birds human language. A Chorus of birds, each one dressed up as a different species with the appropriate colourful feathers, arrive wanting to know why they have been summoned. They are told that they must all set to work to help build a walled city between earth and heaven. Such a city will keep them safe from humans who try to kill and eat them. To have a bird city between earth and heaven will also give the birds an advantage over the gods, as they will be able to block all sacrificial savoury smells from passing them and reaching heaven. From this position of power they will be able to get the gods to do what they want. Equally, they can forbid the passage of the gods when they want to descend to earth; and they can padlock Zeus' whatnot when he is feeling lecherous and lusting after some poor mortal beauty.

Peisetairus sees that there are great advantages in a pair of wings because whenever you get bored by something, or are in a great hurry, you simply take to the air and fly away. And look at how men depend on birds for agriculture: they take their cue from the birds for their farm work as the seasons change. For instance, they know it is time for sowing when they hear the ...*cry of the crane as it flies back to Libya*... *(413)*; or for shearing when the kite is seen, and so on.

By this time Peisetairus and his companion are fitted with wings. The Chorus sings of more advantages in the bird kingdom (Cloudcuckooland). Men, in their anxiety to have good crops, have to thank the birds who kill and eat caterpillars and bugs who are hiding in the leaves of plants, and destroy the harvests.

A Messenger arrives with the good news that the city wall has been built. ... *Thirty thousand cranes flew in from Libya with foundation stones in their crops. The corncrakes shaped the stones with their beaks. Ten thousand storks carried the bricks, and the water was brought up by the plovers and other river birds. (1135-1138.)*

A second Messenger rushes in to say that disaster has struck: one of the gods has flown in. A squadron of thirty thousand archer hawks are despatched immediately to detain the intruder, not to mention the army ...*kestrels, buzzards, eagles, owls, and vultures. Listen, you can hear the whirring of their wings, filling the air with thunder – he must be somewhere quite near. (1180-1184.)*

Iris, goddess of the rainbow, now appears suspended above on a *mechane*; she is dressed in the colours of a rainbow. Peisetairus shouts up to her, and asks what she's doing trespassing on this new city of the birds. He expresses his anger. Has she had her passport stamped? Has she escaped the guards? Death to her! She points out she's immortal.

Several men arrive who want to join them in their city, such as those who really are not wanted down on earth: one who wants to murder his father, another an informer, and a composer of dithyrambs with the ambition to soar on wings of song. Without hesitation they are sent packing.

Next comes Prometheus, the Titan who was chained to a rock in the far beyond by Zeus for being a friend of Man and stealing fire from the gods to help poor mortals. He arrives muffled up and hiding under an umbrella because he doesn't want to be seen by Zeus helping Peisetairus (a man). He is there to let Peisetairus know that the gods are now suffering deprivation because they no longer receive sacrifice from earth, since Cloudcuckooland blocks the passage of the sacrificial savoury smells that used to waft up to them. Zeus, Prometheus says, is prepared to negotiate a peace treaty to get these sustaining aromas back again; his advice is that Peisetairus orders Zeus to hand over the sceptre to him together with a certain Princess.

Prometheus explains that the Princess is in charge of Zeus' thunderbolts and many other things in heaven, and it will certainly be to Peisetairus' advantage to demand that she should become his bride.

Having delivered his message, Prometheus muffles up again, and slinks away hiding under his umbrella hoping to escape detection.

The play ends with a Heavenly Herald calling all to welcome the new king of the birds and his bride: *O feathered race of birds, O lordly ones! Thrice blest are ye this day: tongue cannot name, mind cannot conceive the grandeur and the bliss that now are yours. Receive your king, and bid him welcome in his happy realm. No golden gleaming star, no piercing ray of the sun ever shone with such splendour as he who now approaches; at his side a wife of unmatchable beauty; in his hand the winged thunder of Zeus… Behold, he comes! Now raise your voices in songs of good omen, and let the Muse be heard. (1708-1717.)*

Peisetairus, with the Princess on his arm, arrives holding a clutch of thunderbolts in one hand. And so the comedy ends with the Chorus singing their wedding-song amidst great celebrations. Bride and groom are escorted by a crowd of birds and dance away together up into the sky.

"Like those swallows there!" Fiona says. "I've been watching them, they never pause but are endlessly skimming the trees in figures of eight."

"They are the Procnes of mythology," I say.

"The Procnes, who are they, for goodness sake?"

"Procne in the singular," I correct, "the wife of Tereus (the hoopoe) who raped her sister. The gods changed Procne into a swallow, and her beautiful sister into a nightingale – though some say it was the other way about."

"What other humans were turned into birds, I wonder?" Hilary looks thoughtful.

"Don't ask, or we'll be here all day," Fiona says.

"I'll tell you about where we get 'halcyon days' from, if you like," I say.

"All right. Let's hear it." Fiona puts on her bogus look of deep interest.

"It comes from the name of Alcyone, daughter of Aeolus, king of the island of Aeolia, and controller of the winds. She was so happy with her husband that they believed their love to be the greatest passion ever. But one day he drowned, and poor Alcyone was devastated when she found his body. The gods took pity and turned both her and her husband into kingfishers – not our river kingfishers, but a certain species that nests every winter by the sea. Aeolus (Alcyone's father) helped by making sure that every winter there was calm weather for their nesting period – hence 'halcyon days'."

"So that's where it comes from! That's quite interesting too!" Fiona says somewhat grudgingly.

There's no time for more bird stories because a taxi that Hilary has ordered arrives, and we have to say our farewells to this magnificent spot with its impressive temple. I sit in front by the driver and am relieved to find he is as friendly as the other one was surly. I soon learn that his name is Nikos, he is married and has two small boys; Yes, that tall mountain is where the temple of Zeus is. He points out old monasteries in the hills, and the very old church in the town of Aegina. I learn that the eldest of his two boys is called Georgios after his grandfather which is the custom in Greece, and that his parents come from Crete.

We are put down beyond the column of the temple of Apollo because Hilary and Fiona want to swim. A short walk is all it takes to reach a sandy beach and the sea. I sit and watch the others splashing about, and a few sailing boats tacking silently offshore; a ferry-boat is heading back to Piraeus.

I ponder over Aristophanes' life. His father was well-to-do, and rather strait-laced; he brought up his son to respect his elders, accept conventional beliefs and traditions, and to read, read, read. It is very probable that the young Aristophanes would have read about Pythagoras who, as a young man, had travelled widely and visited Babylon where he'd met the Jewish exiles which included the Prophet Daniel. It must have been this that had made Aristophanes aware of the Babylonian slaves which he'd written about in his comedy *Babylonians*.

As a child, when living in Athens (before going to Aegina), he would have attended the City Dionysia festival and seen the trilogies of tragic dramas by Euripides and Sophocles when they were first performed. But returning to Athens from Aegina as a young man he made the conscious decision that writing tragedies was not for him; instead, he threw himself into comedy, which meant harnessing his wild imagination and adapting his ideas to the disciplines and limitations of the stage.

Athens, after his formative teenage years on the island had, apparently, been something of a culture shock for him. The many young men of his own age in Athens were, by his standards, lacking in morals; but what he thought worse was that some had never read Homer or Hesiod and were, in his estimation, illiterate. Nevertheless, he had the good fortune to meet Socrates and was, no doubt, inspired by the great philosopher. Certainly Aristophanes is present in several of Plato's dialogues.

In Athens he grew rapidly in confidence using his comedies to advance himself in the public eye. In his *Acharnians* which touched on the Peloponnesian War, he couldn't resist the lines: ...*It's not the island* (Aegina) *that they* (Sparta) *want* (but) ...*our poet* (himself).

Little is known about his private life except that he married and had three sons, two of whom followed in his footsteps and wrote comedies, though neither of them were as successful as he was. Setting aside his vulgarity and his lavatorial jokes, what makes his comedies stand out are, undoubtedly, his never failing boisterous good humour, and his kaleidoscopic, bright and colourful ideas.

★

We are on the Flying Dolphin again, making our way back to Piraeus. My mind drifts to Harry and his dramas on the farm at home. He rang me yesterday and told me that his cabbages had been attacked by caterpillars and pigeon. As for the dog! She is in the dog-house for stealing some cold chicken off the kitchen table! Oh, and he's suddenly had an invasion of wasps. Well, that's country life for you! Such small trifles and annoyances would have been experienced by the young Aristophanes living on Aegina. It was dogs and birds and wasps that inspired his greatest comedies! But while all dogs, birds and wasps are doomed to die, his comedies are there to make us smile after two thousand five hundred years – a fact, which frankly, is astonishing.

PART TWO
SECOND TRIP

CHAPTER 8

AULIS

We are back in Greece staying on the long offshore island of Euboea, east of Boeotia (a district on mainland Greece); a suspension bridge connects the island with the mainland. Where we are staying overlooks the sea and we watch as a regular ferry service takes passengers to and from Eretria on Euboea to Skala Oropou, the nearest mainland port.

Today we are going in search of the ancient temple of Artemis at Aulis. It is there that King Agamemnon once assembled the Greek chieftains and their ships in preparation to sail for Troy to retrieve his brother's wayward wife Helen – Helen of the thousand ships? Well, maybe. Unfortunately, the armada was unable to set sail because they were becalmed.

Harry and I had attempted to find it several years ago but without success; it was not surprising as we'd been searching and enquiring on Euboea itself, whereas Aulis was just across the bridge on the mainland, so nobody knew what we were talking about.

Today, with my new found knowledge, we drive off with confidence soon after breakfast; Fiona has a map and her SatNav on her lap, and Hilary is at the wheel.

We cross the suspension bridge and turn left, and soon find ourselves driving beside a long crescent bay. Is this Aulis? There are no ruins to be seen, and I ask Hilary to stop. I get out and stand staring out around the bay. The sea sparkles calmly under the mid-morning sun. To the far left mountains loom, while to the right the coastline is fringed with fir trees and olive groves. It is very atmospheric, and I can picture the thousand Greek triremes lying at anchor here, unable to set sail for Troy because they are becalmed. Today there are no boats, only reed umbrellas and sun-loungers along the beach. We are at a place named Avlida which is sort of Greek for our English word Aulis.

But where are the temple ruins? We drive along the bay and find a taverna where a burly man is very helpful and draws the route we must take on a scrap of paper. He warns us that really it's not worth the bother, just a few stones, he says. Ah, but that's exactly what I want to see, I tell him, and he shakes his head with a sad smile implying that foreign visitors are strange creatures.

"Avoid the shipyards," Fiona instructs, "just keep going along this road and look out for a brown sign which says 'Temple of Artemis'. It won't be yet, though."

At that precise moment I see the sign flash by, and I shout from my back seat. We reverse and turn right; we pass a quarried hillside and head towards a great cement factory complex. I spot the temple ruins on our left, a hundred metres or so from the hideous factory. Only stones? It depends whether you look at them with your physical eyes, or with your mind's eye which is so much more interesting. Yes, there are blocks of stone scattered about, as well as a ruined rectangular wall two stone-blocks high; there are also the drum of a column and a slender pillar; but centrally placed there is a round marble something – could this be the altar on which Iphigenia, King Agamemnon's daughter, was sacrificed?

This ancient site is not beside the sea though; it is the huge cement factory that is beside it. And, oh, how dismal the landscape behind the sanctuary is! Just a hillside with a few scrubby looking trees and, high up, traffic whizzing along the main road to and from the suspension bridge.

So this is Aulis as it is today! I try not to feel a sense of betrayal and great disappointment.

When Euripides set to work on his tragedy *Iphigenia at Aulis* he was over seventy years old. He never saw the play performed, but it was found as an unfinished manuscript amongst his possessions following his death at the court of King Archelaus of Macedonia in 406 B.C.

When the beautiful Helen ran off with Prince Paris of Troy, her cuckolded husband, King Menelaus of Sparta, rallied his allies to set sail for Troy to retrieve her and recover his honour. But there was a big problem; the ships lay becalmed and unable to set sail because his brother, King Agamemnon of Mycenae, had angered the goddess Artemis. It was Calchas, Agamemnon's seer, who informed him that the reason why the army was unable to sail was because

King Agamemnon, some years earlier, on the birth of his youngest daughter Iphigenia, had promised to sacrifice the most beautiful thing he possessed to the goddess but had failed to do so since the most beautiful had been his newly-born baby daughter. Calchas told the king that the fleet would never sail till he had fulfilled his promise to the goddess.

The play begins with Agamemnon summoning a Messenger at dawn. He is in despair: *Not the sound of birds is heard, nor of the sea; the winds are hushed in silence on the Euripus. (10-12.)* The Euripus is the narrow channel of water between Euboea and the mainland, which rather strangely has strong tidal currents which reverse direction four times every day, making sailing there something of a hazard.

Agamemnon's mind is in turmoil. As the newly appointed commander-in-chief he feels the weight of responsibility on his shoulders. His brother Menelaus and Odysseus have told him he must heed his seer and sacrifice his daughter for the greater good of the cause; they warn him that if he doesn't appease the goddess and get the armada under way, the troops will mutiny and shame will descend on Greece.

In the play Agamemnon's wife and daughter Iphigenia (by now a young woman) are already on their way from Mycenae believing that Iphigenia is to become the bride of Achilles, son of King Peleus of Phthia – though Achilles himself has not been told this.

Unable to sleep with the torment of his beloved daughter's impending death, Agamemnon in desperation writes a letter to his wife and, before the first light of dawn, asks his faithful Attendant to go quickly and deliver it into her hands; the letter implores Clytemnestra not to come to Aulis after all, though it doesn't say why there is this change of plan.

Yet the nobles, each with their assembled armies, are waiting here at Aulis, dependent now on Agamemnon's one supreme sacrifice. By now they know the reason for this continual and monotonous delay. Most of them are there because they were once contenders for the hand of Helen, whose father had first made each swear an oath that he would give his full support, if ever he was requested to do so, to whoever won her.

So there they all are, gathered in obedience to their sworn oath, because King Menelaus has requested their help since Helen has run off. Each warrior leader has, no doubt, wrenched himself away from his own family and responsibilities, and each is grumbling because he is fed up with the present enforced inaction.

Agamemnon's letter to stop his wife from coming is intercepted by Menelaus who confronts his brother furiously. They quarrel, and Menelaus points out that since becoming commander-in-chief Agamemnon's character has changed: *...Ill it becomes an honest man, when raised to power, to change his manners... (347-349.)*

Agamemnon retorts in kind: *...Who injures thee? of what art thou in want? A rich connubial bed, is that thy wish? This to procure thee is not in my power. Thou didst possess one, but ill governed it. Shall I, who with no fault have e'er been charged, suffer for thy ill conduct? Is thy heart racked at my honours?... (383-389.)* What more stinging remarks could Agamemnon make to this younger cuckolded brother of his!

The quarrel is interrupted by the Messenger arriving to say that Clytemnestra and Iphigenia, together with Agamemnon's infant son Orestes, have reached Aulis: *...wearied with this length of way, beside a beauteous-flowing fountain they repose themselves... their steeds, unyoked to taste the fresh grass of the verdant mead... (420-423.)*

He describes the peaceful scene where Clytemnestra and Iphigenia are resting; they are looking forward to the joy of the expected marriage between Iphigenia and Achilles. At the news, Agamemnon is overcome with grief and cannot restrain his tears. Menelaus suddenly relents as brotherly love and compassion take over. Let the armies be discharged, he says; the whole campaign can be aborted!

To waver now and turn his back on his disgruntled troops? How can he ignore what he's been told is causing the goddess' anger? No, it is imperative that he himself has the strength and courage to fulfil the demands of the goddess. His wife, however, must never know the truth.

His family arrives, and Iphigenia is overjoyed to see her father again: *Absent so long, with joy I look on thee... (640)* but she notices her father's tears: *A gloom hangs on thee 'midst thy joy to see me. (644.)*

Agamemnon attempts to conceal his deep distress and says: *...I feel my grief too strong, for that I soon shall to Achilles my dear child consign, forgive me: happy is it so to place a daughter, yet it pains a father's heart when he delivers to another house a child, the object of his tender care. (687-692.)*

Clytemnestra also feels the pain of parting from her daughter, but she wants to know about Achilles' lineage. Then, as would the mother of any bride, she asks about what preparations for the wedding have been made – what food, what clothes, what rites? Agamemnon is now on shaky ground. He pretends that since they are surrounded by the troops he doesn't think she should be involved and he will attend to everything: She must return home, he tells her. But she understandably wants to remain: *Of things abroad take thou the charge...but...within the house my care shall deck the virgin's nuptials as is meet. (769-741.)* And she enters Agamemnon's tent to prepare the wedding.

The Chorus take over, singing about the glories of Troy that await the troops, until Achilles arrives and reports the extreme restlessness and growing frustration of the waiting army. Clytemnestra comes out of the tent and, seeing the 'intended bridegroom', is quick to welcome him as her future son-in-law – much to Achilles' astonishment since he knows nothing of it. After some discussion on the matter, Achilles says: *Someone perchance 'gainst thee and me hath framed this mock... (349-351.)*

Then the Attendant arrives who, though faithful to Agamemnon, is even more loyal to Clytemnestra. He tells her of the whole hideous plot to get her and her daughter to Aulis, not for marriage to Achilles, but because Iphigenia has to be sacrificed to get the armada under way; such is the condition laid down by the goddess Artemis.

In her despair, Clytemnestra throws herself down at the feet of Achilles, and appeals to him to protect Iphigenia from such a fate: *...I have no friend but thee: the fell designs of Agamemnon's ruthless heart thou hearest... If thou shalt dare stretch forth thine hand to aid me, I shall find safety: if not, then am I lost indeed. (911-918.)*

So how are we, the audience, affected by all these strands of emotion – this tangled web? Euripides is amazingly good at drawing us in to feel the stresses and anxieties in which all his characters are caught up. Certainly we feel for Clytemnestra and the poignant tragedy of a young and innocent girl who, instead of marriage, is about to be slaughtered because the situation demands it; but we also feel for Agamemnon on whose shoulders this hideous demand has fallen.

The Chorus sing about the situation as they see it. When Agamemnon returns feigning cheerfulness and calling for Iphigenia to come garlanded as for her wedding (he is unaware that the truth has been told to Clytemnestra by the Attendant), he asks: *Why weeps my daughter? Cheerful now no more thy look, nor pleasant: wherefore is thine eye fixed on the ground...? (1122-1123.)*

His wife tells him that they know the truth, and screams accusations against him: hasn't she done everything to fulfil her role as his wife? She continues in full flow: *...Should one ask thee, for what cause* *thy daughter wilt thou kill, what wouldst thou say? Speak; or I must speak for thee! E'en for this, that Menelaus may regain Helen. Well would it be, if for his wanton wife our children made the price... (319.)* And she goes on in despair: *Think what my heart must feel, when in the house I see the seats all vacant of my child, and her apartment vacant: I shall sit alone in tears, thus ever wailing her... (1166-1176.)* And on and on she goes voicing the consequences of her daughter's death, and asking why her? Why not Hermione, Helen's daughter? Why should she, Clytemnestra ... *who to thy bed am faithful, of my child shall be deprived, and she, that hath misdone, at her return to Sparta her young daughter shall bear back? And thus be happy... (1200-1205.)* She has a point.

Iphigenia herself then speaks. If only, she says, she had the voice of Orpheus which had the power to charm the rocks and persuade with words *...But I have nothing to present thee now save tears, my only eloquence; and those I can present thee. On thy knees I hang, a suppliant wreath, this body, which she bore to thee. Ah! kill me not in youth's fresh prime. Sweet is the light of heaven... (1214-1219.)* And she goes on persuasively: *...If Paris be enamoured of his bride, his Helen, what concerns it me? and how comes he to my destruction? Look upon me, give me a smile, give me a kiss, my father, that, if my words persuade thee not, in death I may have this memorial of thy love... (1236-1240.)*

Agamemnon is wretched with the horror of what is demanded of him. His words are bleak and desperate: *...I love my children, else I should be void of reason: to dare this is dreadful to me, and not to dare is dreadful. I perforce must do it. What a naval camp is here you see, how many kings of Greece arrayed in glitt'ring arms: to Ilium's towers are these denied t'advance unless I offer thee a victim, thus the prophet Calchas speaks... (1256-1262.)*

There is a brief discussion regarding the intended wedding, and Agamemnon again tries to persuade his wife she should return home in order to be spared the horror of the impending sacrifice. The play continues with everyone in anguish, helped on by the Chorus. The young Achilles joins them, himself being faced with the fury of his men for what they see as Achilles being influenced by a mere woman. They have even dared to stone him for protecting Clytemnestra and so prolonging their inability to either set sail or return to their families. They are prepared to perform the sacrifice – and so is the great warrior Odysseus, even if he has to drag her by her *golden tresses*.

At last Iphigenia, who has been listening, speaks out. She has heard the arguments and the dilemma they are all facing. She announces that she does not want to be the one to hinder the army, and will freely give herself to be sacrificed for Greece: ...*All the powers of Greece have now their eyes on me; on me depends the sailing of the fleet... To be too fond of life becomes not me; nor for thyself alone, but to all Greece a blessing, didst thou bear me shall thousands, when their country's injured, lift their shields, shall thousands grasp the oar, and dare, advancing bravely 'gainst the foe, to die for Greece? And shall my life, my single life, obstruct all this?... (1375-1392.)* And showing nobility and great courage, she ends: *...for Greece I give my life. Slay me, demolish Troy: for these shall be long time my monuments, my children these, my nuptials, and my glory... (1398-1402.)*

Achilles offers to defend her, while Clytemnestra attempts to persuade her from leaving her bereaved and in mourning for her. But the young girl sees it as her duty: *I suffer not a tear to fall. But you, ye virgins, to my fate attune the hymn, "Artemis, daughter of almighty Zeus." With fav'ring omens sing "Success to Greece." Come, with the basket one begin the rites, one with the purifying cakes the flames enkindle; let my father his right hand place on the altar; for I come to give safety to Greece, and conquest to her arms. Lead me... (1467-1475.)*

And so with the Chorus singing about the glories of Greece and the wonders of Iphigenia's great sacrifice – in her own words to her mother, who asks what she is to do when her daughter is lost, Iphigenia replies: *Not lost, but saved: through me thou shalt be famed. (1440.)* She goes to Artemis' altar (perhaps this same round marble block I'm looking at now).

A time-lapse is assumed because, when a Messenger comes hurrying back to Clytemnestra, he speaks about what he has just witnessed: how Agamemnon, on seeing his beloved daughter advancing as a victim to the grove, groaned and wept aloud. Iphigenia, however, remained calm: ... *"Father, I to thee am present: for my country, and for all the land of Greece, I freely give myself a victim: to the altar let them lead me..." (1547-1555.)*

She refused to be dragged, but bared and proffered her neck. And the Messenger reports how Calchas, the prophet, then placed into the golden basket the *sharp-edged sword, and bound the sacred garlands round the virgin's head. (1567-1568.)*

Achilles was present too, and commended Iphigenia's pure blood to the goddess. The soldiers were silent, fixing their eyes on the ground while the required preliminary rituals took place. The priest then took the sword and *marked where to give the blow. (1584.)* And then a miracle! As the sacrifice took place, Iphigenia vanished! The Messenger

reports: ...*Aloud the priest exclaims, and all the host with shouts rifted the air, beholding from some god a prodigy which struck their wond'ring eyes, surpassing faith when seen: for on the ground in form excelling: with its spouting blood much was the altar of the goddess dewed... (1588-1595.)*
Although it is not reported in the drama itself, legend has it that the goddess substituted a deer.

Oh, how like God ordering Abraham to sacrifice his son Isaac! God wanted to prove Abraham's faith and, when the knife was about to do the deed substituted a ram instead.

Which story came first into the world of imagination? Or were both stories based on fact?

Following the sacrifice in Euripides' drama, wonder of wonders, a wind gets up and *gives a fav'ring gale to swell our sails. (1603.)* The Messenger assures Clytemnestra that he saw it all himself and what he says is true. ...*to the gods thy daughter, be thou well assured, is fled. Therefore lament no more, no more retain thy anger 'gainst thy lord: to mortal men things unexpected oft the gods dispense, and whom they love they save: this day hath seen thy daughter dead, seen her alive again. (1615-1621.)*

And so the drama ends on a note of mysticism.

[handwritten margin note: Aet pre-empts Aesch. Ag. ★ what became of Iph??]

Iphigenia in Tauris describes what happened to Iphigenia next. It was written some several years earlier than his Aulis tragedy (between 414-411 B.C.) It is an extraordinarily powerful James Bond-type drama about the mature Iphigenia who is now serving as priestess to the goddess Artemis at the court of King Thoas of Tauris, thought to be on the Crimean peninsula.

The temple of Artemis is set on a towering rock and, because Iphigenia was sacrificed by the Greeks at Aulis, any Greek who happens to find himself at Tauris is destined to suffer the same fate that she (Iphigenia) had. It is Iphigenia's duty as the priestess to oversee such ghoulish human sacrifice.

The drama starts with Iphigenia haunted by a vivid nightmare that her family home (Mycenae) has fallen, and her brother Orestes (last seen as an infant brought to Aulis by her mother) is dead: ... *Sudden the firm earth shook; I fled, and stood without; the battlements I saw, and all the rocking roof fall from its lofty height in ruins to the ground; of all the house, my father's house, one pillar, as I thought, alone was left, which from its cornice waved a length of auburn-locks, and human voice assumed... (46-53.)* The dream had been so vivid, she was convinced her brother must have perished.

However, he is very much alive. After being acquitted of the murder of his mother Clytemnestra, and the placating of the Furies (see Chapter 4), there are still a few Furies who continue to haunt him, prompting him to consult the Delphic oracle yet again. This time he is told to sail to Tauris and bring back from there the greatly revered statue of Artemis which fell from heaven; only then will he be able to find peace.

In the drama Orestes and his friend Pylades arrive by boat; they anchor at the foot of the towering rock and wonder how to scale it to achieve their goal. Pylades suggests that: *...when the eye of night comes darkling on, then must we dare, and take the polished image from the shrine... In toils the brave are daring; of no worth the abject soul. (110-117.)*

The atmosphere is set and the drama develops as these two young men are spotted on the shore by a Herdsman. The Herdsman reports to Iphigenia the sequence of events as he saw them occur, and tells her how he alerted his fellow herdsmen and they'd discussed what action they should take: *...we judged it meet to seize the victims, by our country's law due to the goddess. (283-285.)* The Herdsman goes on to describe how Orestes was suddenly: *...Convulsed with madness: as a hunter loud then cried: "Dost thou behold her, Pylades, dost thou not see this dragon fierce from hell rushing to kill me, and against me rousing her horrid vipers? See this other here, emitting fire and slaughter from her vests, sails on her wings, my mother in her arms bearing, to hurl his mass of rock upon me! Ah, she will kill me Whither shall I fly?"... (289-297.)* Orestes is the victim of another attack by the Furies.

The two young men are then set upon by the Herdsmen who pelt them with stones. The one reporting to Iphigenia continues: *...And his voice varied, now the roar of bulls, the howl of dogs now uttering, mimic sounds sent by the madd'ning Furies, as they say. Together thronging, as of death assured, we sat in silence: but he drew his sword, and like a lion rushing 'midst our herds plunged in their sides the weapon, weening thus to drive the Furies, till the briny wave foamed with their blood. But when among our herds we saw this havoc made, we all 'gan rouse to arms, and blew our sounding shells t' alarm the neighb'ring peasants; for we thought in fight rude herdsmen to these youthful strangers, trained to arms, ill matched; and forthwith to our aid flocked numbers... (299-313.)*

The Herdsmen manage to close in on these young strangers and they are brought to King Thoas, their sacrificial death now certain. The Chorus take over with their account of the horrors which brought about the sacrifice of Iphigenia. But, despite the numerous despicable things that have and will take place, they say: ...*sweet is Hope, to man's fond breast...(411.)*

And so the play develops. Iphigenia now questions Orestes about his country and, hearing that he is from Mycenae, immediately asks which warriors returned from the Trojan War. She asks about Achilles and is told he's dead. And what of Helen and Menelaus? They have returned to Sparta. And Agamemnon? She learns of his murder, then how their son Orestes avenged his death and killed his mother. Iphigenia tells Orestes (still a stranger to her as she is to him) that since he knows Mycenae, she will spare his life if he will take a letter from her and deliver it. But only one of her two captives can be spared, he or Pylades. Orestes says that if only one of them is allowed to live, then his friend Pylades must be the one, since he was not responsible for this venture: ...*Base is his soul, who in calamities involves his friends, and saves himself: this is a friend, whose life, dear to me as my own, I would preserve. (605-610.)*

Pylades in his turn argues that as his friend he couldn't possibly leave Orestes in the lurch: ...*else shall I obtain the name of a vile coward through the Argive state, and the deep vales of Phocis... (676-678.)*

Orestes urges Pylades to return and marry his younger sister Electra to whom he has already been promised; if they have sons, then his name will live on ...*nor all my father's house in total ruin sink... (697-698.)* And he persuades him to depart and, on his arrival home, to build a sepulchre and monument to him. And so it is agreed.

Iphigenia produces the letter and, of course, Pylades has to know to whom he should deliver it. The answer is to none other than Orestes! What? Is Pylades' friend Orestes of Mycenae? Iphigenia demands proof, and her brother speaks of their forebear Pelops' sword which hangs high on a wall in the palace, to which Iphigenia in astonishment says: ...*What shall I say? 'Tis all surpassing wonder and the power of words. (839.)*

Iphigenia naturally wants to know why Orestes has come to this remote awe-inspiring place, whereupon Orestes tells her of his mission. The final command of Apollo, if he is to rid himself of those few Furies who still molest him, is to bring back the image of Artemis. This throws Iphigenia into a dilemma: how can the image possibly be stolen without severe repercussions on her as priestess? But then she remembers her earlier dream and her sudden longing to see her family again. This she feels to be a sign from on high: *Ere thy arrival here, a fond desire to be again at Argos, and to see thee, my loved brother, filled my soul. Thy wish is my warm wish, to free thee from the toils, and from its ruins raise my father's house; nor harbour I 'gainst him, that slew me, thought of harsh resentment: from thy blood my hands would I keep pure, thy house I would preserve but from the goddess how may this be hid? The tyrant too I fear, when he shall find the statue on its marble base no more. What then from death will save me?... (989-1000.)* of Pelee

The solution, of course, is quite obvious: she must assist them with stealing the image and come with them. She will pretend that the image has been polluted by them and must be purified in the sea. *To form devices quick is woman's wit* says Orestes. Every now and then the great tragedian slips his own views into his dramas: that women, though kept in the background and expected to conform to tradition as child-bearers and chaste carers of the home, are in truth strong characters to be reckoned with.

Orestes is of the opinion that Apollo would never have ordered him on this mission if he had not already known that Artemis (Apollo's twin sister) would agree to it, so they have no need to fear the goddess. But the king? He could kill the king, he suggests? He is, perhaps, becoming too used to killing. He appeals to the women in the Chorus: *One thing alone remains, that these conceal our purpose: but address them, teach thy tongue to melt the heart to pity: thus perchance all things may to our warmest wish succeed. (1050-1054.)*

The king is due to enter the temple, and Iphigenia calls on the Chorus to be faithful to her and assist in her flight. She prays to Artemis, saying that she, the goddess, saved her once at Aulis, and so she can save her now: *...else will the voice of Phoebus* (Apollo) *be no more held true by mortals... (1083-1084.)*

Now comes the James Bond escape-from-the-impossible scenario. The king enters and sees the priestess with the image in her arms. What is she doing with it, he demands? Women's wiles click in, and Iphigenia says the image, of its own accord, suddenly turned on its plinth with its back to everyone. Why, was there an earthquake, she is asked? No, it is due to its dismay at the two Grecian men, one of whom is polluted with the blood of matricide, Iphigenia replies. She goes on to say that not only must the image be purified but also the two men destined for sacrifice. She then tells Thoas that she needs solitude for the purification rites.

Iphigenia demands chains for the prisoners, and for everyone to remain indoors while the purification takes place. Thoas, she says, should draw a veil over his eyes when Orestes and his companion emerge from the temple because they are polluted. As priestess, nobody questions Iphigenia's authority, and they obey her instructions.

She then prays to Artemis, and the Chorus sing the praises of Apollo's oracle. By the time all this has taken place Iphigenia, Orestes and his companion have got away. A Messenger arrives in haste to report that the two young men have escaped in their galley with the sacred image. An angry argument develops between the Messenger, who demands to see the King, and the Chorus. When the King emerges from the temple to see what the rumpus is about, he is told that his priestess and the two Greeks, taking with them the sacred image, have set sail, and that all the talk about purification from his trusted priestess was false.

The Messenger describes their escape: *When to the shore we came, where stationed rode the galley of Orestes by the rocks concealed, to us whom thou hadst sent with her to hold the strangers' chains, the royal maid made signs that we retire, and stand aloof, as if with secret rites she would perform the purposed expiation: on she went in her own hands holding the strangers' chains behind them: not without suspicion this, yet by thy servants, king, allowed. At length, that we might deem her in some purpose high employed, she raised her voice, and chaunted loud barbaric strains, as if with mystic rites she cleansed the stain of blood. When we had sat a tedious while, it came into our thought that from their chains unloosed the stranger youths might kill her, and escape to flight; yet fear of seeing what we ought not kept us still in silence... (1327-1345.)* And the Messenger continues at length to report how he and his men were unarmed and, when a fight broke out, used their fists; but the fifty-man crew fired arrows, and they replied by flinging rocks.

When the King commands that the young men and Iphigenia are caught, the goddess Athena intervenes and tells the King it is Apollo who has sent Orestes to fetch the image of Artemis and bring it back to Greece. A new temple is to be built to house it on the ...*hallowed heights of Brauron.*

The whole attitude of King Thoas alters in obedience to Athena's will. The goddess is well satisfied and tells the king she will accompany Iphigenia, her brother and his friend to Greece, and points out that Artemis is her, Athena's, sister.

And so the play ends. There is a great sense of divine providence.

The characters in the play ultimately are dependent on the will of deity: of Apollo's oracle through whom the will of Zeus (his father) is spoken; of Artemis to whom Iphigenia was first sacrificed; and finally Athena, whose divine intervention brings matters to a happy conclusion.

CHAPTER

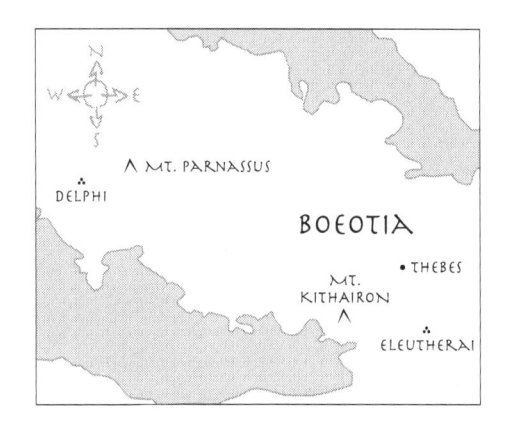

9

THEBES

Map showing Boeotia region with Delphi, Mt. Parnassus, Thebes, Mt. Kithairon, and Eleutherai marked.

The following day we set off for Thebes. Once across the suspension bridge from Euboea, we took the Thebes road, across the extensive, well-cultivated Boeotian plain. As we headed for Thebes, we could see ominous dark clouds gathering in the distance over the ancient city. They gradually grew blacker and more dense, and soon we saw forked lightning zigzagging down from them. Overhead where we were driving, the sky was merely dull and overcast.

Lightning! How appropriate! It was, after all, at Thebes that Dionysos was born; there that Zeus had visited the beautiful Semele, daughter of King Cadmus, founder of Thebes; there that Hera in a jealous fit had persuaded the young girl to ask Zeus to show himself to her in his full glory which reduced her to a cinder; and there also that Zeus had saved the embryo of his unborn child and sewn it into his thigh till the infant Dionysos was ready to be born.

By the time we reached Thebes, the storm clouds had rolled on, though it remained gloomy and spitting with rain. The modern town looked dreary, as though no thought had been given to preserving its historic past.

The road brought us into the centre where almost at once we saw a wire-meshed fenced-off area which looked like a bombed-site. A brown archaeological notice-board informed us it was the Mycenaean Palace of Cadmus, 1400-1200 B.C.

"I don't know about you, but before we start traipsing about I could do with a hot cup of coffee," Fiona said. "It's dismal out here. Come on, let's have something hot to drink and you can tell us about this Cadmus fellow. You know I'm dying to hear!"

We crossed the street under our umbrellas, avoiding the puddles, and darted into a café. Once settled at a rather dingy table I told them briefly about the founder of Thebes.

Cadmus was the son of King Agenor of Tyre and had a sister named Europa. One day Europa was playing with her young friends on the seashore when Zeus spotted her and immediately turned himself into a beautiful white bull. Europa was so intrigued by the beast that she climbed onto its back and immediately Zeus swam away with her to Crete. There he seduced her and she gave birth to Minos who became King of Crete.

I told them how King Agenor, as soon as he realized his daughter was missing, sent his son Cadmus in search of her. Cadmus came to mainland Greece and enquired of the Delphic oracle what he should do. The oracle told him he was to forget his sister and follow a cow with moon-shaped markings on its flank. Wherever the cow lay down, there he was to found a new city.

The cow finally came to rest by a river near here, and Cadmus sacrificed her to the goddess Athena. A dragon was involved in the story which Cadmus killed, whereupon Athena ordered him to remove its teeth and sow them in the ground. As soon as he did this, men sprang up from the earth. These newly-sprung-from-the-ground men began to fight each other till eventually only five remained alive; these five became the first citizens of Cadmus' new city.

Unfortunately, the dragon happened to be the son of Ares, god of war, and, as a penance for killing his son, Cadmus was ordered to be Ares' slave for eight years. After that he was crowned king of Thebes and married Ares' daughter Harmonia. Together they had one son and four daughters, one of whom was Semele, Dionysos' mother.

I'd read that the archaeologist who'd excavated the city's acropolis had been amazed at the intensity of the fire that had destroyed the palace, 'as if it had been the work of a god,' was how he'd described it.

We finished our drinks and set out to explore the ruins of Cadmus' palace. We found steps on the far side of the high wire-mesh fence which led down to the excavated area.

With nothing to tell us what was what – and, mercifully, the area was no larger than a large house, or small palace – we could only imagine that somewhere here was where Semele had been burned to a cinder. I'd read also that somewhere close by was a sanctuary of Dionysos Kadmeios, and nearby a temple of Demeter Thesmophoros. Was it significant that they were both deities of agriculture?

My hope of making sense of anything lay with the Archaeological

Museum which was within easy walking distance. There, although the officials did their best to help, they were quite unable to tell me anything specific. The modern town had been built over its historic past, and the foundations of old temples and sanctuaries, I learned, were buried under churches.

And the city walls with its famous seven gates, I asked? Only the foundations of the Elektrai Gate could be seen at the lower side of the park, I was told. And the Proitides Gate? Just a few stones, came the answer.

I tried to crank up some sort of enthusiasm, but it was fast vanishing. I wished my mind didn't get so numbed by figurines, clay pots, red-figured vases, jewellery and whatnot.

In desperation I asked if they could direct me to a gallery which was of the period of the renowned King Oedipus. I was politely led to another room. There I became more alert with finds from the palace which included lapis lazuli cylinder seals, and a stirrup jar inscribed with Linear B script from Crete – I'd read that Linear B tablets had been discovered here in Thebes. But also on display was a reconstruction of a fresco of female worshippers – were they Maenads worshipping Dionysos in their ecstatic frenzy? They looked too demure. Or were they women worshippers of Demeter at her Thesmophoria festival celebrated by women only?

Did they have anything on ancient drama, I then asked? I was taken to another gallery where a mask was pointed out to me portraying a woman with a fixed expression of dismay with a wreath on her head; I hoped in my dull mood I didn't look the same. There were also ancient manuscripts, but they sent me into a complete bog-eyed state. It seemed that I just had to let the language of the tragedies written by those early dramatists bring Thebes back to life for me.

There were several dramas about the city from the fifth century that have survived, but before embarking on two of them it is important to know something about the unfortunate life of King Oedipus about whom the tragedies were written.

Oedipus was the son of King Laius of Thebes and his wife Jocasta. Laius was the great-grandson of Cadmus. An oracle had declared that Laius would be killed by his son so, when Jocasta gave birth to Oedipus, she had him exposed on the nearby mountain, Mt. Kithairon. The task was given to a herdsman who, not wanting the baby to die, handed him over to a Corinthian shepherd who brought him to the court of King Polybus and Queen Merope of Corinth who were childless.

Oedipus was lovingly brought up in Corinth by the royal couple. However, one day, when Oedipus was a young man, he was teased by a drunken friend who told him that the king and queen were not his true parents. He was so upset by this taunt that he consulted the Delphic oracle and was told the alarming news that it was fated he would kill his father where three roads met, and marry his mother. Believing that his parents were the king and queen of Corinth, he decided not to return there but to continue on to Thebes.

On his journey (where three roads met), his way was blocked by a carriage with an escort heading for Delphi; there the road happened to be narrow, and he was ordered to get out of the way. Oedipus was furious at the arrogance with which he was addressed and refused to move. The carriage then came on and ran over his foot; worse still, King Laius (his true father riding in the carriage) hit him savagely as he passed by. Oedipus was so enraged that he put up a fight and killed him and all those escorting him, except for one man who got away. He then came on to Thebes to find the people in mourning for their monarch, the news of whose death had just reached them.

The original purpose of King Laius' visit to Delphi had been to ask the oracle how to rid Thebes of a winged monster who had been plaguing the city and its surroundings. It was female, with a woman's head and a lion's body, and was known as the Sphinx. She had been devouring every Theban citizen unable to answer a riddle posed by her. The riddle was as follows: 'What creature walks on four legs in the morning, on two at noon, and on three in the evening, and is weakest when it walks on most?'

Creon, brother of Queen Jocasta, was now regent, and offered the throne to whoever was able to answer the riddle correctly. Anything to rid Thebes of this creature who was only prepared to depart when the correct answer was given.

Oedipus solved it with ease. 'It was Man,' he declared, 'because Man crawls on all fours when a baby, and has a stick in old age.'

As a result the Sphinx departed, and Oedipus married the late king's widow Jocasta, not knowing that she was his mother. He ruled Thebes successfully for a number of years during which time he and Jocasta had two sons and two daughters. It was at the point, when their children were young adults, that the story of Oedipus' calamitous life was taken up by Sophocles in his tragedy *Oedipus Tyrannus*, produced c.428 B.C.

THEBES 103

★

The scene is set before the palace at Thebes. The citizens remember their terrors with the Sphinx, but are at present suffering from a devastating plague from which many are dying.

Oedipus is on stage and calls on the gods to help him find the cause of this plague; he believes it might be due to the killing of the former king on his way to Delphi, so he rallies his people to find the killer of King Laius – he, of course, is unaware the man he killed in the carriage was the king. He stresses that, if anyone knows who the murderer is, then he must come forward fearlessly.

It is decided to ask the blind seer Teiresias *who has in him the tongue that cannot lie.* He is brought on stage led by a boy, and Oedipus tells him that it's his belief that the plague is the result of the murder of King Laius.

Teiresias speaks out courageously: *Alas! How terrible it is to know where no good comes of knowing! Of these matters I was full well aware, but let them slip me; else I had not come hither. (359-362.)*

Oedipus is shocked that his seer knows the truth but will not speak. Is Teiresias in some way involved in the murder then? Driven to it by Oedipus' anger, Teiresias responds bluntly: *I say that you are Laius' murderer – he whom you seek. (413)*

Enough! He must face punishment for saying it! *Then shall I say something more, that may incense you further? (417.)* And he hints at Oedipus' incestuous marriage and his children by Jocasta. But Oedipus thinks he's raving – Teiresias is not only blind but deaf and has lost it altogether. Oedipus retorts: *You cannot hurt me, your life being all one night. (432-433.)*

Knowing all, however, Teiresias says that it is not he who will do harm to Oedipus but Apollo who *will bring it all to pass.*

But now Oedipus, in his uneasiness, accuses Teiresias of being in collusion with Jocasta's brother Creon. With some anger Teiresias cries: *...Go, trample on Creon, and on this mouth of mine; but know, there is not one of all mankind that shall be bruised more utterly than you. (487-489.)*

How dare he accuse Oedipus! Yet Teiresias remains calm and persistent: *...he shall be found related as a brother, though their sire, and of the woman from whose womb he came both son and spouse; one that has raised up seed to his own father, and has murdered him... (520-524.)* So saying, Teiresias departs, led off by the boy who brought him. The Chorus prepares the audience for the fact that Apollo will hunt down and find the murderer. Creon enters and Oedipus rages at him – wasn't it Creon who'd asked him to send for Teiresias? Yes, it was. And how long since Laius was murdered? Wasn't it many years ago? So why didn't the seer voice his so-called knowledge then? Why did he stay silent? And he accuses Creon of plotting with Teiresias to bring the blame for the murder on him, Oedipus.

The two throw accusations at each other with increasing anger. Creon states that he is not jealous by nature and doesn't want the crown, which would make demands on him to do much that he'd find dull and irksome. But Oedipus is not convinced: *When he who plots against me in the dark comes swiftly on, I must be swift in turn. If I stay quiet, his ends will have been gained and mine all missed. (692-696.)*

So what is it that Oedipus wants, Creon demands? Must he go into exile? No, Oedipus wants him dead because he is a traitor.

And suppose Oedipus to be wrong in his judgement, Creon asks? Ah, but he, Oedipus, is king *and must be ruler*.

At this point Jocasta comes from the palace wanting to know what the row is about: *Unhappy men, what was it made you raise this senseless broil of words? Are you not both ashamed of stirring private grievances, the land being thus afflicted... (709-712.)* And she learns that the blind seer has informed Oedipus that he was the slayer of Laius. Jocasta, who thinks Oedipus is the son of the king of Corinth and his wife, asks Oedipus how that can possibly be since the Delphic oracle had stated clearly that the king would be murdered by his son and, since Oedipus is not his son, that alone exonerates him. But she then adds that King Laius was murdered where three roads meet. And because she and her former husband had the infant's ankles pinned together and the child exposed at birth, Teiresias' accusation that Oedipus is the murderer is clearly false.

Oedipus seizes upon the 'where three roads meet' and the 'pinned ankles'; a dawning of the truth begins to gleam through his former belief in his innocence. He cannot bear not to know the true facts. How did Jocasta hear about the three roads meeting? Jocasta replies that it was a servant of the former murdered king who escaped with his life. But when Oedipus became King of Thebes, that same servant had implored Jocasta to send him to work in the fields away from the city. Oedipus demands that the servant be brought to him. His need to know the truth however shocking is overwhelming! But what does Oedipus expect to learn from him, Jocasta asks? Oedipus tells her that, although he believed his parents were King Polybus and Queen

Merope of Corinth, a drunkard once called him a changeling. Despite questioning his parents who'd reassured him, yet the matter had at the time troubled him to such an extent that he'd gone to Delphi to enquire of the oracle. And Oedipus tells Jocasta how the oracle had warned that he would kill his father and marry his mother which was the reason he'd refused to return to Corinth but had continued on to Thebes. It was where three roads met that he'd been confronted by a herald who'd commanded him to get out of the way of an approaching carriage. The man riding in the carriage hadn't waited for Oedipus to move, but had come on and struck him whereupon Oedipus had reacted violently and, in his fury, killed him and his attendants.

He is deeply troubled. What if that man who'd struck him was his father? Then – and he hardly dares say it – Jocasta is his mother.

One of the Senators wisely advises Oedipus not to jump to conclusions but to wait for the labourer to come and have his say, whereupon Oedipus and Jocasta depart. When Jocasta returns she carries garlands, intending to call on the gods *...for Oedipus lets his mind float too light upon the eddies of all kinds of grief... (1001-1002.)*

Her monologue is interrupted by a Messenger arriving and asking for Oedipus. He has come from Corinth where King Polybus has just died – surely then, Jocasta thinks, Apollo's oracle has been proved wrong – Oedipus' father has died of natural causes, therefore Oedipus can rest assured, as he cannot kill his father who is already dead.

Yet Oedipus is fearful of returning to Corinth because of the other oracle which warned that he would marry his mother. When the Messenger assures him that he is really worrying about nothing because, in fact, the king and queen of Corinth were not his true parents, Oedipus is incredulous. How does he know that? Because, the Messenger declares, it was he himself who had brought him as an infant to the palace in Corinth.

What? Yes, he was brought from Mt. Kithairon where he'd been exposed – well, not exactly, but where another herdsman had been ordered to expose him (the soles of both his tiny feet bored through and pinned together). The shepherd found him (the baby) in distress and the herdsman had allowed him to take the infant back to his childless monarch.

Who was this herdsman then? He is told that he is the man he has already ordered to be brought to him.

Meanwhile Jocasta, who has been listening, turns on Oedipus and implores him not to delve further into the matter. But Oedipus persists: *No, it cannot be that having such a clue I should refuse to solve the mystery of my parentage! (1160-1162.)* To which Jocasta despairs: *For heaven's sake... don't seek it! I am sick, and that's enough! (1163-1164.)* And, tormented by the thought, she departs in anguish into the palace, crying: *Woe, woe, unhappy! This is all I have to say to thee, and no word more, for ever! (1176-1177.)*

The old Herdsman arrives and Oedipus immediately questions him, asking if he ever met this shepherd from Corinth? Bit by bit he gleans the information he dreads to hear from the Herdsman who would much prefer to remain silent. But Oedipus needs to know the worst however much it hurts ...*to have wedded whom I ought not – and slain whom I might not slay! (1308-1309.)* He finally departs in a state of agonized horror.

The Chorus sing their woes with an increased sense of impending doom. They only cease when another Messenger arrives hurriedly with the shocking news that Jocasta has hanged herself. And there is even more horror because Oedipus, on discovering her body, had immediately snatched two gold pins which adorned her dress ...*lifted them, and smote the nerves of his own eyeballs... that they should see no more... (1403-1409.)*

The newly blinded Oedipus comes from the palace, crying out in his distress: *Thou horror of thick darkness overspread, thou shadow of unutterable dread not to be stemmed or stayed, fallen on my head. (1450-1452.)* One of his men consoles him, and Oedipus says: ...*full well I know that voice of thine, all darkling though I be. (1460-1461.)* If he'd only been left to die on Mt. Kithairon, he would not have become his father's murderer, ...*nor wedded her I have my being from. (1494.)*

His feelings of helpless guilt are interrupted by the entry of Creon. He has not come to mock, he says, but to offer advice. Oedipus must ...*revere the royal Sun-god's all-sustaining fire, not to parade, thus flagrant, such a sore as neither earth nor day can tolerate, nor dew from Heaven!... (1560-1565.)* He mustn't make public his crimes, but keep the knowledge only in the family.

Oedipus asks him one favour, to banish him from the kingdom. Creon answers by saying they must ask Apollo what is his will. He points out that since the words of Apollo's oracle have come to pass he, Oedipus, must believe what Apollo advises him to do next.

The tragedy closes with Oedipus preparing to leave Thebes and go into exile. He asks Creon to bury Jocasta, and to take care of his daughters, his sons now being old enough to look after themselves.

Before leaving, though, he would like to say farewell to his daughters: *...let me, above all else, touch them with hands, and weep away my troubles! ...If but my hands could feel them, I might seem to have them still, as when I still could see. (1606-1612.)*

And so a bitter farewell is made as Oedipus mourns over his fate: *...Your father slew his father, and became father of you – by her who bare him. So will they reproach you; who will wed you then? No one, my children; but you needs must wither, barren – unwed... (1639-1645.)* And again Oedipus appeals to Creon to take care of them.

They leave the stage, and the drama ends with the Chorus lamenting: *...a prince of men... how deep the billows of calamity above him roll... (1680-1684.)*

How vivid are the words of this great tragedy by Sophocles! How the drama towers over the modern buildings of today's dull provincial town which is built over the ancient city, once the kingdom of this still remembered tragic king!

Back to the present moment. I meet up with the others and, when we emerge from the museum we find the sun is shining. We are planning to drive up into Mt. Kithairon to ancient Eleutherai to see the remains of a fourth century B.C. fortress known as the Fortress of Eleutherai. We are by now hungry, and we plan to have a picnic up there. With the sun out and a clear blue sky, things are looking good again.

★

Leaving the modern town on the Lamia road, it became clear that Thebes was indeed founded on an acropolis – an acropolis large enough to build a powerful city fortified by defence walls with seven gates. Thebes had once been the capital of Boeotia and it commanded extensive views over the plains which surrounded it.

We'd been told by a member of the museum staff that along this road we could see on our right the Mount of the Sphinx where the monster had once lurked. We kept our eyes open for a sign-post or notice-board to indicate its whereabouts but saw nothing. There were, though, several prominent mounds and pointed hills rising from the plain, any one of which could have been the creature's lair.

The road began to ascend from the plain as we approached the Kithairon mountain range forested in bottle-green pine-trees. We stopped at a solitary roadside taverna, and almost at once Hilary spotted a sign on the left pointing up a narrow concrete track through the trees – the Fortress of Eleutherai, it said.

It was a steep drive up, the concrete soon petering out to become a dirt-track. After a hundred metres or so we reached a grassy parking area, after which we had to climb up a narrow path till we reached the fortress on the summit. Most of it lay in ruins except for its formidable north wall of massive blocks of stone which stood solid against the skyline with what remained of its six watchtowers. The views from there were stunning – a three hundred and sixty degrees vista around the plains, to distant mountain ranges. I felt triumphant.

The wind whistled and buffeted us and we clung onto our sunhats. We set out our picnic; we buttered our rolls, sliced cheese and tomatoes, and ate succulent peaches.

It was here on Mt. Kithairon that the infant Oedipus had been exposed at birth; here that the women worshippers of Dionysos (the Maenads) would come in their frenetic wildness, possessed with superhuman powers, and tear apart the wild beasts of the forest; here too that the unfortunate descendant of Oedipus, the young King Pentheus, met his death as a direct consequence of denying Dionysos' claim to be a god. Divine vengeance was indeed harsh and final, and a warning to all doubters of the truth of deity. His story was told by Euripides in his *Bacchae* (see Chapter 12).

Interestingly, it was from Eleutherai that the sixth century B.C. ruler of Athens, Peisistratus, had brought the olive-wood image of Dionysos Eleuthereus to Athens and had initiated the first City Dionysia drama festival. A notice-board beside the north wall of the fortress stated that it stood where there had once been a more ancient building. There was, however, no other information, and Dionysos was not mentioned. But the words 'a more ancient building' than the fourth century B.C. fortress? I liked to think it had been a sacred site to Dionysos in which the image had been kept.

Dionysos, god of drama! In 467 B.C. Aeschylus wrote a tetralogy, the only surviving drama of which is *Seven Against Thebes*. The three lost ones must have touched on Oedipus, the titles being *Laius*, *Oedipus*, and *Sphinx*. Aeschylus' *Seven Against Thebes* describes yet another tragic incident in the life of the blind king.

According to Aeschylus, Oedipus didn't immediately go into exile, as Sophocles would have it in his *Oedipus Tyrannus*, but remained in Thebes. His two sons brought down on themselves the wrath of their blind father because, so it was said, they insulted him on two occasions. Firstly, they served up food on the royal platter belonging to their grandfather Laius whom Oedipus had unwittingly killed, and secondly, they took advantage of his blindness and gave him an inferior cut of meat instead of the best joint as befitted royalty. Because of these two incidents, Oedipus cursed his sons and prayed they would destroy each other. He then left Thebes for good to live out the rest of his life in exile, accompanied by his daughter Antigone who gave up everything to care for him.

When Oedipus' two sons, Eteocles and Polynices, were old enough, they both claimed the throne, and finally agreed to take it in turns every other year. But after his year was up Eteocles refused to step down, whereupon Polynices (the elder, who by then was married to the king of Argos' daughter), persuaded his father-in-law to raise an army to lay siege to Thebes. There were six hand-picked men to lead a massed assault on six gates of the city, leaving Polynices to attack the seventh which his brother Eteocles was defending. There they both killed each other as victims of their father's curse.

Seven Against Thebes is filled with Aeschylus' powerfully descriptive language. The play begins with Eteocles exhorting the Thebans to rise to the occasion and fight off the attackers: *...Each to his post in panoply go forth. Line well the ramparts, mount the flanking towers, meet them undaunted at the gates, nor fear their foreign numbers. God shall guide the event... (31-34.)*

A Messenger hurries on with the latest news. He has just overheard orders given to six chieftains to attack six of the seven gates in Thebes' fortifications and urges Eteocles to man the bulwarks *...ere the blast of war descend on her: full loudly yonder surge roars from the land. Seize thou the present hour... (63-65.)* Eteocles prays to the gods: *...Let Cadmus' town still live at liberty from foreign domination; nor impose on Thebes the yoke of bondage... (75-77.)*

A Chorus of women enter having seen the approaching army *... streaming hither, horsemen in the van, a mounted multitude... The tramp of hoofs upon the nearer plain falls on mine ear, threatening captivity. It hovers close at hand, the heightening roar as of wild waters irresistible rending the hills... Why do we groan and linger? Hear ye not the smitten shield? When, if not now, should supplicating robes and wreaths be in request? The sound is clear, nay visible! the clash of many a spear!... (83-90, 99-103.)* And they call on the gods to save them. Eteocles implores the women to hold their nerve for the sake of the men. Their senseless hurrying to and fro sets up panic *...a noise that genders heartless fear;*

whereby the foreigner's advantage grows, and Thebes is ravaged inly by ourselves... (193-195.)

The women barely listen to him, so caught up are they in their panic. Each outcry from them produces a call from Eteocles to control their nerves, but they are overwrought: *Lo, there! I hear the charger neighing high!... The town's foundations groan. They close us round! Battering at gates grows loud! I am full of dread! (243, 245, 248.)* They are deaf to Eteocles' command to cease their *vain repeating of wild babblement.*

The Chorus of women can only imagine the horrors of defeat. ... *While tender cries resound from infant throats... Young captive maids find for their earliest grief a sorrow past relief, the rude lust of an overbearing lord. What help can hope afford?... (348-349, 363-366.)*

The Messenger only adds to their terror as he announces the peril Thebes is in, listing the six gates which are under attack, each one stormed and breached by troops led by an Argive chieftain. He describes the emblazoned shields designed to strike terror in the Thebans. Finally, he tells Eteocles that the seventh gate is being stormed by his own brother Polynices whose shield is embossed with the personification of Justice. Eteocles is alarmed; his father's curse is about to be fulfilled. *...Yet ill would it beseem me here to weep; lest tears give birth to heavier cause of woe. (656-657.)* Justice! In his view *...Unjustly would she bear the honoured name of Justice, to consort with that rash mind. Whereon relying, I will go forth and stand myself to oppose him:- who more fit than I? ...If ill must come, let honour be secure; no other gain accrues to men when dead... (671-674, 684-685.)*

There passes an exchange between the Chorus of women and Eteocles; the women urge him not to fight his brother, but he knows it is his Fate and his courage must not fail him. He leaves to fulfil his destiny, and the Chorus bewail the situation and all that the future holds. A second Messenger arrives with the good news: *...Thebes hath escaped the yoke of threatened bondage; her impetuous foes are fallen from their pitch of vaunting pride, while she sails onward under smiling skies, no water shipped from that sore buffeting, no breach in all her towers, no part unsure: So firm the warrant of those bulwarks set singly to guard them. All but all is well – all in six gateways. But the seventh... (795-808.)* And the Messenger tells them the calamitous news that the curse of Oedipus has been fulfilled, both brothers are dead, each killed by the other: *... and with one stroke consigns to nothingness that hapless race. Thus joy and weeping mingle. We rejoice for Thebes faring gloriously, but weep for her* *two chieftains, generals of this war. Who with the hammered strength of Scythian steel have so divided their inheritance, that, carried headlong by their father's curse, ill-fated, each inherited so much earth as in his burial he may occupy. Thebes is rescued: but her princes twain by mutual slaughter fratricidally are perished: their own land hath drunk their blood. (814-826.)*

The Chorus sing their joy at victory, but sorrow at the death of their king and his brother. Antigone and Ismene arrive deeply distressed by the death of their brothers, and the end of their father's kingdom. Their grief is interrupted by the arrival of a Herald. The High Council of the Theban state has put out a decree that Eteocles, who died defending the city, is to be buried with due honours, but Polynices, who came as an enemy to claim the kingdom, is forbidden any burial rites. His ... *corpse graveless shall be cast forth for dogs to tear, as minded to lay waste our Theban land, had not some god stood in his path and foiled his spear: dead though he be, his country's gods shall ban him, since he brought in their despite a foreign host to invade and subjugate their city... (1018-1025.)*

Antigone is horrified by this declaration, and refuses to obey. She herself will see to the proper burial of her brother. Nothing will stop her. *...I, though a woman, will prepare his mound, carrying the earth in this fine garment's fold. I will cover him, let none think otherwise. (1042-1044.)*

And with much bewailing, cautioning and determination on the part of Antigone, the drama comes to an end.

Her strong sense of family duty is also the subject of Sophocles' play *Antigone* (see Addenda). *Antigone* was one of Sophocles' earliest tragedies – produced a decade or so before his *Oedipus Tyrannus*.

Tomorrow we are travelling on to Athens; I want to see Colonus where Sophocles was born and grew up, and where another of his Oedipus tragedies is set, namely *Oedipus Colonus* which describes the final hours of that tragic king.

CHAPTER 10

ATHENS
SOPHOCLES - *OEDIPUS AT COLONUS*

COLONUS

We were back in our Athens hotel, and I felt foolish as I asked the young man in reception if it was possible to get to Colonus. "King Oedipus of Thebes died there," I said. "Sophocles," I explained, trying to make light of it.

The young man was polite and answered my question solemnly by spreading out a large street plan and, with a black felt pen, ringed around the area. He then pointed to the nearby streets and warned that it was a dangerous part of Athens and I should stay clear of it. He marked it with a big black cross. "You take taxi?" he enquired. He pointed to the Colonus area and said: "Colonus it is all right, but here there are bad people."

Hilary came with me. Our hotel was close to the Acropolis and there was a taxi-rank nearby.

"You speak English?" I asked the first driver in the rank. "So, so," came the gruff reply. He was a stocky middle-aged fellow with thinning grey hair. I wasn't sure if he looked genial or had a cussed streak to his character. "Where you want to go?" he asked.

"How much?" I asked, pointing to the ringed area on my map. "I want to see Colonus, and you wait, please. Then you bring us back."

He shrugged. "Maybe twenty-five euros," he said.

"Twenty-five? O.K." I said. "Not more."

I sat in the front beside him. A little Greek conversation, I thought, would justify the extravagance. I told him I was interested in ancient Greek myth and legend and, instead of changing the subject, he said: "Colonus, it is close to Plato's Academy. I show you."

"Plato's Academy?" I queried. "I thought that was in the Agora."

"No, it is near where I take you."

"Twenty-five euros," I insisted.

"Yes, yes. I take you." I was beginning to like him.

We joined a crush of cars and, by the time we reached the uninspiring suburbs, I'd learned that our driver preferred freedom to being shackled to a wife; that he'd had a number of jobs which included running a jewellery business and dealing in antiques. He also used to gamble on the horses and had lost a lot of money. He was aged sixty-four, and he'd been driving a taxi now for twelve years. Such was his story. But best of all he didn't pooh-pooh my interest in Colonus.

Eventually, driving along a widish thoroughfare beside a small municipal park, our driver drew up at the kerbside and waved an arm indicating we'd arrived. He would wait there while we took a look, he said.

So this busy street with buses, cars and motor-bikes had, over two and a half thousand years ago, been a village outside the city walls of Athens! There was nothing to recommend it now.

We got out of the taxi and walked into the small park with its tarmac pathways and central large concrete fountain scrawled with graffiti with no water in it. A few schoolboys of African origin were kicking a football nearby; other children carrying satchels were walking home from school.

Here then was where Sophocles was born and spent his life. In his day there would have been views from his village to the distant mountains that ringed Athens: Mt. Parnes to the north, the Hymettos mountains to the east; to the north-east the Pentelikon range from which the marble was quarried and used for the construction of the Parthenon and other buildings on the Acropolis. And there would surely have been an unobstructed view to the south-west, to the distant sea and the port of Piraeus?

Sophocles was born here at Colonus 486 B.C. His father was a wealthy manufacturer of armour who gave his son the best possible education. Apparently the young Sophocles excelled at music. He was given private lessons and won prizes for singing and playing the cithara; at the opposite extreme he also won prizes for wrestling.

Aged sixteen he led the chorus of boys in the paean commemorating the victorious Battle of Salamis in 480 B.C., the year of Euripides' birth. Little did he know that twenty or so years later he would be competing at the City Dionysia against the infant born on the day of that triumphant victory; nor that at the end of his long life, when news reached Athens from Macedonia in 406 B.C. of the death of

Euripides that he, Sophocles, would again lead a chorus singing an elegy in praise of Euripides in the theatre of Dionysos. By then Sophocles himself was ninety and was to die later that same year.

It is said that Sophocles acted in many of his own early dramas. He was twenty-eight when he produced his first play (now lost) with which he won first prize at the City Dionysia, beating none other than Aeschylus. Overall he is thought to have written more than a hundred and twenty plays, producing a trilogy every other year, of which only seven dramas have survived.

As a talented musician he composed his own music for his productions. What a shame we have no recording of Sophocles singing and playing the cithera. I imagine a soft-voiced, gifted artist with an amiable temperament. If he excelled at everything he set his mind to, his charm and self-deprecating humour endeared him, so it is said, to all who knew him. Apparently, Aristophanes had attempted to poke fun at him in one of his comedies but had failed completely, such was Sophocles' standing in the public eye.

His last tragedy *Oedipus at Colonus* was written in 406 B.C., the year of his death; he died a couple of years before the end of the Peloponnesian War and final defeat of Athens by Sparta. While he was writing it, he must have been suffering (as everyone in Athens and Attica would have been) from the stresses and strains of the extended war with its destruction, deprivation and starvation.

In his lifetime Sophocles was appointed to several positions of authority in Athens, including managing the finances of the city. He'd seen Pericles as a rising statesman, whose dream of beautifying Athens was realized by the construction of the Parthenon and other temples on the Acropolis. But, over his long lifetime, he also saw Athens overreach herself, and her reputation and splendour begin to ebb away. At the age of ninety he must have been aware that death would soon claim him. Perhaps he saw himself in the shoes of the aged and blind Oedipus who, in his new tragedy *Oedipus at Colonus*, was fated to die at Colonus.

Here, somewhere close by this dry fountain, was the site of the Grove of the Erinyes. It was near here that the blind Oedipus was led by his daughter Antigone, who was now a young woman.

Imagine, not a laid out park with paths, geometric patches of grass and trees, but a well-watered grove. Where today I saw a long, grimy white block of marble serving no purpose so far as I could make out, there was once a bronze threshold leading to the subterranean home of the Erinyes, the ancient chthonic deities (commonly known as the Furies). They were the same goddesses whom Athena, at the trial of Orestes on the Areópagus, re-named the Eumenides (the kindly ones).

In the *Oedipus at Colonus* drama, the tragedy begins with a Citizen seeing the blind Oedipus approaching through the grove, led by Antigone. He warns them they are trespassing here on sacred ground *...the dread goddesses hold it, the daughters of the earth and gloom... this same spot where you stand is called the brazen threshold of this land – the holy rampart of Athens... (45-46, 67-69.)* And he points to a statue of their local hero, the horseman Colonus, honoured by the local farmers (hence the name Colonus for the village).

Oedipus asks who is the ruler of the land, and is told that it is Theseus, king of Athens. Somewhat audaciously, considering his own fall from power and his present state of destitution, Oedipus commands that Theseus be brought to him. When questioned as to why Theseus would want to see him, Oedipus replies: *...to gain much by a small act of kindness. (87.)*

Left alone with Antigone, Oedipus speaks of this as being his final resting place as predicted by a recent oracle. He believes he has been divinely guided here, and prays: *...Now therefore, goddesses, bestow on me, according to Apollo's oracle, some... quick finish of my life... (124-126.)*

But before the 'quick finish of his life' comes, a lot happens. His other daughter Ismene arrives with the urgent news that her two brothers have fallen out because Eteocles is refusing to step down from the throne to allow Polynices his year as king (as described in Aeschylus' *Seven Against Thebes,* Chapter 9). A new oracle calls for Oedipus to return home. Oedipus, however, is come here to die, and he is full of resentment against his two sons.

Rather surprisingly Theseus does come at Oedipus' bidding. He is generous-hearted and speaks reassuring words to this fallen and disgraced king, saying: *...for by thy garb and thine afflicted presence we perceive that thou art really he; and pitying thee, thou forlorn Oedipus, I would enquire with what petition to the city or me thou and thy hapless follower wait on us?... (624-629.)* And he goes on to tell Oedipus how he himself has known what it is to be on foreign soil and friendless.... *wherefore no foreigner, such as now thou art, would I turn aside... (636-637.)*

Oedipus pours out his problems, how he has suffered wrongs upon wrongs, to which Theseus offers to *replant him in our country.*

They are interrupted by the arrival of Creon from Thebes; he has come to inform Oedipus that the citizens of Thebes want him to return. And he remarks on how wretched Oedipus looks, and how terrible for Antigone to have to lead him everywhere.

Oedipus and Creon exchange angry words. Why on earth, Creon asks, would Theseus want to give shelter to one who is the killer of his father, and the husband of his mother?

Oedipus turns on him furiously. Just because he sees that Theseus is welcoming him *...you try with your soft cruel words to part us!... (878-879.)*

Creon responds in kind: *...Do you hug reproach to your old age? (917-918.)* There is a skirmish and Antigone and Ismene are taken hostage by Creon's men, and Oedipus cries out to the Citizens of Colonus to save them. Theseus turns on Creon in anger for behaving in such a manner in his, (Theseus') domain. Creon retorts in similar vein. How can Theseus, king of Athens with the Areópagus and all that it stands for, offer sanctuary to Oedipus who is both guilty of patricide and incest, he asks? But Oedipus cries out: *O front of impudence! ...Who has spit forth out of thy mouth at me murders and marriages and accidents, which to my grief, not of free will, I suffered... I shall not be silent, you being grown to such a monster of outspokenness!... (1095-1121.)*

Theseus takes command of the situation and orders Creon to help him retrieve Oedipus' daughters. He tells Oedipus to stay where he is till he returns with them. They depart leaving the Chorus to describe the search. When Theseus arrives back with the two girls, Oedipus is overjoyed and filled with gratitude: *...And may the gods bestow as I desire on you, and on this land; since among you alone of men did I find piety.... (1275-1277.)* And he adds: *...Only the man who has experienced it can sympathise with misery such as mine... (1287-1288.)*

At this point Polynices, Oedipus' son, arrives in a highly emotional state. He weeps at seeing his father and sister destitute and wandering like vagrants. He then proceeds to pour out his own troubles to his father, and implores his help because his brother refuses to relinquish the throne.

Oedipus, however, feels no sympathy for him, and has no inclination to cooperate. What has Polynices ever done for him when he most needed him? He erupts with resentment: *...I disown thee, reptile! Of base souls basest! And take with thee this doom of mine, never to win thy native land in fight, nor to return to Argos... but by a kindred hand thyself to fall, him having slain, who was thy banisher. This is my curse!... (1567-1574.)*

Polynices is dismayed by his father's outrage and turns to Antigone, imploring her that if he dies she, at least, will bury him. But Antigone asks: ...*Do not ruin yourself – and Thebes! ...Where is your profit in overthrowing your country? (1606-1612.)* Why in heaven's name put himself in the situation where he and Eteocles will die ... *each from the other's hand? (1619.)* She is dismayed by the thought of losing both brothers.

The Chorus sing of imminent disaster and foresee doom and death. The sound of thunder adds to the drama, and Oedipus has a premonition of finality; he declares his wish to be buried here where Theseus has given him sanctuary in his realm: ...*Nay, do not touch me; let me for myself search out the hallowed grave where, in this soil, it is my fate to lie... Already I creep upon my way to hide my last of life in Hades... May you live happy, and to your happiness fortunate ever, think of me, you dead! (1753-1764.)* And Oedipus walks into the Sacred Grove alone.

The Chorus pray to Hades and Persephone of the underworld and the impending gloom intensifies till a Messenger arrives hurriedly to announce the demise of Oedipus. *Truly the event is meet to wonder at...First, in what fashion he set forth from hence, you must have seen, being present, even as I; none of his company conducting him, but he himself showing to us all the way...having reached the threshold of that chasm whose root is in the brazen stairs below...he stood still... (1797-1806.)* And he relates how Oedipus threw off his dirty clothes and called to his daughters to bring him water from a stream. They washed and clothed him in fresh garments. ...*And when, now, nought remained unsatisfied of all that he desired, sounded from Hades thunder, and the maids, as they heard, shivered; and at their father's knees fell down and wept, beating their breasts, and raised wailings prolonged, unceasing. He the while, soon as he heard their bitter note of woe, folding his arms about them, said: "For you, my girls, this day there is no father more; for all things now are ended that were mine; and now no longer need you bear for me the burden of your hard tendance, hard indeed – I know it, my children; but one single word cancels the evil of all cares like this: Love..." (1818-1831.)*

The Messenger describes how ...*suddenly some voice shouted his name; so that the hair of all stood up for fear; for a god called him – called him many times from many sides at once... (1836-1839.)*

But before obeying the voice, the Messenger reports, Oedipus had first requested Theseus to swear to take care of his two daughters. to which Theseus had agreed. Oedipus had then groped around blindly till he'd found and embraced his daughters for the last time, saying:

"...bear up in spirit, as befits your nobleness; look not on the sights you may not see...with all speed depart..." (1861-1864.)

Obediently they had left the scene. The Messenger continues: ... *When we had gone apart, after short space we turned and saw far off – the man, indeed, was nowhere visible – only the king* (Theseus) *holding up his hand over his face... as if some sight of terror had appeared, awful, intolerable to gaze upon; then, in a moment, without interval, we saw him kneel, worshipping earth, and heaven the abode of gods... (1869-1877.)*

The Messenger had seen nothing more, no sudden visible wonder such as a thunderbolt or whirlwind taking Oedipus off. It was as though there was ...*some guide sent from above, or depth of the earth beneath opening to take him, friendly, without pain. For not as of one mourned, or with disease grown pitiable, was his departure; but if any ever was so, wonderful... (1882-1883.)*

Antigone and Ismene, shedding tears of misery, ask to see their father's grave; but Theseus tells them about the solemn oath he swore that the whereabouts would be kept for ever secret. ...*And he* (Oedipus) *said that if I kept my pledge I'd keep my country free of harm for ever. I swore it, and the powers heard my vows, and Zeus' son above all, the guardian of our oaths who sees all things. (2002-2011.)*

Antigone requests that she and Ismene should now be allowed to return to Thebes swiftly, hopefully in time to prevent the war between her two brothers. Theseus agrees, and so the drama ends.

Unlike Aeschylus and Euripides who in their dramas often had the gods actively engaged in human activities, Sophocles preferred a more subtle approach; his gods were unseen but their presence felt. He wove into his tragedies an eternal divine law of justice and right behaviour. Those who broke the law or did evil could expect to be divinely punished. If some virtuous people seemed to suffer undeservedly, it was due to the sins of their forefathers – something that could have been picked up from the Jewish Old Testament.

It has been suggested that with his *Oedipus at Colonus* Sophocles was predicting his own death, something he didn't regard as a finality but as a moving on to some new existence. He never lived to see the play performed; instead, it was produced posthumously by his grandson (also named Sophocles, and also a writer of tragedies). It was staged in 401 B.C. though whether it won an award or not, or whether it was performed at the City Dionysia or the Lenaia, is not known.

There are several stories regarding Sophocles' death: some say he died by choking on a grape at a Dionysos festival; others that he died of happiness at winning first prize at the Great Dionysia, though with which play remains a mystery; another story is that he expired trying to recite a long sentence from his *Antigone* without drawing breath.

I have a last look around Colonus, at the park with its graffiti-covered dry fountain, and the oblong block of marble, then turn my back on it.

Hilary, who's been perched on the edge of the fountain, joins me, and says: "It's not exactly inspiring, is it? – hardly spiritually uplifting!"

I'd briefed Hilary about the Colonus tragedy and had read some of it to her the evening before. I suppose she's sadly disillusioned as there are no well-watered grove of trees or brazen threshold.

Our taxi-driver makes no comment when we return to him, but merely says he will take us now to Plato's Academy. I hope he isn't going to up the fare considerably, but I'm keen to see it. "They still work there and discover new things," he says. "Come, I show you."

About three minutes later we arrive at a larger park with trees and paths and stretches of grass on which archaeologists have been at work revealing rectangular areas of stone blocks.

Our driver stumps ahead leading the way to the excavations. It occurs to me that this might be the dangerous quarter I was warned about; it's possible that this stocky fellow is leading us into the bushes where who knows what might happen. I am reassured when we pass a newly married voluptuous bride in a tight fitting white satin wedding gown seated on a park bench with her bridegroom; they are kissing for a wedding photo. We see the photographer darting about, arranging her white satin train in an artistic swoosh around her feet.

Before Plato's day, a nearby river had been diverted so that what originally had been dry and barren, had become well-watered with trees and shady walks. Plato then took it over for his Academy where he taught his students.

So what's exciting about these ruins? Well, absolutely nothing except that it has the name of the great philosopher. The word 'Academy', I am later to discover, comes from the local hero Hekademos. The story is as follows: Theseus had once abducted Helen of Troy when she was only a child, and had placed her in the care of his mother Aithra till she was old enough to become his bride. Hekademos, knowing her whereabouts, told Helen's twin brothers, Castor and Polydeuces. They immediately rescued her, and returned her to her home in Sparta. As a consequence, throughout the Peloponnesian War the Spartans, in gratitude to Hekademos for saving their beautiful, legendary Helen, made a point of never ravaging this region which was his (Hekademos') home.

Hilary picks an olive leaf from a tree and the taxi-driver, spotting her doing this, says: "Pah! just one leaf? You want olive? Take!" and he breaks off two good-sized twigs, which he presents to each of us. "These trees they come from the olive of Athena on the Acropolis," he informs us. "When the Persians come many years ago they burn everything on the Acropolis including the holy olive tree of Athena. But the roots they grow again and from her tree they plant here twelve olive trees."

"The olive is symbolic of peace," Hilary says. "That's what olive branches represent – peace."

"It is used for many things," says our driver. "It is used to crown the winners of the Olympic Games. The wood is also good for building boats."

"And for cooking," Hilary adds.

"And for lamps, for burning fire, for olive-oil, for eating in salad. The olive has many uses."

On our return the driver passes through the area which must be the one our hotel receptionist warned me against. He points to the many immigrants, and holds forth volubly about Greece's impending explosive situation. There is nothing politically correct about him, and what he says is alarming.

Back at our hotel I bravely take out thirty euros, and say: "Twenty-five you said, and here is another five but only if you do not gamble with it."

He looks happy. "I stop gambling six months now. No, I will not gamble more," he says.

So the notes pass into his hands with gratitude.

I've seen all I hoped to and more, thanks to his own interest in his historic past, and his wish to share it with us.

PART THREE
THIRD TRIP

CHAPTER 11

MACEDONIA: PELLA & AIGAIA

It was early May when we flew in to Greece again, this time to Thessaloniki in the north. On this occasion I was on the trail of Euripides' last years. When he was in his seventies, he was invited by King Archelaus of Macedonia to his court at Pella. For a long time the king (413-399 B.C.) had been aware of Athens' flourishing culture: her talented and inspired dramatists, musicians, artists, poets and suchlike, and was determined to have such men around him also.

For this purpose he moved his capital from ancient Aigaia and founded a new capital at Pella, some eighty kilometres further north. For trade he needed good land- and sea-routes, and chose the location because at the time Pella had easy access to the sea through a lagoon. An ambitious monarch, Archelaus was determined to prove wrong the pervading Greek view that all Macedonians were uncouth and drunken barbarians – the word 'barbarian' comes from the Greek word *bárbaros* meaning 'foreign', 'ignorant'.

Having built his new capital, Archelaus invited Euripides, together with other men of intellect and culture to come. It is believed that Socrates was also asked, but declined.

My first planned destination for this trip was the king's new capital, some forty-five kilometres west of Salonika. Despite Fiona's faith in her Satnav and navigational skills, Hilary, as driver, still managed to screw things up, and it was some while before we eventually escaped from the interweaving roads in the extensive suburbs of Salonika and found the right one we wanted for Pella. Throughout it all Hilary remained supremely calm however wrong she was. Maybe everyone (as she had) should spend a few years in a convent or monastery to learn patience and serenity.

As we drew nearer to Pella, we saw snowy peaked mountains veiled by a gossamer haze looming as a distant backdrop to Archelaus' new city, and the sight filled me with excitement and expectation.

★

What, no palace? The museum attendant looked chagrined and apologetic. It had yet to be excavated, he said. So where was this unexcavated palace, I asked? I was informed that it was thought to be several hundred metres behind the museum on a plateau of land, itself a kilometre or so away from the main Pella archaeological site.

We discussed the matter over a salad lunch on the museum terrace. I badly wanted to see the site where the palace was thought to be. Fiona wasn't keen and said: "You guys go off and find your palace while I stay here. I'm expecting Bob to ring any moment." Bob was her latest internet dating contender, and had said he would phone every afternoon at two, Greek time. As we drove off, Hilary told me she thought this new man sounded promising, and she just hoped it wouldn't end in tears.

We drove along a minor road for several hundred yards till we saw a footpath. We left the car, and followed a rutted track to where we thought the palace was supposed to be. Wild flowers and grasses grew in profusion, and here and there were drifts of bright red poppies. A few small powder-puff clouds hung suspended against the blue sky.

So it was here, if indeed it was the palace site, that Euripides had come as a guest of King Archelaus in 408 B.C. Here, that it is said he wrote *Iphigenia at Aulis* and his *Bacchae*. It would have been from here too that Euripides would have looked out over the navigable lagoon which gave access to the Thermaic Gulf and the Aegean sea. The lagoon, though, had long since silted up, and the sea no longer visible, being now some forty or so kilometres away.

We returned to the museum and picked up a beaming Fiona (she'd had her phone-call), and drove on down to the ancient city and the main archaeological site. Dutifully, I walked around and saw the sanctuary of Aphrodite, the public archives, the agora, the House of Dionysos, and the House of Helen – the two latter so-called because of their pebble-mosaic floors: the former of Dionysos riding naked on a panther (now exhibited in the museum), the latter (still in situ) depicting the Abduction of Helen. They were made from tiny sea pebbles, outlined with clay or lead. An information board told me the one in the House of Helen was not of Paris abducting Helen, but of Theseus who'd caught sight of her as a child playing beside the river Eurotas at Sparta – a moment of woeful lust and abduction tarnished his otherwise unblemished, noble character.

From the agora, Hilary pointed out in the far distance, a building and near to it a rise in the landscape. "That, surely, is the museum?" she said. "And on that plateau to the right of it must be where the king had his palace, do you see?"

Certainly I saw. The mind's eye took over and a sense of enthusiasm surged suddenly. If Euripides had looked down from there to this new city of King Archelaus (now no more than ruined walls in squares and rectangles), equally, from these houses the king's subjects would have gazed up at the palace in its monumental splendour rising from the plateau.

So what about a theatre here at Pella? There was no indication that there had been one, nor had the museum staff said anything about a theatre. Strange. Yet King Archelaus had invited the dramatist Euripides to live at his court; surely there would have been a theatre where he could present his work?

We turned our attention back to the pebble-mosaic floor and the Abduction of Helen. Little did Helen realize that her life story would inspire artists and writers down the ages. That her one act of infidelity would impact on her family and friends, and members of the royal family in Troy, every son of which would die (including Paris), and every female member be reduced to penury and slavery.

To look on the bright side, without Helen's passionate love-affair, Euripides would never have written his *Trojan Women*, or *Iphigenia at Aulis*; nor would he have written *Helen* four years before coming to Macedonia. Interestingly, in it he had Helen, not in Troy as Homer had her, but in Egypt throughout the ten year Trojan War. He had, it is believed, picked up on the idea of a phantom Helen in Troy from a lyric poet named Stesichorus who'd lived in the seventh to mid-sixth century B.C. But let me start at the beginning of the drama, and allow the play to speak for itself.

★

Helen, in Egypt, is alone on stage and introduces herself. She explains how she was born as a result of her immortal father Zeus who, disguised as a swan, had it off with her mortal mother Leda. She goes on to speak about the Judgement of Paris. Paris had been asked to choose who was the fairest of three goddesses: Aphrodite, Hera or Athena. Aphrodite tried bribery, promising him the most beautiful woman in the world if he chose her; Hera promised him power, and Athena victory. Paris, a virile young man, scorned the latter two tempting bribes in favour of the most beautiful woman in the world.

Piqued at losing to Aphrodite, Hera played a trick on Paris and, in Helen's words: *...in my semblance formed a living image composed of ether... (46-47.)* She explains how it was this phantom image of her that Paris had had with him in Troy all this time, while the real her had been brought here to the palace of Proteus in Egypt so that *...undefiled I might preserve the bed of Menelaus... (65.)* Well! Fancy having a gruesome ten year war fought to retrieve only a phantom! Fortunately an audience is very willing to be transported to the realms of fantasy.

According to Euripides in the drama, Proteus (an ancient sea-god) is the recently deceased king of Egypt, with a palace on the island of Pharos at the mouth of the Nile. The action of the play takes place outside his sepulchre at the entrance to the palace where his son Theoclymenus now lives as king. To confuse matters, Theoclymenus is determined to make Helen his bride. She tells us that she has never been unfaithful to her husband Menelaus, king of Sparta – something I find difficult to accept since her whole raison d'être in history is her adultery. But let's continue with the realm of fantasy.

Ajax's brother Teucer arrives on the scene, having been banished by his angry father Telamon because he's returned home to Salamis without bringing back the body of Ajax. The real Helen in Egypt rather naturally wants to know what has happened to her phantom self in Troy. Teucer tells her how, at the fall of Troy and the triumphant Greek victory, Menelaus seized her by her hair and dragged her away. She then learns that both Menelaus and she (except the real she is there) have drowned at sea having been shipwrecked in a storm. So Menelaus, her beloved husband to whom she has remained faithful all these years, has died? After all her patient fidelity that has lasted seventeen years (ten years of war, and seven more when the Greek warriors, with the gods thwarting them, were attempting to sail back to Greece).

Helen asks Teucer about her mother Leda and is told that she hanged herself for shame of what Helen had done. And her twin brothers, Castor and Polydeuces? They both fell on their swords because of the disgrace Helen had brought on the family.

Teucer then explains he is there to consult the king's sister Theonoe, a prophetess, on how he can best get to Cyprus. Helen warns him that the king kills any Greek who sets foot on Egyptian soil, and advises him to flee before he is discovered. Teucer departs leaving Helen alone bewailing her lot.

How overwhelmed she feels! Her mother dead, her brothers too, and now Menelaus! And all those wagging tongues when all the while she's been here in Egypt remaining faithful to Menelaus! ...*It were a lesser evil...to sin than be suspected falsely... (373-376)* she wails.

And in another long soliloquy she remembers her daughter who *...in the virgin state grows grey, still... unwedded... (389-390.)* She blames it all, not on herself and her amorous adventure (which never happened, apparently), but *...to the power of adverse fortune... (395.)*

"What would you say," I'd asked Harry, when we'd been discussing the play one day, "if I'd run off with some handsome youth, and pretended it wasn't really me, but a phantom image of me gone off with him?"

"Hum. Well, if you were sitting here with me, then I wouldn't worry about it, would I?" he'd replied reasonably.

"But I'm not with you," I said, trying to cajole him out of his sense of a happily secure marriage. "The real me is – well, in Egypt, let's say, and you think the real me is with him."

"Well, it's not really an issue," Harry'd remarked. "You haven't gone off." Then he'd added, "And you never would go off."

For some reason his certainty niggled, and I'd said: "How do you know I never would?"

"Because – just because – well, you're no Helen!"

That riled.

"You mean I'm no beauty?"

"No. I mean, yes. I mean – Oh, you know what I mean!"

I'd eyed him silently while he'd unsuccessfully tried to extricate himself, then I'd added: "Some people thought me beautiful when I was younger. I could have gone off with – " and I named several rather attractive men Harry knew, then added: "Maybe I'm just the phantom me, sitting here. Maybe the real me is with my lover!"

But Harry was not to be rattled. "All I can say is, if it's been a phantom you all these years, then I'm perfectly content with the phantom, thank you." And that was the end of the subject.

To get back to Euripides' drama. Helen ends her long monologue of woes, with the mild complaint: *...For beauty renders other women* *blessed, but hath to me the source of ruin proved. (419-420.)*

The Chorus, consisting of Helen's attendants, try to cheer her up. What if these rumours of Menelaus' death are untrue, they suggest? They advise Helen to ask Theonoe, the prophetess, since she knows the answer to all things.

With Helen and the Chorus gone, Menelaus himself appears, having survived the shipwreck along with his phantom Helen and many of his crew who are all hiding in a cave while he comes to the palace for help. A Woman Servant comes from the palace. When he asks her for assistance, and tells her he is a shipwrecked Greek mariner, she warns him that no Greek is allowed on Egyptian soil, then explains that it is because the Greek Helen, whom the king intends to marry, lives in Egypt. Menelaus is bemused. The Greek Helen? How? Has she been found in the cave where she and his men are hiding? He is told that Helen has been there since before the armada set sail for Troy!

Left alone, Menelaus ponders aloud his bewilderment: Helen hiding in the cave? Helen who's been living in Egypt? Helen, whom the king wants to marry? The wretched Menelaus groans with confusion, a victim always, he realizes, of the curse of the House of Atreus.

Helen and the Chorus arrive having consulted Theonoe, the prophetess. They have learned from her that Menelaus is still alive. Helen and Menelaus, who is bedraggled and in dire straits after being nearly drowned, meet. They admit that they recognize each other but are puzzled. How can it be, Menelaus asks, when his Helen is in the cave?

Eventually, Helen confesses: *To the domains of Troy I never went: it was my image only. (872-873.)* And she explains how Hera made a phantom replica of her. But poor Menelaus becomes more and more mystified. How can she be there and here all at the same time? And, much to Helen's distress, he prepares to leave.

A Messenger arrives from the cave with alarming news. It's Helen! *Borne to the skies your consort from our sight hath vanished, in the heavens is she concealed… (858-859.)*

Little by little Menelaus and Helen realize that each is the real, living reality and, despite all these years and all the distress they have suffered, they fall into each other's arms.

So how come Helen came to Egypt, Menelaus finally asks? The goddess Hera brought her here: *…from my country in an evil hour, from my loved native city, and from you, me hath the goddess driven, a wretch*

accursed in that I left our house, and bridal bed, which yet I left not…
(915-919.)

And by the time Helen has told her sorry tale, Menelaus is reassured that everybody is to blame except for Helen herself.

The Messenger helps by saying: *…Oh how variable is Zeus, and how inscrutable! For he with ease whirls us around, now here, now there… (930-932.)*

Menelaus instructs the Messenger to return to the cave and tell them the good news that the vanished Helen was an image only, and he has found the real Helen at last.

At this point Helen remembers the dangers facing Menelaus, and tells him he must leave or risk being killed because he is Greek. Oh, poor Menelaus! How he is thrown from one dilemma to another – to flee now, when he has just found her? The Helen he's retrieved from Troy just a phantom image of her now vanished to the skies? The real Helen now reunited with him whom the king of Egypt has set his heart on?

Helen feels that their best solution is to supplicate Theonoe, the prophetess and king's sister. Since she knows everything as she is a seer, they must implore her to keep their plans a secret.

To cut a long drama short, Theonoe agrees to say nothing, and Helen comes up with a solution on how best to escape. She suggests they pretend Menelaus is dead and he can act the part of a messenger bringing her the news of his death: he will tell her how he drowned when his ship foundered on rocks, although he (the messenger) managed to survive. She herself will play the part of a grieving widow having just learned of her husband's death. She will cut off her golden locks, and persuade the king that it's compulsory that she undertake certain funeral rites. For this she will need a ship so she herself can perform the rites at sea, as is required by the Greeks of a drowned monarch's widow.

Her cunning plan convinces King Theoclymenus who is happy that Helen agrees to marry him now she knows Menelaus is dead. By all means let the funeral rites take place, he says.

A passage of time is marked by the Chorus singing an account of Helen and Menelaus aboard their ship. Another Messenger arrives and describes how the ship was prepared and how the 'Messenger', who'd accompanied Helen, called on his fellow survivors of the shipwreck to come from their cave for the funeral rites of their drowned king. … *Simulated tears they shed, and went aboard the ship, carrying the presents to be cast into the sea for Menelaus... (2052-2055.)* Although the Egyptian crew's suspicions were aroused, since the king had entrusted the Greek Messenger (Menelaus) to do the necessaries, they hadn't liked to voice their doubts. A bull had been brought on board to be sacrificed. ...*he bellowing rolled his eyes around, bending his back and low'ring betwixt his horns, nor dared we to approach and handle him. (2064-2067.)* But when Menelaus ordered his men to carry the beast aboard, they had obeyed. The Messenger described how all the Greek survivors, together with Helen, had embarked; the Egyptian crew strained at their oars, and the ship had moved off. But – oh, horrors! Later, while sacrificing the bull and calling on Poseidon, Menelaus and his men had seized their swords which had been concealed under their garments, and overpowered the crew: ...*on their feet all now stood up; our hands with nautic poles were armed, and theirs with swords: a tide of slaughter ran down the ship... (2117-2121.)*

King Theoclymenus is understandably furious at having been duped by Helen and Menelaus. He wants to pursue them, punish them, kill them, everything a king who's been made a fool of wants in order to recover his dignity. The Chorus try to pacify him, pointing out that Helen has returned to her rightful husband, but he remains irate.

The drama ends with Helen's twin immortal brothers, Castor and Polydeuces, speaking from the heavens: *Restrain that ire that hurries thee away beyond the bounds of reason, oh, thou king of Egypt's realm... Thou rashly hast indulged thine anger, for the loss of her whom Fate ne'er destined to thy bed... (2199-2201, 2204-2206.)* And they advise Theoclymenus not to be angry with his sister Theonoe for saying nothing for she has done him no injury. No, it was ...*the immortal powers, who had ordained that these events should happen... (2219-2220.)*

And her immortal brothers now pronounce that she, the good and righteous Helen, is destined to become a goddess. ...*after you have finished life's career, you shall be called a goddess, shall partake with us the rich oblations, and receive the gifts of men: for thus hath Zeus decreed... (2031-2034.)*

And it is true. After her death Helen took on a divine role and was evoked as a goddess at numerous cult shrines. Amazing!

The play ends with Theoclymenus accepting what he cannot change. He will not punish his sister for not revealing what she knew, nor will he pursue Helen but will let her sail for Sparta since the gods decree it must be so.

The Chorus sing the final lines: ...*A thousand shapes our varying fates assume the gods perform what least we could expect, and oft the things for which we fondly hoped come not to pass; but Heaven still finds a clue to guide our steps through life's perplexing maze, and thus doth this important business end. (2061-2066.)*

★

Two days after visiting Pella we drove to Aigaia. We expected it to be dismal since King Archelaus had abandoned it as his capital in order to found Pella. To my surprise we were captivated by the ancient city. It was there at Aigaia (today's Vergina) that archaeologists had excavated the tumulus tomb of Alexander the Great's father Philip II. The tumulus was a wide grassy mound, the base of which was surrounded by trees. It was in the tomb that a hoard of exquisite gold artefacts had been found. The astonishingly beautiful exhibits were displayed with great effect in a subterranean museum built around the tomb itself. Spellbinding in their gold-wrought beauty were the exquisite gold wreaths depicting paper-thin oak leaves with acorns and bees hidden in the foliage – they could only have been the workmanship of the most highly skilled craftsmen. Had King Archelaus been alive, he would have felt nothing but pride that his endeavours to bring culture to his kingdom was so evident by the fourth century B.C.

The palace at Aigaia covered an extensive excavated area and was, certainly at the time we were there, undergoing reconstruction work. It dominated a wide protruding shelf of land at the base of a low mountain which was bright with flowering yellow broom. The palace overlooked a well-cultivated plain – on our way to Aigaia, we'd passed many fields of cotton, aubergine and maize, as well as paddy-fields of rice and acres of cherry trees.

About two hundred metres below the palace, cut into the hillside, was the city's theatre. So Aigaia had a theatre, though Pella didn't? That seemed odd. Visible from the road, we could see the theatre's tiered seats outlined under turf and partly hidden by a glade of mature olive trees. A high wire-mesh fence prevented us from taking a closer look.

Maybe it was here that King Archelaus had watched a production of Euripides' work? Here that he'd seen the drama *Helen*? Or even Euripides' much earlier tragedies, not forgetting the works of Aeschylus, Sophocles and the comedies of Aristophanes.

One drama that had definitely been acted out here was a shocking real-life one which took place in the fourth century B.C. It was one that was to alter the course of history.

I turned to Hilary beside me. "The father of Alexander the Great was murdered here," I told her.

"Who was murdered?" Fiona, who may have been dreaming of Bob, was suddenly all attention.

"What happened?" Hilary asked, her kind blue eyes showing concern.

I told them how on the wedding-day of Philip II's daughter Cleopatra (Alexander's sister), the king had arranged a great pageant to be held in this theatre. The guests were gathered and, in order to make his own entrance the more spectacular, Philip had ordered statues of the twelve Olympian gods to be carried ahead of him along the processional way which descended to the theatre from his palace. His idea had been to follow behind and appear as the thirteenth Olympian god. To impress his guests even further, Philip commanded his bodyguard to keep well back. But, as he was making his majestic appearance, disaster struck. A member of his bodyguard seized the opportunity, drew his sword, rushed forward and killed him.

"On her wedding-day, her father killed! Poor girl!" Hilary said.

I told them how it was afterwards whispered that the gods had been displeased and were wreaking their revenge – the king the thirteenth Olympian god? He had overstepped the mark to compare himself to deity when he was but mortal! What presumption!

"Can you imagine how awful it must have been for Alexander the Great, aged only twenty, to see his father felled like an ox at his sister's wedding?" I said.

In fact, it was rumoured that Alexander's mother Olympias had been behind the assassination. Olympias had been a somewhat strange woman, fiercely ambitious for Alexander her only son. Her marriage to Philip (long ended) had been arranged as a diplomatic alliance between the Macedonians and the Molossians (a Greek tribe from Epirus). It is said that on the eve of her wedding, Olympias had dreamed that her womb had been struck by a thunderbolt, and there was a fire which flared and had then died down. And with the consummation of the marriage, Philip had dreamed that he had set a seal on Olympias' womb in the shape of a lion; this was explained, by those who knew how to interpret such things, that Olympias would give birth to a son who was destined to be as brave as a lion.

Olympias was not the easiest of women, and her marriage to

Philip had been a stormy one, doomed from the start, though not before she also bore Philip a daughter whom they named Cleopatra.

The final straw, so it is said, was when Philip caught Olympias with snakes in her bed. Snake handling, it has been suggested, was something she introduced into the cult of Dionysos. Apparently, she had been a devout follower of Dionysos and a Maenad.

True or false, one thing is certain: after Philip remarried, Olympias was determined to see her son crowned king, and she could only achieve her ambition by the death of Philip. So it was whispered that she'd been the brains behind his assassination.

Philip II's body had been burned on a pyre, and his ashes and bones placed in an impressive large golden urn with the 'Sunburst' symbol of the Macedonian kingdom on its lid. We'd seen it in the museum along with a smaller, similar urn with a 'Sunburst' in which the bones of his second wife had been placed after she'd followed him onto the pyre.

So Olympias got her wish, and the twenty-year-old Alexander ascended the Macedonian throne. All the portents which had suggested a great leader were proved correct. But what could he do without the gods? Alexander felt the need for their divine protection.

The ancient city of Dion had always been the religious centre of the Macedonian kingdom; it existed at the time of King Archelaus, and certainly it is known that Alexander the Great came there in order to honour and offer sacrifice to Zeus before setting out on his campaigns. It was to Dion we were going next.

CHAPTER

12

DION

Dion was spread over a wide area and fed by many springs. The great bulk of Mt. Olympus loomed snow-crested in the near distance, its foothills less than seven kilometres away – Mt. Olympus, home to the twelve Olympian gods! The word Dion is a corruption of the name Zeus.

Dion was ninety kilometres from Salonika where we were based for the week. Hilary and Fiona had begun to feel edgy (maybe traumatized was a better word) about getting out of Salonica in a hired car. As ninety kilometres was a long drive in one day (there and back) and, as Fiona whispered to me, Hilary's driving was erratic under the best of conditions, her nerves couldn't stand seeing her go off yet again on the wrong road; it was driving her mental. I was all right, she pointed out, because I was sitting in the back and oblivious to the dangers. And, as Hilary also confided: Fiona's map-reading was atrocious – she was always sending her off on the wrong road and blaming her for it! Far better, it was mutually agreed, to hire a taxi for the day – and damn the expense! At least that way we could all enjoy the outing.

So there we were at Dion, all relaxed and in good humour, having been driven by a pleasant, bearded young man called Kostas.

Soon after entering the site, we came to a lake fed by springs. Around this area was the Sacred Grove of the Muses. The nine Muses were the daughters of Zeus and Mnemosyne (Memory) – and, let's face it, without Memory how could drama, art and culture have blossomed, or been appreciated?

Close by the Grove of the Muses, where I stood under tall trees, was a sanctuary of the goddess Demeter where sacred objects had been found. A well, encircled by a wall, was Dion's equivalent of Demeter's Kallichoron well at Eleusis where her Greater Mysteries had been celebrated. Interestingly, her Thesmophoria festival (women only) had also been held here in October to promote fertility in Macedonia.

Eager to host their own Olympic Games, the Macedonian kings had introduced an Olympic nine-day festival at Dion, each day named after one of the Muses. King Archelaus was delighted when the greatest athletes and artists took part, not only from Macedonia but from all over Greece. Apparently, King Archelaus himself had competed and won several times in the tethrippon (the four-horse chariot race).

Here at Dion there were birds, butterflies and insects fluttering and sheltering amongst the abundant shrubs and trees, nourished by the springs, though the river, which was once navigable, was now only a stream.

I left the others who were more interested in identifying butterflies, and went on alone to the temple of Zeus Olympias, the sacred centre of this ancient site. Here, sacrifice had been offered to the supreme god of the heavens before all major events. In particular, Alexander the Great had come to honour Zeus before setting out on his campaigns. Alexander, who'd had the good fortune to be tutored by Aristotle, was a great admirer of Homer and his *Iliad* which, it is said, he took everywhere on his campaigns and kept under his pillow at night. He'd also admired the Greek dramatists of the fifth century – no doubt Aristotle had guided him in this. He especially loved the tragedies of Euripides, long passages of which, it is said, he could recite by heart.

I asked a stranger to take a photgraph of me at the sanctuary of Zeus with Mt. Olympus looming snow-crested as the backdrop. I then walked along the tarmac pathway to the theatre. It was a large reconstruction over what was originally a much smaller, semi-circular structure of tiered seats built against a manmade embankment.

It was there that King Archelaus held dramatic competitions during his nine day Olympic festival. Euripides himself might well have come here to a festival and watched a drama. It was while in Macedonia that he was inspired to write his famous *Bacchae*; but he was never to see it performed because he died in 406 B.C. The tragedy was produced posthumously by his son in 405, and won first prize in Athens at the City Dionysia.

The plot of the *Bacchae* revolves around the return of Dionysos as god to his native Thebes; the setting is before the palace of Cadmus.

In the drama, Cadmus has recently abdicated in favour of his grandson Pentheus. This newly crowned young king, however, is arrogant, and jeers at the idea that the newly returned Dionysos is the god he claims to be.

A Chorus of ~~women~~ Maenads, wearing the customary fawn-skins, and carrying thyrsi (the ivy-clad wands topped by a pine-cone), have followed Dionysos from Asia Minor where he has been living and acquiring many followers.

Teiresias, the old, blind seer, enters asking to see Cadmus who, recognizing Teiresias' voice, comes from the palace to join him – they both wear crowns of ivy and fawn-skins. Cadmus says: ...*I come prepared, in all the guise and harness of this God. Are we not told his is the soul of that dead life of old that sprang from mine own daughter?* (Semele) *Surely then must thou and I with all the strength of men exalt him... (180-185.)*

And, as they begin the rites of worship, their aged bodies are filled with a mysterious superhuman power ...*heaven's high mysteries... (200)*, as Teiresias puts it.

Pentheus, cocky with his own self-importance, strides out from the palace accompanied by his soldiers, and the two older men quickly draw back out of sight. Pentheus is furious on hearing that the women worshippers of Dionysos have taken to the mountains ...*with dance and prayer to adore this new god whoe'er he be... (219-220.)* The idea that Dionysos is divine is laughable, and Pentheus is full of derision. Catching sight of Teiresias, he asserts his newly acquired powers as monarch. If it wasn't for the old seer's silver hair, he warns, he'd have him ...*sitting chained amid thy crew of raving damsels... (258-259.)* New gods, indeed!

But Teiresias cautions him: *Good words, my son, come easily when he that speaks is wise, and speaks but for the right. Else come they never! Swift are thine, and bright as though with thought, yet have no thought at all... (266-269.)* And he draws attention to the fact that Dionysos introduced the vine (and, therefore, wine) which ...*giveth sleep to sink the fretful day in cool forgetting. Is there any way with man's sore heart, save only to forget?... (281-283.)* And Teiresias also warns him against arrogance; he must not be angry that they themselves accept Dionysos as god, declaring that he and Cadmus ...*Will wear his crown, and tread his dances! Aye, our hairs are white, yet shall that dance be trod! I will not lift mine arm to war with God for thee nor all thy words... (321-325.)*

Cadmus also warns his grandson to beware and ...*bear thee humbly in God's sight.* He makes to crown Pentheus with a Dionysian wreath but is turned on angrily with the warning not to ...*smear on me thy foul contagion! (243.)* He will have none of it and orders his soldiers to seize and take Dionysos prisoner. Questions and answers are exchanged between Pentheus and Dionysos, the former becoming increasingly irritated by Dionysos' quiet and reasonable responses. Eventually, losing all patience, Pentheus orders his soldiers to cut off Dionysos' curly hair, and to seize his thyrsus, which Dionysos calmly hands over. Pentheus is enraged and orders him to be locked up. But Dionysos only says that his divine father will release him: ...*Even now he stands close here, and sees all that I suffer. (498-499.)* Such confidence! Pentheus retorts: *Where is he? For mine eyes discern him not. (501.)* Dionysos answers: *Where I am! 'Tis thine own impurity that veils him from thee. (502-503.)* Pentheus explodes: *The dog jeers at me! At me and Thebes! Bind him! (504-505.)*

And so Dionysos is marched off to a dungeon; his hands are bound, his hair is shorn and his thyrsus removed from him. His voice is heard calling his Maenads. Then, from inside the palace comes the sound of an earthquake, followed by lightning on Semele's tomb ...*hot splendour of the shaft of God. (600.)*

Dionysos comes from the palace unbound, and is welcomed by the Chorus. He asks them why they were so quick to despair since nothing can hold him; he goes on to describe how Pentheus hurried back to the prison with his sword drawn and, seeing a miraculous image of Dionysos, sliced through air but *smote emptiness.* He now ... *lies outworn and wan who dared to rise against his God in wrath, being but man... (639-641.)*

Pentheus returns, beside himself with rage at Dionysos, this so-called god. He sees him and comes in to the attack, but Dionysos stands his ground peacefully. Pentheus calls to his guards to imprison him again, but Dionysos asks: *What? Cannot God o'erleap a wall? (654.)* How similar that is to Peter when, four or five centuries later, in the Acts of the Apostles, is released from prison by divine intervention! (Acts 12:5-10.)

Scathing exchanges are interrupted by a Messenger arriving ashen faced with terror, to report the extraordinary events he's witnessed on Mt. Kithairon. He saw the Maenads asleep on the mountainside, and had watched as Pentheus' mother Agave had woken, startled by the sound of grazing cattle. She'd sprung up and called out to her fellow Maenads to wake and dress for action; whereupon they'd put on their fawn-skins, their ivy wreaths and seized their wands. Then, quite unaccountably, one of them had struck a rock with her thyrsus and out had gushed a jet of water.

"Just like Moses in the wilderness," I'd told Harry when reading the passage to him at home. "But better still another struck the ground and up came a fountain of wine!"

The Messenger, continuing with his amazing story, tells Pentheus that the women then all cried out "Iacchos, Bromios, Lord, God of God born!" – And all the mountain ...*worshipped with them; and the wild things knelt... (728-730.)* Didn't Jesus have animals who bowed down and worshipped him as a newborn baby lying in the manger?

The women had then with their bare hands been empowered to fall on the herd of cattle and tear them apart. ...*Yea, bulls of pride, horns swift to rage, were fronted and aside flung stumbling, by those multitudinous hands dragged pitilessly... (743-746.)* And other great feats and wonders were seen and reported by the Messenger. He now advises Pentheus to believe in Dionysos who first brought them the grief-assuaging vine. He must be allowed to live: *For if he die, then Love herself is slain, and nothing joyous in the world again! (775-777.)*

Pentheus, however, remains unmoved. Dionysos is too proud and lacks respect for his royal status. ...*This needs an iron hand!* is how he sees it.

He calls for action and declares war against these foolish women. *Before God, shall women dare such deeds against us? It's too much to bear! (784-785.)*

Dionysos responds with quiet firmness; he warns Pentheus not to fight against divinity: *Better to yield him prayer and sacrifice than kick against the pricks, since Dionysos is God, and thou but mortal... (794-796.)*

Despite his fury, Pentheus gradually falls under the spell of Dionysos who lulls him into submission to his will; he cautions him from rushing off to the mountain in anger, warning that any such rash action will result in him being set upon by the women.

No, let him first disguise himself as a woman, then he will be able to merge with them and observe their strange behaviour. During the next dialogue, without realizing it Pentheus, the young arrogant king, is persuaded by Dionysos to wear a frock, to pin on tresses of hair, don a fawn-skin, and take up a wand. Dionysos then says he will lead him to the mountain, and Pentheus agrees, *Aye, indeed! Lead on. Why should we tarry? (812-813.)*

Dionysos' gentle persuasion, however, belies his ruthless intention to punish the young king. When Pentheus eventually presents himself dressed as a Maenad, Dionysos assesses his disguise; he arranges a stray lock of his/her hair, arranges his gown, shows him how to walk like a woman, and how to hold the thyrsus correctly. And so they set out for the mountain.

A passage of time elapses as the Chorus sing of what is about to take place. In due course they are interrupted by a Messenger who comes running back to report the shocking and unexpected death of Pentheus. He describes what occurred on the mountain. Pentheus, wanting to see the Maenads but not wishing to be seen himself, climbed up into a pine-tree. Dionysos, posing as his friend and appearing to assist him, *...touched the great pine-tree's high and heavenward crown, and lower, lower, lower, urged it down to the herbless earth. Round like a bending bow, or slow wheel's rim a joiner forces to, so in those hands that tough and mountain stem bowed slow – oh, strength not mortal dwelt in them! to the very earth. And there he set the King. And slowly, lest it cast him in its spring, let back the young and straining tree, till high it towered again amid the towering sky with Pentheus in the branches!... (1064-1074.)*

So there Pentheus perched with his bird's eye view. But Dionysos now wreaked his revenge. He warned the Maenads they were being spied on, and the intruder in the trees was theirs to avenge. *And ...a pillar of high flame... rose from the earth to the sky. And silence took the air, and no leaf stirred in all the forest dell...(1083-1085.)* And, when they heard the voice again and they recognized their god's clear call, they all came running. When at last they saw Pentheus, they were outraged and tried to stone him *...And there he clung, unscathed, as in a cage caught... (1104.)*

So many arms reached up till the tree was uprooted and fell to the ground. Pentheus tore off his tresses shrieking to his mother Agave (also a Maenad). But in her frenzy *...with lips a-foam and eyes that run like leaping fire... (1124-1125)* his mother was unable to recognize him: *...Round his left arm she put both hands, set hard against his side her foot, drew...and the shoulder severed! – Not by might of arm...but easily, as the God made light her hand's essay...Yea, all the air was loud with groans that faded into sobbing breath, dim shrieks, and joy, and triumph-cries of death. And here was borne a severed arm, and there a hunter's booted foot; white bones lay bare with rending; and swift hands ensanguined tossed as in sport the flesh of Pentheus dead...And, ah, the head! Of all the rest, his mother hath it, pierced upon a wand, as one might pierce a lion's and* *through the land, leaving her sisters in their dancing place, bears it on high... (1127-1131, 1134-1140, 1144-1148.)*

Such was the Messenger's report. Agave now returns from the mountain bearing her trophy. She is still blind to what she's done, and holds what she thinks is a lion's head which she raises triumphantly for the Theban citizens to see. Everyone is aghast and cries out: *...See, these palms were bare that caught the angry beast, and held, and tore the limbs of him... (1210-1212.)*

Agave calls for her father to come and see her prize. Cadmus arrives back from the mountain with attendants bearing the body pieces of Pentheus on a bier. He is devastated by his daughter's madness. But she herself is still unaware she is possessed, and says: *My father, a great boast is thine this hour. Thou hast begotten daughters, high in power and valiant above all mankind – yea, all valiant, though none like me! I have let fall the shuttle by the loom, and raised my hand for higher things, to slay from out thy land wild beasts! See, in mine arms I bear the prize that nailed above these portals it may rise to show what things thy daughters did! Do thou take it, and call a feast... (1233-1242.)*

Cadmus is grief-stricken; he sees his daughter is deluded. Unaware of what she has done, Agave speaks of Pentheus with disappointment: *...Would that my son likewise were happy of his hunting... Father, thou shouldst set him right... Will no one bring him hither, that mine eyes may look on his, and show him this my prize! (1251-1253, 1256-1258.)*

Oh, the horror of her hallucination! Bracing himself to accept the fact that his daughter is deranged, he begins by asking her what she sees when looking at *...yon blue dome of air! Is it the same, or changed in thy sight? (1264-1266.)* She answers that it is *More shining than before, more heavenly bright! (1267.)*

Cadmus asks her more searching questions and she answers them correctly. She gradually emerges from her trance, and Cadmus gently asks: *Thou bearest in thine arms an head – what head? (1277.)* She hardly dares to look, but replies: *A lion's – so they all said in the chase. (1278.)*

When Cadmus firmly says: *Look upon it full, till all be clear! (1281)* she is bewildered, then dismayed and horrified when she sees she holds the head of her son. Who could have done this, she demands, stupefied. *Answer! My heart is hanging on thy breath! (1288.)* And Cadmus feels compelled to tell her truthfully: *'Twas thou. Thou and thy sisters wrought his death. (1289.)* But she remembers nothing of it – not even going to the mountain. Why had her son Pentheus gone there?

Cadmus replies: *To mock the God and thine own ecstasy, (1293.)* And, to the immense distress of all, it dawns on them that it is Dionysos who has brought this disaster on them, due to Pentheus' scorn and denial he was divine.

Euripides ends his tragedy by highlighting the far-reaching consequences of denying deity. Agave is overwhelmed by what she's done, and her father Cadmus feels compelled to live the rest of his life in exile.

Apparently, several pages of the surviving *Bacchae* manuscript are lost. But the final lines are of Dionysos speaking from a cloud, pronouncing judgement on the Theban royal family. Agave begs forgiveness for her and her son's sins but Dionysos is unforgiving: *Too late! When there was time, ye knew me not. (1345.)* Agave accuses him of being ...*proud in his rage*. But Dionysos answers: *'Tis my sire, Zeus, willed it long ago. (1349.)* And so the drama ends with the warning to mortals of the misfortunes awaiting those who dare deny the existence of the gods.

Some say that Euripides wrote the *Bacchae* as the consequence of some last-minute conversion. Although he'd often questioned the existence of the gods, his tragedies, nevertheless, had in them frequent divine interventions, which suggested a decided belief of some kind.

In the fifth century B.C. there were no biographers, so little was known about Euripides' private life except that he was married twice and had three sons by his second wife. Both wives had been unfaithful, leaving Euripides morose and seeking solitude in his cave on Salamis.

Whether Euripides departed from his beloved Athens due to his private life and personal problems, or because of the continual threat from Sparta and her allies in the Peloponnesian War (Athens was finally defeated in 404 B.C. four years after Euripides' departure), is not certain. In fact, some think Euripides was driven to live in Macedonia because of Aristophanes' ceaseless jokes at his expense. For example, in his *Women at the Thesmophoria*, which had been produced 411 B.C. only three years before Euripides' departure, a character in the comedy complains about Euripides ...*writing his tragedies and persuading people there aren't any gods... (479.)* Such a truth spoken in jest was dangerous at that time.

The word 'atheism' in those days hadn't the same meaning as it has today but comes from the Greek *atheos* – an 'a' before a word in Greek being a form of negating it, and *théos* meaning 'god'. To be *atheos*, therefore, implied someone who didn't believe in the accepted gods of the city-state with their established cults. Less than a decade after

Euripides' departure, his friend Socrates was accused and sentenced to death for being *atheos*; he too had been the butt of Aristophanes' jokes regarding his unorthodox view of the gods.

There was a rumour that Euripides hadn't died of natural causes here in Macedonia, but had been savaged by King Archelaus' hunting-dogs. If so, it would have been devastating for the king that the great dramatist had lost his life while a guest at his palace. But it was only a rumour and might well have been a deliberate whispering of misinformation begun by the Greeks themselves to promote the idea of the gods wreaking their revenge on non-believers; or even to emphasize their long-held view that the Macedonians were nothing more than barbarians.

I caught sight of Hilary and Fiona waving to me from the footpath leading to the theatre. Fiona called out: "We've time for Mt. Olympus if we leave NOW!" And she pointed to her watch. Kostas had already said he'd be happy to drive us to Litochoro, the small town which served as a base for those wanting to climb or explore the mountain; he had, however, to be back in Thessaloniki by about four o'clock, so our time was limited.

Certainly I wanted to pay my respects to the mountain of the gods.

CHAPTER

13

MT. OLYMPUS

Our taxi winds its way up the steep streets of the small, picturesque town of Litochoro; we are heading for a restaurant located beside the Enipeas gorge at the foot of Mt. Olympus.

Why do I find the mountain so atmospheric – but, oh, so threatening! I suspect it is the myths and legends that enchant me, in direct contrast to its numerous precipices and deep ravines which fill me with alarm.

Our young driver Kostas joins us for a salad lunch. During the meal we tell him that the evening before, we'd watched from our balcony a protest march with people carrying flags, and we'd frequently heard the word 'Macedonia!' being shouted.

"Ah, Macedonia!" he says. "It is bad what they do!"

"What are they doing?" I ask. It's not a subject I've given any attention to, supposing that today all the ancient cities of the Macedonian kingdom are in Greece.

"The people north of our borders call their land Macedonia!" he says, his eyes flashing.

"Does it matter?" I ask thoughtlessly.

"It matters very much!" he says briskly. The sudden sharpness in his tone rings alarm-bells.

"Like you wouldn't like it if people in Scotland called part of England Scottish," Fiona remarks.

"No, I wouldn't," I agree.

"They want to steal our Macedonia from us! They want our sea! They take our Macedonia flag and put the sun on red instead of blue like we have it! It is very bad!"

"Yes, we saw the blue flags yesterday, don't you remember?" Hilary says. "They had the sunburst emblem on a blue background. We saw the sunburst on Philip II's gold urn at Aigaia, you remember?"

A young man who has just entered the restaurant shouts a greeting. Kostas looks in his direction and immediately rises from his seat; the sensitive subject of Macedonia is instantly forgotten.

They slap each other on the shoulder, and speak rapid Greek which is quite incomprehensible. When his friend rejoins his companions, Kostas returns to his seat all relaxed and smiling again. He tells us that he and his friend, some several years back, had run the Olympic Marathon. The Olympic Games, I ask? No, no, the Olympic Marathon here on the mountain, he says proudly. He tells us that the Marathon is held annually, and the starting point is Dion. The runners have to be exceptionally fit because their route includes the Plateau of the Muses on Mt. Olympus, then climbs as far as Refuge Hut A, then round and down again, passing the Monastery of Agios Dionysios, and from there back here to Litochoro. Well, well! That puts what Harry and I had once done to pathetic shame!

Some thirty years ago, Harry and I had set out confidently to follow the trail back to Litochoro from the ancient Monastery of Agios Dionysios. It is interesting that this early monastery had been dedicated to a saint whose name was similar to the god Dionysos! The latter had been worshipped in the locality, so it surely must have been to ease the transition from honouring the pagan god to honouring the god turned Christian saint.

It had been one of our more arduous walks. We'd followed red arrows painted on trees which pointed sometimes alongside the Enipeas river, and sometimes across it. The trek, which should have taken four hours, had taken six. We'd had to cross and re-cross the river, leaping from boulder to boulder, sometimes where the river ran deep, sometimes where it was shallow. The walk had been both wonderful but at times for me hair-raising.

We'd finally come to a halt where the deep waters had swirled around protruding boulders which were just too far apart for me to feel brave enough to take the mighty leap required from where I stood marooned midstream; a waterfall cascaded perilously a few metres further downstream. Harry had made the jump successfully, and had then held out an arm for me to grab; but I'd lacked the confidence, and felt I'd only unbalance him and we'd both be swept away to our deaths. As we'd already been over three hours on the trail, it seemed a far worse option to turn back. So what to do? The situation had been miraculously resolved by a strong young man coming up from Litochoro, bold and positive and alone. He'd helped Harry across to the far bank, had then leapt nimbly from boulder to boulder and, oozing confidence, had grabbed my arm and swung me over.

"Dionysos to the rescue!" I, the agnostic, said to Harry when the young man had gone on.

"Nothing of the sort." said the God-believer. "He was just a young student."

"Or a miracle performed by Agios Dionysios?" I, the agnostic, persisted.

"Gods and saints, my foot!" said the God-believer with a snort. "Coincidence is more like it – a matter of luck!"

Here now at the restaurant Fiona's mobile rings – the time is two p.m. exactly. Her face lights up. "Ah!" she says, and allows it to ring several times before she grabs it. She tosses her ebony hair back and puts the mobile to her ear. "Hi!…Ah, I thought it might be you!" Her whole being becomes animated as she speaks, while gesticulating with her free hand for us to set off on our walk, mouthing at us that she'll catch us up. As we leave, I hear her say: "Where are we? I'm not sure where we are!…Oh, yes, we're on Mt. Olympus…no, not the top, the bottom…"

As we set off alongside the gorge, Hilary says: "I'm so glad he's rung today. Poor Fiona was worried she'd put her foot in it yesterday by jokingly saying she was after his money! I think she genuinely fancies him."

We pause to look at the gorge filled with deciduous trees fresh with the pale green leaves of spring. The sky is a deep blue with cooling, billowing white clouds above us casting their shadows. I'd like to walk far enough along this path till we are alongside the river with its crystal clear rock-pools, but I know time is against us.

But oh, how tranquil it is as we intrude into this the territory of the gods! We can't see the river through the trees, but we can hear it murmuring to us. Neither can we see the Throne of Zeus, but I know the great scallop-shaped rock is up there on the summit somewhere.

It is easy to imagine the immortal goddesses bathing in a secluded corner of the river. There is a story that Teiresias, the blind seer and friend of Cadmus, lost his sight here on Mt. Olympus when he came across the goddess Athena bathing naked in a rock-pool and she'd struck him blind.

"You can feel their presence, don't you think?" Hilary remarks, a look of wonder on her face. "Twelve Olympian gods – twelve disciples – I wonder if that's just coincidence?" Before I can say anything, she goes on: "I was reading about Orpheus the other day. He came from around these parts. You know, Orpheus and Eurydice?"

I'm pleased she's mentioned him because certainly there are stories here on Mt. Olympus regarding him. Orpheus was a mystic who came from Thrace, north-east of here, and was said to be a devotee of Dionysos. He was renowned for playing the lyre and the beauty of his voice. In fact it was said that his singing was so divine that mountains bowed down to hear, animals would gather round, and fish would jump from the sea to listen.

Yet he met his death here on the mountain at the hands of Dionysos' Maenads. The legend is that on the death of his beloved wife Eurydice, and following his failed attempt to rescue her from Hades, he'd shunned the company of women. The Maenads greatly resented this so one day in anger, in a combined frenetic ecstasy, they'd torn Orpheus limb from limb and thrown his head into a river (not the Enipeus but another on Olympus). The Maenads had then washed their blood-stained hands in its waters but, horrified, the polluted river vanished underground, and didn't resurface till it reached Holy Dion. It was also said that the head (unaffected by death) had floated across the Aegean sea still singing till it was washed up on the island of Lesbos where it floated up a river and ended in a cave. From there it had delivered oracles to the locals till Apollo put an end to such audacity as oracle pronouncements were his exclusive province together with his father Zeus.

"Such a strange story," Hilary muses when I tell her about this legend. "To have his head still singing! It beggars belief!"

"You know he sailed with Jason and the Argonauts?"

"Did he really? But then all the great heroes sailed with Jason. I know Heracles did," she says.

"Yes. And King Admetus of Pherae, whose wife Alcestis became the subject of Euripides' first surviving drama *Alcestis*."

"Oh, *Alcestis*! Such a tragic play, though not without some humour in it also. I saw a production of it years ago and I still remember it. Where is Pherae, I wonder?"

"Not too far from here," I say.

And since King Admetus and Heracles are at the centre of the plot, I will introduce the drama here.

MT. OLYMPUS 151

★

The lovely young woman Alcestis was the daughter of King Pelias of Pherae, the king whom Medea had murdered while pretending to rejuvenate him with her herbs and magic – the one who usurped the throne from Jason's father and who refused to step down unless Jason brought back the Golden Fleece from Colchis.

Far from being cunning and evil like her father, Alcestis was gentle and faithful, and all that a husband could wish for in a wife. She was even prepared to sacrifice her life for her husband King Admetus when the Fates decreed that he must die. Apollo at the time had been serving as a slave to King Admetus, on the order of Zeus, as a penance, either for having killed the Python/dragon at Delphi, or for killing the Cyclops who'd made the thunderbolt which Zeus had flung at *eh* Asclepius for resurrecting Hippolytus.

When Apollo heard what the Fates had decreed, he persuaded them to allow the king to live on condition that someone else forfeited his or her life instead. The Fates agreed to this, but the only person in the king's household prepared to die for him was Alcestis. One might wonder why Admetus wasn't himself prepared to die rather than allow this to happen, but evidently it never occurred to him.

The play begins with Apollo outside the royal palace of King Admetus. It is still dark but dawn is breaking, and a radiant light shines around Apollo. For the benefit of the audience, the god explains the crisis that has arisen.

The crouching, black-haired and winged figure of Thanatos (Death) enters, and he and Apollo discuss the situation. Alcestis' agonizing farewell to her husband and young children is excessively prolonged before she finally draws her last breath. The harsh reality of his wife's death now hits King Admetus who is devastated (hadn't he realized he would be?) The Chorus take up their farewells to their dead queen as she is carried into the palace, and they only cease when the great hero Heracles turns up wearing his lion-skin and carrying his club. He is in a cheerful mood and on his way to fulfil his eighth Labour, to bring the man-eating horses belonging to a certain Diomedes of Thrace back to King Eurystheus.

The newly bereaved Admetus comes from the palace and, for some inexplicable reason, welcomes him without saying a word about Alcestis' death, though he is clearly in deep mourning. To Heracles' enquiries as to whose funeral is about to take place, Admetus cannot bring himself to speak the truth. Heracles offers to leave if it's inconvenient as it clearly is, but Admetus will have none of it; to turn a visitor from his door? Certainly not! And Heracles enters the palace. The Chorus does its bit to indicate a passage of time and then the funeral cortège leaves the palace.

To prune back the drama somewhat, before leaving for the funeral Admetus and his father have a fierce argument. Admetus is outraged that his elderly parent allowed his wife to die since he was at the end of his life anyway. Far from agreeing with his son, his father reminds him angrily that he has given him everything over the years: *...Say, how have I wronged thee? What have I kept away? "Not died for thee?"...I ask not thee to die. Thou lovest this light: shall I not love it, I?...(689-692.)*

Meanwhile, Heracles is drinking wine inside the palace and can be heard becoming boisterous. The Servant attending him is shocked as Heracles shouts: *...Let this stupid grieving be; rise up above thy troubles, and with me drink in a cloud of blossoms. By my soul, I vow the sweet plash-music of the bowl will break thy glumness...(793-797.)*

At last Heracles learns from the shocked Servant the truth of the matter, that it is Alcestis who is being buried. Heracles reacts with appalled anger. Why was he not told the truth at once? He demands to know where exactly they have gone to bury her, and is told it is close by the straight Larissa road. Harry and I once travelled that road when driving to Mt. Pelion, and I'd noticed a sign pointing to Pherae. The landscape had nothing picturesque or significant about it and we didn't stop to investigate as we needed to get to our destination before dark.

In the drama Heracles sobers up; his one purpose now is to recover the dead Alcestis and return her alive to Admetus. With great daring he descends to Hades, wrestles with Thanatos (Death) and succeeds in rescuing Alcestis. As the mourners return to the palace, he arrives accompanied by a veiled young woman; she doesn't speak (apparently the newly resurrected take time to adjust to light and life again, and for a while they remain silent). Heracles insists on handing her over to Admetus but, in his grief, he is in no mood to have a strange woman thrust on him. Before dying, Alcestis had made him promise never to re-marry as the children might not take kindly to a step-mother. Heracles, without saying it is Alcestis, persists in telling Admetus he mustn't turn his back on this woman he is offering him and, in due course, the king notices that the veiled figure has the same height and shape as his cherished wife.

After several more pages of dialogue, Admetus at last realizes that although she remains silent, it is really, really, really Alcestis come back from the dead. But Heracles speaks: ... *She hath dwelt with Death. Her voice may not be heard ere to the lords of them below she pay due cleansing, and awake on the third day... (1145-1148.)*

Awake on the third day? I am at once rivetted. How Christian does that sound! Jesus rose on the third day. He could have risen on the fourth, fifth or sixth, or any day at all, but he rose on the third day – four centuries later! The moon too is not seen but is visible again as a thin crescent on the third day. Interesting!

Alcestis is led into the palace, and Heracles tells Admetus that he himself must now leave to attend to the Labour he had originally set out to do. Admetus is left full of hope and happiness at the return of his much loved wife.

The drama ends with the Chorus of Elders singing of their amazement: *There be many shapes of mystery; and many things God brings to be, past hope or fear. And the end men looked for cometh not, and a path is there where no man thought. So hath it fallen here. (1162-1167.)* These lines are surprisingly similar to the final lines sung by the Chorus in Euripides' *Helen*.

It is curious that Euripides, who questioned the truth of the Olympian gods, nevertheless saw men being manipulated by them, or somehow perceived that they were interwoven with them in some way. Though a sceptic, he was curiously intent on introducing the gods and goddesses into his tragedies, seeing them as other-worldly presences circulating amongst humans, and taking part in their affairs. *Alcestis* was produced in 438 B.C. and was awarded second prize competing, it is believed, against Sophocles' *Antigone* (see Addenda).

"Ah, there you are, folk!" a cheerful voice calls. We turn and see Fiona coming up the track. She is clearly elated and in high good humour.

"All good between you and Bob?" Hilary asks, relieved from Fiona's expression that there are no hairline cracks in this new relationship that she need tiptoe around.

Fiona crosses her two index fingers and playfully holds them prominently before Hilary's eyes then, with a comical grimace holds them crossed before her nose and looks defiantly at me; I'd told her when she'd first shown me a photo of Bob that he looked nice but – well – he might have a temper; it was his mouth, I said. But she assured me that they had a good laugh, and for the time being –

She turns and looks down at the trees in the gorge in their pale green spring foliage, and the rugged grey rockface that soars up from the opposite bank. "So what wild stories do we have here?" she asks cheerfully. "What dramatists or dramas are we supposed to know about here on Mt. Olympus?"

"Actually, Aristophanes wrote a crazy comedy set on Mt. Olympus," I tell her.

"Go on. I suppose we'd better hear about it!" she remarks.

So I tell them about *Peace*, one of his many anti-war comedies which was produced in 421 B.C. Using his extraordinary imagination, Aristophanes has an Athenian farmer named Trygaeus who, fed up with all he's had to endure over the years of the Peloponnesian War, hitches a lift on the back of a dung-beetle and flies up to the peaks of Mt. Olympus to consult the gods.

"A dung beetle! What made Aristophanes think of a dung beetle, I wonder?" Hilary remarks.

"Yes, why not a dragonfly, or a bird?" Fiona asks.

I ignore them and continue with the plot of *Peace*. Trygaeus reaches Zeus' palace where he alights from his beetle, only to be told by Hermes that the gods themselves, sick and tired of seeing men at war... *set up house as high in heaven as they could get, so they couldn't either see you fighting each other or hear you praying to them. (214-219.)*

Trygaeus then learns that Peace has been buried in a cavern. However, with the help of the Chorus, he manages to dig Peace out of her dungeon, together with her two close companions Cornucopia and Festival, and brings them out into the daylight. Trygaeus promptly falls in love with Cornucopia and wants to marry her. Festival he hands over to the Council.

Trygaeus prepares for his wedding and sacrifices a lamb. He sprinkles holy water and purifies the audience with a generous amount of it, and the comedy closes with great celebrations. He marries Cornucopia, and from now on food will be plentiful; better still, there'll be no need for helmet-makers, spear-, breastplate- and bugle-makers, who will have to find other lucrative employment.

"Well, there you are! Lucky Try-whatever marrying Cornucopia! I don't want to hurry you guys, but Kostas is quite anxious we don't dawdle out here as he's on a tight schedule."

I feel mildly cheated that we haven't reached a waterfall that can only be a short distance away. But I have to remind myself that at least Kostas brought us to the mountain, which is something I wasn't sure he'd agree to.

I say a final silent farewell to the mountain. I doubt that I will ever see it again. It has been responsible for so many, just so many wonderful and imaginative stories and is forever speaking to me; and I'm not alone in being drawn to it. People like iron filings to a magnet come from all over the world because of the extraordinary tales that have been passed down over the millennia. Olympus is a drama in itself, and we small mortals are the audience gathered at its feet.

But every drama must perforce have an ending; there has to be a final curtain. And so I turn around and, with the others, reluctantly, I take my leave.

EPILOGUE

One evening while in Athens, we'd gone for a stroll behind our hotel, following a footpath through a wooded area. We could have taken the path in various directions but had forked right, as if the powers-that-be were guiding us, till we came to a wide open space with extensive views. Here the ground was hard-packed and stony. There was a raised area and with excitement I read a notice saying we were on the Pnyx. Here was where democracy had been born, where orators had addressed assembled Athenian citizens who'd then cast their votes for or against the proposals put to them. Close by were the remains of a sanctuary of Zeus Eleutherios which added solemnity to the site.

It was there that Pericles, the great fifth century statesman, had swayed the masses with his oratory. It was he whose inspiration, energy and vision had slowly turned Athens into a rich and powerful city-state.

From where I stood on the Pnyx that evening the views were fantastic: to the east was the Acropolis where the Parthenon so-called because it was dedicated to Athena Parthenos (Athena the Virgin) – towered majestically with eye-catching beauty. To the far north was Lykabettos, a tall solitary and lonely hill which rose up from Kolonaki, a well-to-do residential area of Athens. In the near north-east was the Areópagus where Orestes had stood trial before the Athenians; and looking south from the Pnyx I could see the Hill of the Muses with its long evening shadows, and the great marble Philopappos Monument rearing up through the trees.

While there on the Pnyx, as the sun sank below the skyline to the west, I turned east again and watched the Parthenon slowly become floodlit from the base upwards. What more glorious sight on this my last full day in Athens?

I sat on a boulder in the twilight facing the direction of the Areópagus as the lights began to twinkle around Athens. It was there in 52 A.D. that St. Paul had preached the Resurrection to the Athenians. ...*Now when they heard of the Resurrection of the dead, some mocked; but others said, "We will hear you again about this." So Paul went out from among them. But some men joined him and believed, among them Dionysius the Areópagite... (Acts 17:32-34.)*

Dionysius was, apparently, a judge on the Areópagus but, more interestingly, the Greek New Testament spells his name Dionysios, and at that time it denoted that he was a follower of the god Dionysos.

I let my mind drift back to the influence of the early dramatists, their view of the gods, of women and society. How extraordinary it was that the city blossomed in the fifth century B.C., and when I say the city, clearly I mean the people who had the intellectual ability to help her to blossom. Athens flourished as a cultural centre with its dramatists, poets, artists, sculptors, philosophers, architects and so on.

The floodlit Parthenon in full view was symbolic of the eternal mystery of the divine, but also of human excellence and ability; the Hill of the Muses, symbolic of human creativity, and divine inspiration; the Areópagus of law and justice. And there I sat in the NOW of history, absorbing all that I could see around me. For the fifth century B.C. citizens of Athens to be aware of the invisible and transform it into the visible was sheer genius.

But it all began with language. Without the use of words nothing would have been achieved. The past would never have been brought into the present without speech. The great philosophers chewed over the meaning of life with words; the politicians debated, orated and laid down laws with words; but the great lyric poets and dramatists used words and powerful language to fire the imagination and transfix their audiences; actors before massed audiences portrayed the consequence of words and action. And into all this was the belief that the gods were at the centre of human life. Gods who had to be honoured, appeased and kept on side – divine wills at work on human wills, sometimes clashing, sometimes in harmony. Words! Drama!

It was the power of language which began it all. Homer first, then several centuries later Aeschylus closely followed by Sophocles, Euripides and Aristophanes. It was a slow, tortuous unravelling of the conscious mind, and the gradual dawning of what was good and right from its primordial sleep. The inspired Greek intellects of the fifth century B.C. brought culture and a great awakening to the still dormant Western world.

ADDENDA

AESCHYLUS
PROMETHEUS BOUND

To understand the tragedy of *Prometheus Bound* it is helpful to know the legend of this Titan/god. According to ancient sources, man was fashioned out of clay by Prometheus. This greatly angered Zeus as he was himself thinking of creating man, and he quickly found fault with those moulded by this young upstart.

Prometheus had already annoyed Zeus in another matter. Appearing to be generous-spirited, he had asked Zeus to choose which part of an ox would be the most acceptable to him when men offered him sacrifice. He showed Zeus two parcels: one of succulent fat which he'd craftily wrapped around the entrails of a bullock, the other of the best cuts of beef well concealed within the stomach. Zeus, confident he knew all things, failed on this occasion and chose the fat covered entrails. Some say he knew all along and his choice had been deliberate so he could take his revenge on Prometheus for trying to deceive him. Whatever was the truth, thanks to Prometheus, whenever men sacrificed to the gods, they benefited because they were able to feast on steak and the best joints of beef; every sacrificial event became a communal banquet and a great celebration for mankind.

For these two misdemeanours Zeus decided to get his own back. As a thorn in the flesh for the man Prometheus fashioned out of clay, Zeus created a woman whose name was Pandora (meaning 'all gifts'). The goddesses gave her beauty and garlanded her, and Aphrodite bestowed on her womanly wiles. Zeus then sent her into the world with a box which was under no circumstances to be opened.

Prometheus, whose name means 'forethought', had a brother called Epimetheus (meaning 'afterthought'). With his forethought, Prometheus warned his brother not to accept gifts from the gods. But with his lack of thought till it was too late, Epimetheus welcomed Pandora and took her for his bride. Zeus was well aware that Pandora would not be able to resist opening the box and, sure enough, her curiosity overcame her and she raised the lid just a little to peer inside, enough for all the sins of the world to fly out. She closed it just in time to keep Hope from escaping. Since then, whatever happens and whatever sufferings men have to endure, they always have Hope.

At some point Zeus, who was a harsh despot and gloried in his power, withdrew fire from men, thus depriving them of heat and light and the wherewithal to work with metal – these nonentities of human beings needed to know who ruled the heavens and the earth! Prometheus, however, supported them and managed to steal a little fire from Hephaestus, god of fire and metal-work. He placed his stolen fire (some say it was only a spark) in the hollow stalk of a fennel plant, and carried it back down to earth. That same night, when Zeus saw men with their myriad lights, he was enraged, and commanded Hephaestus to clamp iron manacles on Prometheus' wrists and ankles and pinion him to a crag in the Caucasus. To compound the torment, an eagle was sent by Zeus to attack him. Daily it hovered over Prometheus, beating its great wings while it clawed and pecked at his liver. Although by day the eagle tore at it with its talons and devoured it, every night the liver grew again because Prometheus was a Titan/god and, therefore, immortal.

By some good fortune Prometheus held secret information concerning Zeus which he realized he could use to his advantage. He would reveal his knowledge only when Zeus freed him from the iron fetters clamping him to the crag. Anxious to know what the secret was, Zeus eventually allowed his hero son, the great Heracles, to shoot the eagle and release him.

Such was the myth that Aeschylus drew on for his *Prometheus Bound*.

In the drama Zeus sends Power (personified) to make certain his command to Hephaestus to secure Prometheus is implemented. Power revels in his role, but Hephaestus feels only compassion for his victim: ...*My heart shrinks from this task – to bind a kindred god with violent hand to yon storm-cloven ravine! Yet must I steel my spirit to this deed: slackness is dangerous where Zeus commands... (14-18.)* Having accomplished what they are there for, Hephaestus and Power depart, leaving Prometheus to his fate. He has nobody, no human or divine contact and can speak only to the void around him: *Ether of heaven and winds untired of wing, rivers, whose fountains fail not, and thou sea, laughing in waves innumerable! Oh earth, all-mother! – Yea, and on the sun I call, whose orb scans all things – look on me and see how I, a god, am wronged by gods. Behold how torn with outrage here I must remain through countless ages wrestling against pain... (88-95.)*

But Prometheus is not alone for long and is joined by a gathering of Ocean Nymphs who make up the Chorus. They tell Prometheus they have come because *...deep within our cave the echoed clang of smitten steel amazed us as it rang... (132-133.)*

They see Prometheus' plight as he cries out to them *...look! Behold how, clasped to towering cliffs with fetters hard, o'er this ravine I mount unenvied guard. (143-145.)*

Their father Oceanus arrives. He too sympathises with Prometheus' plight and offers to do whatever he can to help. Despite his great distress, Prometheus warns Oceanus not to attempt to help him *...till the heart of Zeus be lightened of its angry load... (375-376.)* But Oceanus won't be deflected from doing what he can, and departs on a flying griffin to confront Zeus.

Prometheus is left alone with the Ocean Nymphs who sing of their compassion and the dreadful power of Zeus, not only over men but over the gods. Prometheus informs them of the various benefits he himself has bestowed on humans: he has opened their eyes to possibilities they had never dreamed of: *...All their works were wrought without perception, till I made them know the risings of the stars... writing and spelling...from my thought, they learned to mingle kindly healing drugs, that guard them from all illness...in one word, know this: Prometheus gave all arts to men. (456-504.)*

The Chorus cry out their astonishment that after all such kindness, there he is clamped to the rock and helpless. Prometheus tells them that despite everything he still has Hope because of his secret knowledge. The Chorus weep for his misfortune and are interrupted by the arrival of Io.

Io is the unfortunate former priestess of Hera who had served her at her great *Heraion* near Argos. Zeus, however, had become enamoured of her, and in anger Hera had turned her into a heifer (or it may be that Zeus turned her into a heifer to escape detection). In time, Hera set a gadfly on her from which she was unable to escape or settle anywhere but was constantly fleeing from it. She now comes across Prometheus. Io consoles him while mourning her own plight. She asks Prometheus with his foresight to tell her when her own agony will cease. He recites a catalogue of woes she must first endure as she travels over land and sea.

I have myself only just discovered why the Ionian islands on the west coast of Greece are called Ionian; it is because Io (the heifer/

priestess) was pursued there by the gadfly; and why the Ionian sea on the east coast is so-named: because poor Io swam up it, and so across the Bosphorus which is also named after her because of her passage across it (*bous*, meaning 'ox', *poros*, meaning 'ford').

Prometheus finally informs her she will eventually come down to Egypt where Zeus, by a mere touch of his hand and nothing more, will impregnate her, and she will bear a son – an immaculate conception of a pagan pre-Christian sort.

He goes on to tell her that her descendants will become legendary: there will be fifty daughters who will one day come to Argos to marry fifty male cousins, who on their wedding-night will be murdered by their wives except for one. From that wife's progeny there will come the kings of Argos, and from one of them Heracles will be born who, so it is ordained, will release him. It seems that the unfortunate Prometheus has many centuries of agony and torment ahead of him if he is not to be released before the birth of Heracles.

And so Io learns what lies in store for her. *Oh, horror untold! Yet again, yet again, I am smitten within by the nerve-rending pain that maddens my spirit... My heart throbs and knocks at my fear-laden breast, and mine eyeballs whirl round in a rage of unrest... (876-882.)* And the poor priestess/heifer is driven on her way by the tormenting gad-fly.

Addressing the Ocean Nymphs, Prometheus tells them of his foreknowledge that Zeus will be brought down ...*let him reign securely, trusting to his thunder's noise and wielding there aloft his lightning brand! Nought shall they warrant him from that sure fall, intolerable, unhonoured, unreprieved... a portent huge in might, the weapons of whose forging shall o'er-blaze his lightning and outblaze his thunder-blast... (915-923.)*

The Ocean Nymphs implore him not to speak so rashly regarding Zeus who may wreak ever greater revenge on him. But Prometheus no longer cares: ...*Less than the least care I for Zeus' will. Let him exploit his strength even as he may, for this brief hour. His reign will soon be o'er... (936-938.)*

His defiance is interrupted by the messenger-god Hermes arriving. He has been sent by Zeus to prise the secret of his downfall from Prometheus. What is it that makes it worth his rebelling '...*gainst the sons of heaven, dispensing their prerogatives to men who are born and die, frail creatures of an hour, thou thief of fire – the Father bids thee tell what marriage 'tis thou vauntest, or what hand forsooth must hurl him from his place of power... (943-948.)*

Prometheus, however, will reveal nothing till he is released....*Young gods, young pride of unproved majesty! Ye think, your eminent souls shall ne'er know pain. Have I not from those very towers beheld two monarchs headlong hurled?...* (Zeus' grandfather Ouranos was overpowered by his son Kronos, Zeus' father, who was himself overthrown by Zeus) – *Ay, and erelong the third* (Zeus), *who now wields lordship unalloyed, will follow. I shall see it with mine eyes. Deem'st thou these youngling deities o'erawe and daunt me?... (950-962.)*

Hermes can only retort with the warning: *This haughty spirit and reckless speech of thine have landed thee where now thou art in woe... (965-967.)*

Warnings and defiance continue with Prometheus lashing out: *I would not change it for thy servitude. Better to grieve than be a lackeying slave. (968-969.)* Hermes despairs of Prometheus' obduracy: *What madness past belief thy words disclose. (979-980.)* But Prometheus stays firm: *If hatred of a cruel foe be madness. Let me be mad. (981-982.)*

Hermes finally turns to the Ocean Nymphs and warns them to cease supporting Prometheus because they might well suffer also from the blast of Zeus' fury. They, however, are staunch in their resolve to stay by his side, and the drama ends with an ever defiant Prometheus whose last words are: *Oh, earth, thou beholdest my wrong! (1094-1095.)*

It is generally thought that the 'great secret' which Prometheus refused to impart till he was released, was that Zeus would be overthrown by the son of the semi-divine sea-deity Thetis with whom he was enamoured. When Zeus finally learned this, he saw to it that Thetis was put out of temptation's way by arranging a marriage between her and King Peleus who ruled over the Myrmidons on Mt. Pelion. The result of that union was Achilles who became far greater than his father ever was.

That Zeus was eventually overthrown – or maybe the word eclipsed might be a better word – came finally with the coming of Christianity. There was no sudden overthrow of the Olympian gods; it took nearly four hundred years before they were ousted, thanks largely to the Roman Emperoror Theodosius the Great who issued a decree forbidding all pagan worship.

Prometheus Bound was the first of a trilogy written 460-456 B.C. The other two, *Prometheus the Fire-Bringer* and *Prometheus Unbound*, are lost.

AESCHYLUS
SUPPLIANTS

Aeschylus' drama *Suppliants* is about the descendants of Io (Hera's priestess-turned-heifer). Many generations have passed since Prometheus was chained to his rock, and twin sons have been born whose names are Aegyptus and Danaus; Aegyptus eventually fathers fifty sons, and Danaus fifty daughters (known as the Danaids). It is Aegyptus' wish that his fifty sons marry their fifty female cousins, but Danaus, suspecting that his brother has ulterior motives and has his eyes on his kingdom, rejects the idea. He, therefore, builds a ship and sails with his fifty daughters from Egypt to Argos in the Peloponnese, his forebear Io's homeland.

In *Suppliants*, Aeschylus focuses on the arrival by sea of King Danaus with his fifty daughters. The daughters make up the Chorus and sing of Epaphos, their ancestor, the son of Io and immortal Zeus:
...*Divine protector, now beyond the sea, son of the highest, the wandering heifer's child – for while she roamed, and cropped the flowery lea, Zeus breathed on her, and, ever undefiled, she felt the touch that filled her veins with thee, and made her to be mother of us all; Epaphos...on thee we call!...* (44-50.)

It is a picturesque passage of Io as a heifer grazing quietly, unmolested by the gadfly for a short while. They then sing of the will of Zeus: ...*What thing his nod hath ratified stands fast, and moves with firm sure tread, nor sways, nor swerves, nor starts aside. A mazy thicket, hard to thread, a labyrinth undiscovered still. The far-drawn windings of his will...* (90-95.)

Aeschylus was interested in the gradual evolution of morality in mankind, in the choices humans had to make, and the reality of their mortality interwoven with the gods. The choices before them were stark – they had to choose between the good and the bad, between kindness and cruelty, compassion and indifference.

Arriving at Argos with his fifty daughters, Danaus seeks shelter in a sanctuary of the gods; they carry boughs wreathed with white wool, a sign that they are suppliants seeking refuge.

King Danaus sees the approach of chariots, and wonders if they are going to be welcomed to this land or regarded as the enemy. King Pelasgus of Argos is the first to address them. He can see by their clothing and the colour of their skin they are not Greek but are come as suppliants because of their wool-wreathed boughs. He asks their reason for coming to his shores. The Chorus of Danaus' daughters eagerly tell him that they are descendants of Io who was once priestess at the goddess Hera's temple here at Argos.

Pelasgus tests them on the facts regarding the priestess. He asks them what action Hera took when learning of her husband Zeus' new infatuation? And the Chorus recount how Hera sent Argus to keep watch over Io the heifer/priestess. Argus had a hundred eyes of which only two closed at any one time. Zeus, however, had outwitted this plan of his dear wife by sending his messenger son Hermes to use his cunning. Hermes had disguised himself as a fellow herdsman and joined Argus as though seeking companionship. He then told him long and boring stories, and played lullabies to him until one by one all his eyelids drooped and finally closed, whereupon Hermes cut off his head. It was then that Hera had set the gadfly on the poor, unfortunate priestess-turned-heifer, causing her for ever to flee from one place to another to escape its torment.

King Pelasgus is satisfied that these suppliants who have just arrived on his shores, are indeed who they say they are and in need of his protection. But he fears repercussions from Aegyptus and his fifty sons. He counsels them to ...*take in thine arms those wool-wreathed boughs, and lay them before another sanctuary, where all the dwellers in our city may behold these visible tokens of your sure distress, lest my report of you should pass for nought... (481-486.)*

Danaus is relieved to find the king is prepared to help. He asks him to find him an escort to lead him to the sanctuary he speaks of. The king orders an attendant to show him the way and they depart.

The daughters are anxious of their fate without their father's presence, but Pelasgus reassures them. *Though your pursuer have wings we will not yield you. (510-511.)* And he also departs, assuring them first that he is going to speak to his people and put them in a friendly mood. A show of hands will tell him what is best. Perhaps this reflected the beginning of democracy Aeschylus was witnessing in Athens.

Danaus eventually returns with the good news that the majority of Argive men have voted to give sanctuary to them. They will even fight on their behalf if need be: ...*The bright sky bristled with right hands in air, from that great crowd, confirming this decree; that we should share the freedom of their soil, and none should seize or claim our persons here... (607-610.)*

But Danaus' relief is short-lived because he spots a ship on the horizon approaching swiftly: ...*And now the men on board are plain to see, dark limbs appearing out of garments white, nor less remarkably her convoy swarms with smaller craft around her. She herself their leader, now approaching land, hath lowered her canvas, and all hands are at the oars ... (724-729.)*

His daughters are terrified, knowing that Aegyptus and his sons are in pursuit. They cry out at what they see: ...*In that firm-timbered black-eyed bark they come, rowed by dark throngs of warriors and impelled with headlong rage...Madly intent are they with godless fury, frenzied with insolence, ignoring heaven... (744-746, 762-763.)*

In due course a Herald arrives from Aegyptus and his sons. He shows no mercy and orders the women to board their ship. At the distress he sees, he merely says: *Howl as thou wilt, and rend thy robes, and call thy gods to aid! Thou shalt not overskip the limiting bulwark of Aegyptus' bark. Ay, howl and cry, out-wailing thy distress; thou hast thy name conjoined with wretchedness. (872-877.)*

The situation is saved by the return of King Pelasgus. He rounds on the Herald in anger for treating his kingdom as his own. ....*Much folly and no judgement, sure, is thine... (917),* and he accuses the Herald of lacking respect for the Argive gods, to which he retorts that he respects the gods of Egypt, and complains of King Pelasgus' lack of courtesy to him, a stranger. To this he is told by Pelasgus that he has no intention of showing courtesy to sacrilege, and tempers rise.

The Herald declares that King Pelasgus' defence of the women means war. The king, however, says he is well able to wage war if necessary, and the Herald departs. The drama ends with Danaus returning and advising his daughters to show gratitude: ...*acknowledge your preservers here. Ye owe to the Argives, as to gods in heaven, rich drink-offering, and prayer and sacrifice; your saviours without controversy are they...Respect me then the more, since I have won this favour through persuasive friendliness... (983-994.)*

And they sing their father's praises and put their faith in Zeus who ...*with that healing touch, that with kindly force Divine, founded our ancestral line. (1067-1069.)* From being the ruthless and unyielding god in *Prometheus Bound*, Zeus has become almost benign.

As with Aeschylus' *Prometheus Bound*, *Suppliants* could well have had two other dramas, because the legend continued with Danaus having to give in to the sons of Aegyptus, who'd been ordered by their father not to return so long as their uncle remained alive.

Legend has it that his daughters were forced to marry, but Danaus gave each daughter a dagger and ordered her to kill her husband on her wedding night. This they all did except for the eldest (if she was the eldest of fifty she must surely have been in her seventies!) who found herself in love with her new husband. She told him of the plot and urged him to escape. In due course he returned to his wife (his name was Lynceus, and his wife was called Hypermnestra). The forty-nine daughters who'd murdered their bridegrooms had then to be purified of their sin, and eventually they each married an Argive. Each young Argive willingly took one as a bride when he was told he didn't have to present gifts to Danaus but that each would be rewarded with riches.

As for the eldest daughter's husband Lynceus (Aegyptus' only remaining son), tradition has it that he avenged the murder of his forty-nine brothers, by killing Danaus.

If Aeschylus was interested in influencing the Athenian audiences, he may well have done so. From his dramas he reveals the good that spreads widely when kindness and compassion are shown to the distressed; and when overweening arrogance and harshness rear their ugly heads, then to stand up in defiance can only be a virtue.

SOPHOCLES
ANTIGONE

Antigone was written c.442 B.C. It is believed to have won first prize but whether at the City Dionysia or the Lenaia is not known. The setting is Thebes.

With the death of Antigone's two brothers, Eteocles and Polynices, the curse put on them by their father Oedipus was fulfilled – for the curse see Sophocles' *Oedipus Colonus* (Chapter 10).

Their death came about because, when their father Oedipus stepped down from the throne, the two brothers agreed to reign alternate years. At the end of his first year, however, Eteocles refused to relinquish the crown. Polynices, having spent that year in Argos, and having married the king of Argos' daughter, raised an army of Argive chieftains and attacked Thebes, with the fatal consequence that he and his brother died by each other's hand. Following their death Creon, their uncle, was crowned king.

The play begins at this point when Creon, as monarch, decrees that, because Polynices is the one who raised an army against Thebes, his body is on no account to be buried but left for the birds and wild beasts to devour. Eteocles, on the other hand, as reigning monarch, has been buried with due honours, but anyone caught attempting to bury Polynices, will be stoned to death.

Antigone refuses to accept Creon's ruling against her brother, and asks her sister Ismene to assist her with the interment of his body. Ismene is reluctant to disobey her uncle: *What, would you bury him, against the proclamation? (52-53.)* When Antigone remains defiant, her sister warns: *Your heart beats hotly for chilling work! (102.)* But Antigone has no doubt at all what her duty is; she is prepared to die rather than neglect what she believes is necessary for her brother. If she forfeits her life doing what she knows is right, then at least she herself will die with honour. They both depart, leaving the Chorus to elaborate on the attack on Thebes by Polynices, which resulted in this mutual fratricide.

Creon enters and voices his determination that the body of Polynices is to be left to rot. Since he is king, he must be obeyed or the consequence will be death. He holds forth at length, only to be interrupted by a Sentinel who arrives in a state of great anxiety. Polynices has been buried by an anonymous hand; it is possible that a supernatural power did it. The news causes Creon to shout the poor man down *before I choke with rage.* To have his orders so wilfully disregarded? Only the payment of money could have persuaded a man to dare disobey his express orders. *...no such ill currency ever appeared, as money to mankind; this is it that sacks cities, this routs out men from their homes, and trains and turns astray the minds of honest mortals, setting them upon base actions... (335-340.)*

After an exchange of accusations and denials, King Creon and the Sentinel depart, leaving the Chorus mulling over who could be the culprit. Eventually the Sentinel returns with Antigone, whom he declares he's caught in the act of burying her brother.

Creon arrives, and is informed by the Sentinel how he and his fellows had cleared the light covering of earth from the body and had kept watch. A strange storm had filled the air and when it had ceased *...there stands this maiden in sight, and wails aloud, shrill as the bitter note of the sad bird, when as she finds the couch of her void nest robbed of her young; so she, soon as she sees the body stripped and bare, bursts out in shrieks, and calls down curses dire on their heads who had done it... (470-476.)* And the Sentinel goes on to describe how Antigone deliberately set about covering the body with earth again.

Antigone confesses gladly that she is guilty. Creon confronts her in anger: *And you made free to overstep my law? (498.)* Antigone is unrepentant; Creon's law, perhaps, she agrees, but not the law of Heaven. *...This is not of today and yesterday, but lives for ever, having origin whence no man knows: whose sanctions were loath in Heaven's sight to provoke, fearing the will of any man... (505-509.)*

Creon is irate, and shouts in anger: *...Truly if here she wield such powers uncensured, she is man, I woman!... (541-542.)* The situation is intolerable! Women should know their place and never take the initiative in such matters – and certainly never disobey a king's orders! And the verbal tussle continues with the King accusing and Antigone quietly determined to fulfil her duty to a brother – a brother, but a foe to Thebes, as King Creon sees it.

Ismene comes from the palace to join them, and claims that she too helped Antigone in the rites. But Antigone denies it – she herself is alone to blame and her sister played no part in it, she says. But Ismene insists she is as much to blame as Antigone. Creon loses patience and declares Antigone must die. What? Is Creon to deprive his son Haemon of Antigone, his intended bride? She is unworthy of him, Creon shouts, and anyway he can easily find somebody else. In a fury, Creon orders the two sisters to be taken off to be executed.

The Chorus discuss the laws of heaven until Creon's son Haemon enters. He fawns on his father, saying *...you guide my steps with your good counsels, for which for my part I will follow closely... in the path of honour. (709-713.)*

To this Creon retorts that Antigone is not a fit bride for him. ... *Better to spurn this maiden as a foe! Leave her to wed some bridegroom in the grave!... (729-730.)* Never let it be said that *a woman worsted us.*

Haemon begins to question his father's so-called 'honour'. Antigone was right to bury her brother, defying his orders. His father must listen to others and not insist that what he thinks and says is always right. *...Do not persist, then, to retain at heart one sole idea, that the thing is right which your mouth utters, and nought else beside. For all men who believe themselves alone wise, or that they possess a soul or speech such as none other, turn them inside out, they are found empty... (788-794.)* He could not speak more plainly! And he goes on to implore his father to relent *...Let thy wrath go!*

But his words increase the anger of his father. They are at loggerheads as Creon stands his ground and his son accuses him: *A city is no city that is of one man only. (824-825.)* And Creon retorts: *Is not the city held to be his who rules it? (826-827.)* To that Haemon says: *That were brave – you, a sole monarch of an empty land! (828-829.)* And he goes on to warn his father that if Antigone dies, he will die too. But Creon is not listening and explodes with anger: *...If thou revile me, and find fault with me, never believe but it shall cost thee dear!... (849-850.)*

So speaks the king as his son in blind fury departs, declaring he never wants to set eyes on his father again. Following this fierce argument, the blind seer Teiresias is led on stage; he foresees trouble ahead for the king. The birds and dogs have begun devouring Polynices' body and, therefore, the gods are displeased. He urges Creon to change direction: *...thou shalt not tell many more turns of the sun's chariot-wheel, ere thou shalt render satisfaction, one from thy own loins in payment... for that thou hast...sent a living soul unworthily to dwell within a tomb, and keep'st a corpse here, from the presence of Powers beneath...wherefore the late-avenging punishers, Furies, from Death and Heaven, lay wait for* *thee, to take thee in the evil of thine own hands... (1181-1197.)* And, having delivered his warnings, Teiresias departs, leaving Creon with a touch of fear, but still stubbornly determined not to appear weak.

He will not yield, yet he has been warned of the gods' displeasure. He asks the advice of a Senator who suggests he goes and frees Antigone, even to build a tomb for her dead brother. And Creon in alarm says: ...*You deem that I should yield? (1226.)* The Senator's answer is clear: ...*Sir, with all speed. Swift-footed come calamities from heaven to cut off the perverse. (1227-1228.)* And Creon at last relents: ...*I cannot fight at odds with destiny. (1229-1231.)*

But it is already too late. Creon's son Haemon has found his beloved Antigone dead and has himself joined her in death. Creon's wife Eurydice appears, is told the awful truth and, instead of breaking down, shows no emotion but returns silently into the palace. The Messenger says to those around that he supposes she ...*would not choose, hearing her son's sad fate, in public to begin her keening cry... (1376-1377.)*

With the arrival of King Creon bearing the body of Haemon, the king now learns that his wife too has committed suicide. With this double blow, the king has been taught the harsh lesson that none of this would have happened but for his own stubborn pride.

In despair Creon cries out: *Lead me forth, cast me out, no other than a man undone; who did slay, unwitting, thy mother and thee, my son! I turn me I know not where for my plans ill-sped, and a doom that is heavy to bear is come down on my head. (1460-1465.)* And with these words he departs, leaving the Chorus singing: *Wisdom first for a man's well-being maketh of all things. Heaven's insistence nothing allows of man's irreverence; and great blows great speeches avenging, dealt on a boaster, teach men wisdom in age, at last. (1466-1470.)*

EURIPIDES
SUPPLIANT WOMEN

Euripides' *Suppliant Women* is an exercise in grieving, of agony and woe. Its storyline is about the mothers of the seven Argive chieftains who were killed at the seven gates of Thebes. It may be remembered that Polynices, son of Oedipus, raised an army against his brother Eteocles because they had agreed that each would be king of Thebes on alternate years. When, however, it was Eteocles' turn to step down, he refused. The two brothers killed each other as predicted in the curse laid on them by their father.

The six other Argive chieftains, who attacked the seven gates of the city, also died in the attempt, and the Thebans refused them burial or to give up their bodies. Because of this impious treatment, the Mothers of these Argive warriors come to supplicate Theseus, king of Athens, who at this time is still young and inexperienced.

The setting for the drama is the sanctuary of Demeter at Eleusis (see Chapter 6). This site symbolizes the agony of Demeter's loss of her daughter and the joy of recovery; it reflects Demeter's daughter Persephone's abduction by Hades, and her eventual return to the upper world.

Theseus' mother Aithra is present, and a Chorus of Argive Mothers implore Aithra to plead with Theseus on their behalf to help get the bodies of their dead sons restored to them: *Reverend Queen, with aged lips do we implore thee; in our suppliance at thy knee we fall before thee. Oh, redeem thou unto us from that assemblage of the dead our beloved... (41-43.)*

And from one Mother comes the cry on behalf of all: *...What should I do but mourn, who have laid not out my dead unto his burial to be borne, and who see not any heaping of the earth-mound for his tomb?... (52-54.)*

Drawn to the sound of anguished mourning, Theseus arrives. He is relieved to find his mother there since she's been missing from home for some while. But why are these women here with suppliant boughs, and Adrastus, king of Argos, lying prostrate before the temple, he asks? Aithra explains their plight: *My son, these are the mothers of the… chieftains who fell in battle by the Cadmean gates. And with suppliant boughs they hold me captive as thou seest. (101-103.)*

There is a rapid exchange of words between Theseus and the unfortunate Adrastus who is on his knees in supplication. Theseus reprimands him, saying he should never have gone to war with Thebes in the first place. As he points out: *Valour instead of wisdom thou favoured. (161.)*

Adrastus regrets his action and feels only shame: *…Oh, king of Athens… to fall to earth, and to embrace thy knee, a grey-haired king in time past prosperous. Yet to mine evil plight I needs must bow… (164-167.)* And he begs Theseus to help him restore the sons to their grieving Mothers: *…Who have endured to come… no mission to Demeter's mysteries, but seeking burial for their dead… (171-174.)*

The young Theseus regards King Adrastus with barely concealed contempt; he lays the blame squarely on him: *…Thou led forth the Argives to war, though seers spake heaven's warning… so ruined thy state, by young men led astray… (229-232.)*

Adrastus replies that he hasn't come to him to be criticized, but to seek assistance. Since he has clearly failed to move him he instructs the Mothers to depart. Aithra regards Theseus' lack of compassion as dishonourable, and insists that, as king, he must show not only strength and courage but kindness. She is quite frankly appalled by his callousness, and cries out: *I will not hold my peace, to blame hereafter myself for cowardly silence… My son, I bid thee look to this first, lest thou err, despising their appeal to heaven. In this alone thou err'st… (297-302.)* And she implores him to show compassion, warning that *…God bringeth low the proud. (391.)*

Such a reprimand from his mother brings Theseus up short. Her words weigh heavily on him as he wants only her approval, not chastisement. He quickly corrects himself, and says he will do as she advises; he will himself march on Thebes and bring back the Argive dead. But first, he insists, he must consult the Athenian citizens and seek their assent as democracy demands. Theseus and his mother depart while the Chorus of Mothers sing of their new hope that their prayers will be answered.

Sure enough, Theseus eventually returns with an Athenian Herald whom he instructs to go to Thebes and inform the ruler there that he, King Theseus of Athens, demands that the Argive bodies be returned;

that if they refuse his army stands ready to attack. His words are interrupted by the arrival of another Herald, this one from Thebes. He has messages from Creon who has become ruler of Thebes since both sons of Oedipus are dead. He asks to see the 'despot', to which Theseus is quick to say ...*Our state is ruled not of one man only: Athens is free... (404-405.)*

The Theban Herald is not impressed. How can that be sensible? ...*How should the mob which reason all awry have power to pilot straight a nation's course?... (417-419.)*

Theseus speaks of the benefits of democracy: ...*No worse foe than the despot hath a state, under whom, first, can be no common laws... But when the laws are written, then the weak and wealthy have alike but equal right... (429-434.)*

The Theban Herald brings warning from Creon. He forbids Theseus to allow King Adrastus of Argos to set foot in Athens. Nor will he allow that the Argive dead be given up. If Theseus shows friendship to Argos Thebes will declare war.

Theseus is quick to respond: ...*It is not I that launch upon this war... but lifeless bodies – harming not your state... lo, all Hellas' law do I uphold. How is not this well done? ...If one shall rob the dead of rightful dues, and hold them from the tomb: this shall unman even heroes, if such law shall be ordained... (522-527, 539-541.)* Force will be used if necessary ... *For never unto Greeks shall it be said that the Gods' ancient law was set at nought... (561-562.)*

So war it is. The Theban Herald departs, leaving Theseus blatantly defiant of the terms set by Creon. His departing words are that he has the gods on his side: ...*for where these are, they give victory. Naked valour nought avails to men, except it have the Gods' good will. (594-597.)*

The Chorus of Argive Mothers divide and sing alternately of their hopes and fears: they appeal for divine intervention, and their prayers mark a passage of time.   At last a Messenger arrives to tell them of Theseus' success. He describes the battle in graphic detail: ... *Of thousand horrors there... of men, by tangling reins snatched from the cars, flung earthward – of the murder-streams of gore – men falling here, and there, as crashed the chariots, with violence hurled head downwards to the earth, and battered out of life by chariot-shards... (686-693.)* And he describes how he'd heard Theseus shout out to the Thebans: ... *"Not to destroy the town came I... but to reclaim the dead." (723-724.)* He speaks highly of Theseus: ...*Well might men choose such battle-chief as this, who is in peril's midst a tower of strength... (725-726.)*

King Adrastus, still at Eleusis since Theseus insisted he remain, asks what has happened regarding the bodies of the dead Argivian chieftains. The Messenger reports how Theseus showed excessive humility by personally washing the wounds of the bodies (a task usually performed by slaves) and adds: ...*Hadst thou but seen his ministry of love! ...And spread the biers, and veiled the bodies o'er. (765, 767.)*

Soon Theseus himself returns, accompanied by Athenian soldiers carrying the biers on which the bodies of the fallen are laid. The Chorus of Mothers weep and wail: ...*But to see my son's corpse! Sight bitter for me, yet proud, for the day that I hoped not to see... earth's ghastliest misery. (782-785.) Oh, my son! Bitter word for a mother's lips to moan! I cry on thee, in ears that do not hear. (802-804.)*

King Adrastus praises the dead with eulogies designed to bring comfort to the bereaved Mothers: one who, though wealthy, preferred moderation; another who had no wealth but was *rich in honour*, and so on. Adrastus asks Theseus what is to happen to the body of Polynices, and is told by Theseus that he has a sepulchre prepared for him there in the sanctuary. Adrastus is about to call on the Mothers to come to view the bodies of their sons, but Theseus intervenes. He knows their battle wounds will distress them beyond endurance, and insists they wait till the bodies have been consumed on funeral pyres; each can then pour her grief out over her son's ashes. *'Twere death to look on them so sorely marred... Why then would'st add fresh anguish to their grief? (944-946.)*

Seven pyres are lit; the bodies are cremated and the Mothers cry out their laments. The attention of the audience is then drawn to Evadne, one of the wives of the seven dead. This young widow is beside herself with grief; she is suddenly to be seen on a cliff overlooking the sanctuary, and cries out: ...*Oh, love, I rush to thee from mine home, raving, seeking thy tomb, thy pyre, longing with strong desire to end in that same fire... (1000-1004.)*

Her father fails to stop her, and the overwrought widow throws herself from the cliff onto her husband's pyre. So, with much weeping and wailing, this doom-laden drama becomes ever more depressing as a procession enters (a second Chorus of the young Sons of the dead). Each Son makes a short despondent speech to which his grandmother (from the first Chorus) responds. If anything comes from this tragedy it is its glaring revelation of the harsh and painful consequence of war in which young men are slaughtered. The seventh young Son appears holding the urn containing his father's ashes: *By this my burden am I all undone!* he cries. His grandmother responds in tears: *Let me embrace the ashes of my son!* To which her grandson sobs: *I weep to hearken thy piteous word – my heart dies in me.* And his grandmother wails: *Oh, my son, thou art gone: never more will your glorious face gaze on thy mother! (1160-1161.)*

The drama ends with King Adrastus for ever grateful to Theseus for dealing with the Argive dead and giving them a ritual burial. Theseus replies that, as a result, he hopes that Argos will ever remember his help and live in peace with Athens.

At this point the goddess Athena, as protectress of Athens, appears on the temple roof. She demands that the alliance be sealed with an oath ...*that never Argive men shall bear against this land the arms of war; if others come, their spear shall bar the way... (1191-1193.)* And if the oath is broken and Argos does declare war on Athens ...*call down on Argos miserable ruin... (1195.)*

To make the oath doubly binding, Athena insists it must be sworn over a bronze tripod, into which the blood must flow from three sheep whose throats are slit as they are sacrificed; the tripod is to be kept in the sacred hearth at Delphi, and the knife used for the sacrifice is to be buried in the ground beside the pyres of the Seven here at Eleusis. This knife will be for ever a symbol, to be shown to the Argives if ever they come in arms against Athena's city; it will act as a reminder of the oath they have just sworn.

And so the tragedy ends on a note of hope with Theseus calling on the goddess, saying: ...*only thou guidest me in justice. If thou look kindly on us we will remain safe ever more. (1230-1231.)*

This drama was written between 423 and 420 B.C. and it is unknown for which festival it was entered.

EURIPIDES
MADNESS OF HERACLES

The name Heracles (Roman Hercules) immediately brings to mind an indomitable hero possessing superhuman strength, courage and tenacity with which to overcome his near impossible Labours. Most people are oblivious of the fact that Heracles had a spell of madness during which time he murdered his wife and three young sons.

Before writing about the *Madness of Heracles*, I will give a few brief details of Heracles' birth and early life.

Lord Zeus, knowing that it was ordained that one day there would be a great battle of the gods and giants, was determined to conceive an exceptionally courageous hero on a mortal woman who would have the strength to help the gods overthrow the enemy. For this purpose he chose the beautiful Alcmena, wife of King Amphitryon of Tiryns. If some legends claim Heracles was born in Thebes it was, no doubt, because the city, hearing of his great achievements, wanted to boast he was their citizen (or maybe it was the other way about).

To conceive such a son Zeus waited till Alcmena's husband King Amphitryon was absent on some campaign then, taking on the guise of her husband, he was welcomed to Alcmena's bed. Later that same night, King Amphitryon happened to return home and immediately went in to his wife who told him that he had already made love to her. Teiresias (the renowned blind seer) pronounced the true facts, and the king felt greatly honoured that his wife had been chosen by Zeus. The result of that night's double impregnation was the birth of twin boys to the queen.

Zeus' wife Hera was enraged by her husband's infidelity (what was new?) and did all she could to harm the babies. She sent a pair of serpents to kill them and, because one infant screamed at the sight of them but the other seized and strangled them, it was immediately evident which was the son of Zeus, and which was not.

The goddess Hera, however, remorselessly continued her jealous attacks on Heracles, irate that this prodigy of her husband Zeus had been born to a mere human and not to her, his true immortal wife. In her rage she saw to it that Heracles' birthright, which should have been the Argolid kingdom which included Mycenae and Tiryns, passed to Eurystheus, who became Heracles' arch enemy. It was due to King Eurystheus' hatred of Heracles that he tried to rid himself of the hero by setting him the Labours for which he became famous.

In his twelfth and final Labour, Heracles was ordered by King Eurystheus to capture and bring back Cerberus, the dog who guarded the entry to the underworld. Undaunted, Heracles persuaded Hades to let him take the dog for a short period. This he was allowed to do on condition he used no weapons that might harm Cerberus and to return him safely. Showing his usual indomitable courage, Heracles picked up this loathsome canine monster and carried him bodily to the palace of King Eurystheus. Terrorized by the sight, Eurystheus jumped into a large brass tub, a place where he always took refuge when frightened. Having completed this last Labour, Heracles returned Cerberus to Hades as promised.

It should be said that by now Heracles had married Megara, the daughter of King Creon of Thebes, and they'd had three sons. It is at this point that in one of Hera's jealous rages she struck Heracles with a bout of madness and, while deranged, he killed his family.

The tragedy takes place outside the royal palace in Thebes while Heracles is absent, returning the loathsome dog Cerberus to Hades.

In the drama Megara's father Creon has recently been murdered by a certain Lycus who has usurped the throne. King Lycus (his name means 'wolf') gloats over the hapless plight of Heracles' family with murder in mind. He taunts them that Heracles is neglecting them when he is most needed.

Megara prays that her husband will arrive back in time to save them. But she knows she must yield to her destiny. Her father declares he has no fear of death but requests that he and his daughter are killed first so that ...*we see not the boys gasping out life*... *(323-324.)*

To their surprise and joy Heracles does arrive. When he learns that Lycus has usurped the throne having murdered Creon, and that his wife and sons are to be his next victims, he urges his family to stay strong: ...*rally thou, my wife, thy fainting spirit. From trembling cease*... *(626-627)* and he turns to his small sons: ...*and ye, let go my cloak. I am no winged thing, nor would I fly my friends... Even must I lead them clinging to mine hands, as ship that tows her boats*... *(627-632.)*

And with these words he departs with them into the palace in full confidence of his ability to prevent disaster.

The Chorus sing the praises of Heracles and all that he's achieved *...whose toils gave peace to humankind, slaying dread shapes that filled man's mind with terrors ceaseless-haunting. (698-700.)* And they question the gods who seem unable to differentiate between good and evil *...no line clear-severing 'twixt good and bad the Gods have drawn... (669-670.)*

They cease their song as Lycus enters with Heracles' mortal father Amphitryon. Lycus is unaware that Heracles has returned and commands Amphitryon to bring out Megara and the three boys, even if they are supplicating the gods, because they are wasting their breath. But Amphitryon courageously says that to fetch them would make him an accomplice to murder, to which Lycus retorts that in that case he will get them himself. He departs declaring that their death will *gladden my heart*.

Amphitryon is, of course, aware that Heracles is with his family in the palace and, confident that all will now be well, he follows Lycus muttering: *...Joy it is to see an enemy die, suffering vengeance for his ill deeds done. (732-733.)*

The Athenian audience would know what is about to happen, the terrible story of how this son of Zeus was struck down by Madness personified, and murders his wife and children. If Euripides makes the point that the gods see that justice is done in the world of men, he also draws attention to the injustices wrought by them.

And so Madness enters the palace leaving the Chorus to voice their alarm and anxiety. They cry out their terror as they hear Madness take possession of Heracles, and the sounds of horrifying distress that come from within the palace: *...Away, oh, ye children, in flight, for death, death shrieks through her pipe by the blast of her breath!... (984-985.)*

Finally a Servant comes from the palace ashen-faced to report how Heracles, overcome by Madness, has murdered his wife and sons. The Chorus cry out their astonishment. How can the gods do this? ... *Say, say in what fashion the malice of gods hath brought these ills on the house, and the fate with misery fraught on the children that fell. (918-920.)*

Euripides gives full vent to the horrors as the Servant describes Heracles who, *...with rolling eyes distraught, and bloodshot eye-roots starting from his head, suddenly with a maniac laugh he spake... (932-935.)* And the wretched, deranged Heracles, mistaking his own sons for the sons of Eurystheus – the king who has been setting him his

Labours – kills them one by one. The Servant describes his ravings as he savagely set about the murders: ... *Then shouted Heracles, and vaunted thus: 'One of Eurystheus' fledglings here is slain, dead at my feet, hath paid for his sire's hate!' Against the next then aimed his bow, who crouched at the altar's base... the poor child clasped his knees, and stretching to his beard and neck a hand, 'Ah, dearest father,' cried he, 'slay not me! I am thy boy – thine!'– 'Tis not Eurystheus' son!' He, rolling savage gorgon-glaring eyes, since the boy stood too near for that fell bow, swung back overhead his club, like forging-sledge, down dashed it on his own son's golden head, and shattered all the bones... (981-994.)*

The Servant's account of the horrendous scene is unsparing till the unexpected intervention of the goddess Athena who, seeing the wreckage in the palace and murderous slaughter, hurls a great rock which hits Heracles on the chest and sends him reeling backwards against a pillar which knocks him senseless. The rock is supposedly still to be seen, though I never saw it when exploring Thebes, and no one I spoke to at the museum seemed to know about it. In the tragedy, Heracles' father, who has escaped death, helps the servants tie Heracles to the pillar where he remains unconscious. But soon he will recover.

At this point the palace doors are opened to reveal the terrible and tragic scene of the dead boys with their mother, and the bound Heracles. Heracles' father urges the Chorus to be silent for fear of waking Heracles. But he is already stirring, and Amphitryon orders them all to flee for their lives.

Heracles regains consciousness and, finding himself tied to the pillar with the bodies around him, is utterly confused. Why is he trussed up? Why the corpses? Why so much destruction around him? When Heracles sees Amphitryon, he cries out: *Father, why dost thou weep and veil thine eyes, shrinking afar from thy beloved son? (1111-1112.)*

His poor father has the terrible task of drawing his attention to the dead bodies of his family. This he does as gently as he can: they are not Eurystheus and his children, as he'd intended, but his own wife and young sons. Amphitryon unties his bonds calling on Zeus to look down on what Hera has brought about ...*this curse hurled from Hera's throne...(1126)*, and he gently tells Heracles what he did while Madness had taken possession of him.

Heracles is devastated. He cannot believe he is responsible for his beloved family's murder, and he wants now only to kill himself. He can't bear it when he sees Theseus approaching the palace – Theseus, king of Athens, who will see the death and destruction of which Heracles is guilty. ...*Come, let me in pall of darkness shroud mine head; for I take shame for evils wrought of me, nor would I taint him with blood guiltiness – nay, nowise would I harm the innocent. (1159-1162.)*

Theseus has come to offer Heracles his hand in friendship because he's heard that Lycus has usurped the throne and, as Heracles came to his aid in Hades (yet another story), so the very least he can do is to help him now that his help is needed.

With shock he sees the scattered corpses and realizes he has come too late. Whoever could have slain the boys? ...*Some unheard-of outrage here I find! (1176.)*

Amphitryon quietly informs him that Madness is to blame. Heracles hides his face, humiliated and deeply distraught to be the slaughterer of such innocence. Gently his father and Theseus persuade him to face the truth. Here Euripides, having his Athenian audience in mind, yet again portrays this legendary king of Athens as kindly and compassionate. Theseus takes command of the situation and offers his friendship to Heracles where others might well have withdrawn from the scene, fearful of being polluted by the sight of blood and death. What, Theseus asks, is the use of friends who are only there in good times but back away when times are tough: ...*Stand up, unmuffle thou thine hapless head: Look on me, who of men is royal-souled beneath the blows of heaven, and flincheth not. (1226-1228.)* And he gently draws away the cloak that veils the head of his friend.

Has Theseus seen the horrors he is guilty of, Heracles asks? Yes, he has seen. Then he should flee from such pollution, Heracles cries out. Not at all, Theseus replies, he is full of concern for his wretched state: *From earth to heaven reach thy calamities (1240)* are the words he uses. He wants only now to kill himself, Heracles says, to which Theseus answers: *No hero's words be these that thou hast said. (1248.)*

Heracles recoils at this rebuke and points out that Theseus himself is not weighed down by such guilt as his. With friendly reassurance Theseus says he has not had to endure as much as he has; and he draws his attention to how much Heracles has achieved for mankind – his courage and heroism in killing off the monsters that have threatened men. He is their ...*benefactor and their mighty friend. (1252.)*

But Heracles is not persuaded. Although he lists his successes, he is the victim of Hera's everlasting wrath, and see what has happened? She has won. ...*Now let her dance, that glorious bride of Zeus beating with sandalled foot Olympus' floor! She hath compassed her desire that she desired, down with his pedestal hurling in utter wreck the foremost man of Greece! To such a goddess who shall pray now?... (1302-1307.)*

Theseus tells him not to think of killing himself but to suffer and be strong. It is the best way since nobody escapes misfortune. Look at the gods themselves: *...In Olympus still they dwell, by their transgressions unabashed. What wilt thou plead, if mortal as thou art, thou chafe against thy fate, and gods do not? (1318-1321.)*

And Theseus invites Heracles to leave Thebes and come to Athens with him. *Rise, sorrow-stricken; let these tears suffice*, he says, and Heracles replies: *I cannot; lo, my limbs are palsy-chained. (1395.)*

But Theseus is firm: *No more! To a friend, a helper, reach thine hand.* But Heracles warns him: *With this blood let me not besmirch thy robes! (1399)* to which his compassionate friend replies: *On me wipe all off! Spare not. I refuse not! (1400.)*

Heracles' mood begins to change as gratitude floods over him. He now has no sons but Theseus is as a son to him, to which Theseus says: *Cast o'er my neck thine arm; I lead thee on. (1403.)* When Heracles wavers yet again, Theseus accuses him of playing a woman's role, to which Heracles turns on him with the retort that when he was bound in Hades had he not then himself felt as helpless and weak? And Euripides, the great playwright, ends the scene with the two friends trusting each other in loyal companionship. It is finally agreed that Amphitryon will join them in Athens when he has buried Heracles' sons and wife – it is something Heracles cannot do himself being guilty of their murder. The Chorus closes the play with the following lines: *...With mourning and weeping sore do we pass away, who have lost the chiefest of all our friends this day. (1428-1429.)*

Euripides' *Madness of Heracles* was written 416 or 414 B.C., and it is not known whether it was written for the Great Dionysia or for the Lenaia, or whether it won a prize or not.

EXTANT DRAMAS

* Denotes dramas included in this book

AESCHYLUS

*Persians
*Seven Against Thebes
*Suppliants
*Oresteia (Trilogy),
   Agamemnon, Libation
   Bearers, Eumenides
*Prometheus Bound

SOPHOCLES

*Ajax
*Antigone
Women of Trachis
*Oedipus Tyrannus
Electra
Philoctetes
*Oedipus at Colonus

EURIPIDES

*Alcestis
*Medea
Children of Heracles
*Hippolytus
Andromache
Hecuba
*Suppliant Women
Electra
*Madness of Heracles
*Trojan Women
*Iphigenia in Tauris
Ion
*Helen
Phoenician Women
Orestes
*Iphigenia at Aulis
*Bacchae
*Cyclops

ARISTOPHANES

Acharnians
Knights
*Wasps
*Peace
*Clouds
*Birds
Lysistrata
*Women at the
   Thesmophoria
*Frogs
Assembly Women
*Wealth

TRANSLATIONS

Aeschylus: *Oresteia, Persians, Seven Against Thebes, Prometheus Bound, Suppliants*. Translated by Lewis Campbell, M.A.

Euripides: *Cyclops, Trojan Women, Hippolytus, Medea, Iphigenia at Aulis, Iphigenia in Tauris, Helen, Bacchae, Alcestis, Madness of Heracles, Suppliant Women*. Translated by R. Potter, M. Wodhull, A.S. Way.

Sophocles: *Ajax, Oedipus Tyrannus, Oedipus Colonus, Antigone*. Translated by Sir George Young, M.A.

Aristophanes: *Clouds, Frogs, Plutus, Women at the Thesmophoria, Wasps, Birds, Peace*. Translated by David Barrett and Alan H. Sommerstein.

BIBLIOGRAPHY

Aeschylus: *Seven Plays in English Verse, translated by Lewis Campbell, M.A.* Oxford University Press, 1906.

Conacher, D.J: *Aeschylus' Prometheus Bound (a literary commentary).* University of Toronto Press, 1980.

Aristophanes: *Lysistrata, the Acharnians, the Clouds, translated by Alan H. Sommerstein.* Penguin Books, 1973.

Aristophanes: *the Knights, Peace, the Birds, the Assembly Women, Wealth, translated by Alan H Sommerstein, David Barrett.* Penguin Books, 1978.

Aristophanes: *the Wasps, the Poet and the Women, the Frogs, translated by David Barrett.* Penguin Books, 1964.

Aristophanes: *The Complete Plays, translated by Paul Roche.* New American Library, 2005.

Dover, K.J: *Aristophanic Comedy.* B.T. Batsford Ltd, London, 1972.

Euripides: *Plays of Euripides, translated by Shelley, R. Potter & M. Wodhull,* Vol. I. J.M. Dent & Sons Ltd., 1906.

Euripides: *Plays, translated by A.S. Way,* Vol. II. J.M. Dent & Sons Ltd., 1956.

Euripides: *Collected Plays of Euripides, translated by Gilbert Murray.* George Allen & Unwin Ltd., 1954.

Euripides: *Bacchae, Edited with Introduction and Commentary by E.R. Dodds.* Oxford University Press, 1960.

Freyne, Sean: *Galilee, from Alexander the Great to Hadrian, 323 BCE to 135 CE.* T & T Clark Ltd., Edinburgh, 1980.

Grant, Michael & John Hazel: *Who's Who in Classical Mythology.* Weidenfeld & Nicolson, 1993.

Graves, Robert: *The Greek Myths: I & II.* Penguin Books Ltd., 1986.

Greece, the Blue Guide. A & C Black Publishers Ltd., 1990.

Greece, the Rough Guide. Penguin Books, 1995.

Grigson, Geoffrey: *The Goddess of Love*. Constable & Co. Ltd., 1976.

Herodotus: *The Histories of Herodotus, translated by Harry Carter*. Oxford University Press, 1962.

Harvey, Sir Paul: *The Oxford Companion to Classical Literature*. Oxford University Press, 1974.

Hesiod: *Theogony, translated by Richard Clay*. Penguin Books Ltd., 1985.

Homer: *The Iliad, translated by Martin Hammond*. Penguin Books Ltd., 1987.

Homer: *The Odyssey, translated by Richmond Lattimore*. Harper Perennial, 1967.

Kerényi, Carl: *Dionysos*. Princeton University Press., 1996.

Lang, Andrew: *The Homeric Hymns (a new prose translation)*. George Allen, London, 1899.

Murray, Gilbert: *Aristophanes, a study*. Clarendon Press, 1933.

Pausanias: *Guide to Greece, volumes 1 & 2*. Penguin Books Ltd., 1971.

Plato: *The Collected Dialogues of Plato, edited by Edith Hamilton and Huntington Cairns*. Princeton University Press, 1961.

Plutarch: *Greek Lives, translated by Robin Waterfield*. Oxford University Press, 1998.

Radice, Betty: *Who's Who in the Ancient World*. Penguin Books, 1973.

Scully, Vincent: *The Earth, the Temple, and the Gods*. Yale University Press, 1962.

Sophocles: *The Dramas of Sophocles, rendered in English Verse Dramatic & Lyric by Sir George Young*. J.M. Dent & Co.

Sophocles: *The Three Theban Plays, translated by Robert Fagles*. Penguin Classics, 1982.

Thucydides: *The Peloponnesian War, translated by Martin Hammond*. Oxford University Press, 2009.

GLOSSARY

ACHILLES
Greek hero of the Trojan War, son of Peleus and Thetis, a minor goddess.

ADMETUS
King of Pherae, husband of Alcestis.

AEACUS
Son of the nymph Aegina and Zeus.

AEETES
King of Colchis and father of Medea.

AEGEUS
King of Athens and father of Theseus.

AEGINA
A nymph, mother of Aeacus.

AEGISTHUS
Cousin of King Agamemnon and his brother Menelaus, later to become the lover of Clytemnestra, wife of Agamemnon. He helped Clytemnestra to murder her husband when he returned from the Trojan War.

AEGYPTUS
A descendant of Io and Zeus.

AEOLUS
King of the island of Aeolia and controller of the winds.

AEROPE
Wife of King Atreus. She was seduced by his brother Thyestes.

AESON
Father of Jason and rightful heir to the kingdom of Iolchos in Thessaly but Pelias usurped the throne.

AESCHYLUS
One of the three great Athenian dramatists c.525-456 B.C.

AETHRA / AITHRA
Mother of Theseus.

AGAMEMNON
King of Mycenae and brother of Menelaus. He was commander-in-chief of the Greek army in the Trojan War. On his return from the war he was murdered by his wife Clytemnestra.

AGENOR
King of Tyre, nnd father of Cadmus and Europa.

AJAX
Greek hero and son of King Telamon of Salamis.

ALCMENA
Wife of King Amphitryon of Tiryns.

ALEXANDER (the Great)
356-323 B.C. King of Macedonia, son of Philip II and Olympias.

AMPHITRYON
King of Tiryns and husband of Alcmena.

ANDROMACHE
Wife of King Priam of Troy's son Hector.

ANDROMEDA
Married to Perseus who turned a monster to stone when it was about to devour her while she was chained to a rock.

ANTIGONE
Daughter of Oedipus and Jocasta.

APHAIA
Formerly known as Britomartis, a Cretan goddess. She was pursued by King Minos of Crete but escaped by leaping into the sea and ending up on the island of Aegina where she was worshipped as the goddess Aphaia.

APHRODITE
Goddess of love.

APOLLO
Son of Zeus and Leto, and twin brother of Artemis. He was god of music, archery and prophecy.

ARCHELAUS
King of Macedonia 413-399B.C. He was keen to bring Athenian culture to his kingdom.

ARES
God of war.

ARGONAUTS
The heroes who joined Jason on his quest for the Golden Fleece.

ARGUS
A monster with a hundred eyes.

ARIADNE
Daughter of King Minos. She helped Theseus kill the Minotaur then ran away with him to Naxos.

ARISTOPHANES
Great Athenian comic dramatist c.448-c380 B.C.

ARTEMIS
Daughter of Zeus and Leto, and twin sister of Apollo. She was goddess of wild life and hunting.

ASCLEPIUS
God of medicine and healing, son of Apollo.

ASTYANAX
Young son of the Trojan Hector and his wife Andromache.

ATHENA
Daughter of Zeus, goddess of handicraft, and protectress of many cities, but especially of Athens. She was the embodiment of wisdom.

ATOSSA
Wife of King Darius of Persia, and mother of Xerxes.

ATREUS
King of Mycenae and father of Agamemnon and Menelaus.

CADMUS
Founder and first king of Thebes.

CALCHAS
A seer who accompanied King Agamemnon to the Trojan War.

CASSANDRA
Daughter of King Priam and Hecuba. She had the gift of prophecy though no one ever believed her.

CASTOR
See Dioscuri.

CERBERUS
Monster dog with three heads guarding the entry to Hades.

CHARON
The ferryman who was believed to row the dead across the river Styx to Hades.

CHOREGOS
The word for any Athenian of standing and sufficient wealth who was nominated to be responsible for the music, dancing and success of a Chorus in the Great Dionysia or Lenaia drama festivals.

CIRCE
An enchantress with whom Odysseus spent a year on his journey home from Troy. She was Medea's aunt.

CLEMENT OF ALEXANDRIA
Christin theologian c.150-c.215 A.D.

CLEON
Athenian politician and general during the Peloponnesian War. Died 422 B.C.

CLYTEMNESTRA
Wife of King Agamemnon, and sister of Helen. She took Aegisthus for her lover, and murdered her husband on his return from the Trojan War.

CREON
1. King of Corinth, and father of Glauke whom Jason hoped to marry.
2. King of Thebes, Successor to Oedipus and brother of Jocasta.

CYCLOPES
One-eyed giants who made thunderbolts for Zeus. Polyphemos was one of them.

DANAUS
Descendant of Io (priestess of Hera at Argos).

DARIUS
King of Persia, married to Atossa.

DEMETER
Goddess of corn and agriculture, mother of Persephone. Her sacred rites were known as the Eleusian Mysteries.

DIOMEDES
Greek hero of the Trojan War, and son of King Tydeus of Argos.

DIONYSOS
Son of Zeus and the mortal woman Semele, daughter of King Cadmus of Thebes. He was god of wine and drama.

DIOSCURI
Castor and Polydeuces, the 'heavenly twins'. They were the sons of Zeus and Leda, and brothers of Helen and Clytemnestra.

ELECTRA
Daughter of King Agamemnon and Clytemnestra, sister of Iphigenia and Orestes.

EPIMETHEUS
Brother of Prometheus. His name means 'afterthought'

ERINYES
Otherwise known as the Furies. Ancient chthonic goddesses who rose from the ground to torment anyone guilty of family bloodshed.

ETEOCLES
Son of Oedipus and Jocasta.

EURIPIDES
Great Athenian tragic dramatist c.480-406 B.C.

EUROPA
Daughter of the King of Tyre, and sister of Cadmus.

EURYSTHEUS
King of the Argolid, including Mycenae and Tiryns. He set Heracles his Twelve Labours.

FATES
Three female goddesses who supervised human destinies.

FURIES
(See Erinyes.)

GAEA
Personification of the earth.

GLAUKE
Daughter of King Creon of Corinth. Jason wanted to abandon Medea to marry her.

HADES
Brother of Zeus and god of the underworld. His queen was Persephone.

HAEMON
Son of King Creon of Thebes, and engaged to Antigone.

HARMONIA
Daughter of Ares, and wife of King Cadmus of Thebes.

HECTOR
Son of King Priam and his wife Hecuba, brother of Paris. His wife was Andromache.

HECUBA
Wife of King Priam of Troy, and mother of Hector and Paris.

HEKADEMOS
An Attic hero, also known as Academus after whom Plato's academy was named.

HELEN
Daughter of Leda and Zeus. She became the wife of Menelaus, and they had a daughter Hermione. She was seduced by Paris and ran away with him to Troy which triggered the Trojan War.

HEPHAESTUS
Lame son of Zeus and Hera. He was god of fire and a master craftsman in metal-work.

HERA
Wife of Zeus, goddess of women and marriage. Her jealousy at Zeus' extra-marital affairs caused her much suffering.

HERACLES
His Roman name was Hercules. He was noted for his strength and courage, and the Twelve Labours he accomplished.

HERMES
Son of Zeus and the mortal woman Maia. He often acted as his father's messenger, and conducted the souls of the dead down to Hades.

HERMIONE
Daughter of Menelaus and Helen. She was nine years old when her mother ran off with Paris.

HERODOTUS
Historian c.480-425 B.C.

HESIOD
Greek poet c.700 B.C. Author of Theogony.

HOMER
Composer of the two epic poems the *Iliad* and the *Odyssey*. He was believed to have lived c.700 B.C.

HYPERMNESTRA
The eldest of Danaus' fifty daughters, who failed to slay her husband on her wedding night.

IACCHOS
A little heard of deity identified with Dionysos in Demeter's Greater Mysteries.

INO
Daughter of King Cadmus of Thebes and sister of Semele. She cared for Dionysos as an infant till Hera drove her mad.

IO
Hera's priestess at Argos whom Zeus loved.

IPHIGENIA
Daughter of King Agamemnon and Clytemnestra. Her father sacrificed her at Aulis in Greece in order to appease Artemis who was preventing the Greek ships from setting sail for Troy.

IRIS
Goddess of the rainbow and messenger of the gods.

ISMENE
Daughter of King Oedipus and sister of Antigone.

JASON
Son of Aeson, the rightful king of Iolchos whose throne was usurped by Pelias. The latter promised to give up the throne if Jason brought him back the Golden Fleece from Colchis.

JOCASTA
Mother and wife of King Oedipus of Thebes.

KORE
(See Persephone.)

LAIUS
King of Thebes, and great-grandson of Cadmus.

LEDA
Wife of King Tyndareus of Sparta, and mother of Clytemnestra, the Dioscuri and Helen.

MAENADS
Women followers of Dionysos who, under his power, were seized with unnatural strength and, in a state of ecstatic frenzy, ran into the mountains where they tore apart wild beasts and devoured them. They wore fawn skins and carried a thyrsus (a staff crowned with a pine-cone).

MEDEA
Daughter of King Aeetes of Colchis. Thanks to her witch-craft she helped Jason retrieve the Golden Fleece and returned with him to Greece. They married and had two sons.

MEDUS
Son of Medea and King Aegeus of Athens.

MEGARA
Daughter of King Creon of Thebes. She married Heracles and they had three sons.

MENELAUS
Son of King Atreus of Mycenae, and brother of Agamemnon. He became king of Sparta when he married Helen.

MINOS
King of Crete.

MINOTAUR
Half-man, half-bull, the son of Pasiphae, wife of King Minos of Crete and a white bull of Poseidon with whom she became besotted. The Minotaur lived on human flesh till Theseus killed it.

MUSES
Nine daughters of Zeus and Mnemosyne (personification of Memory). Each presided over one of the arts or sciences.

MYRMIDONS
They fought in the Trojan War under Achilles' command.

NEOPTOLEMUS
Son of Achilles, sometimes known as Pyrrhus. He was married to Hermione, and Andromache became his slave-woman after the fall of Troy.

NEREIDS
Daughters of Nereus. They were Sea-deities, one of whom was Thetis who became the mother of Achilles.

NEREUS
A kindly sea-deity and father of Thetis the mother of Achilles.

ODYSSEUS
Son of Laertes of Ithaka. He was married to Penelope and they had one son Telemachus. Odysseus was one of the most courageous and daring of the Greek warriors in the Trojan War.

OEDIPUS
King of Thebes who unwittingly killed Laius, his father, and married his mother Jocasta.

OLYMPIAS
Wife of Philip II of Macedonia, and mother of Alexander the Great.

ORESTES
Son of King Agamemnon and Clytemnestra. After the murder of his father by his mother, Orestes killed his mother to avenge the murder.

ORPHEUS
Son of one of the Muses and a follower of Dionysos. His singing was so divine that mountains would bow down to hear, and fish would jump from the sea. He died at the hands of the frenzied Maenads, and his head still singimg ended up on Lesbos.

PANDORA
The first woman created by Zeus as a thorn in the flesh for mankind. She was give a sealed box and was told not to open it. Curiosity, however got the better of her and on raising the lid all the sins of the world flew out. Only Hope remained inside.

PARIS
Son of King Priam of Troy and Hecuba. It was his selection of Aphrodite at the Judgement of Paris that triggered the Trojan War.

PASIPHAE
Wife of King Minos of Crete and mother of the Minotaur.

PEISISTRATUS
A benevolent Athenian despot 561-527 B.C. under whom Athens developed culturally and economically.

PELASGUS
King of Argos, who gave sanctuary to King Danaus and his fifty daughters.

PELEUS
King of Phthia who married Thetis, a Nereid. Achilles was their son.

PELIAS
King of Iolchos in Thessaly. He usurped the throne and sent Jason, the rightful heir, to retrieve the Golden Fleece, promising him the crown on his return, but then went back on his word.

PELOPS
Son of Tantalus, a forebear of King Agamemnon.

PENELOPE
Wife of Odysseus.

PERICLES
A great Athenian statesman c.500-429 B.C.

PERSEPHONE
Daughter of the goddess Demeter.

PHILIP II
King of Macedonia c.382-336 B.C. and father of Alexander the Great.

PITTHEUS
King of Troezen.

PLATO
c.429-347 B.C. A great Athenian philosopher and pupil of Socrates.

PLUTO
Name for Hades, meaning 'rich one'.

POLYBUS
King of Corinth who, because he was childless, brought up the infant Oedipus who'd been exposed at birth.

POLYDEUCES
One of the twin brothers of Helen and Clytemnestra.

POLYNICES
Son of King Oedipus and Jocasta, and brother of Eteocles, Ismene and Antigone.

POLYPHEMUS
A one-eyed Cyclops and son of Poseidon.

POSEIDON
Brother of Zeus. He was god of the sea as well as of earthquakes and horses.

PROMETHEUS
A Titan. He rebelled against the gods and helped mankind.

PYLADES
A lifelong friend and companion of Orestes.

PYTHAGORAS
Greek philosopher born on the island of Samos c.580 B.C.

SATYRS
Followers of Dionysos. Lustful creatures half-human with the tails of a horse, and legs of a goat. They were equated with fertility.

SCHLIEMANN, Heinrich (1822-1890 A.D.)
A self-made German millionnaire. He was an enthusiastic amateur archaeologist, obsessed with the major sites mentioned in the *Iliad* and the *Odyssey*.

SEMELE
Daughter of King Cadmus of Thebes who was loved by Zeus. She was reduced to a cinder when he revealed himself to her in his full glory. The embryo of Dionysos was sewn into Zeus' thigh till he was ready to be born.

SILENUS
A Satyr noted for his wisdom. He became tutor to the young Dionysos.

SOCRATES
A major Athenian philosopher 469-399 B.C.

SOPHOCLES
One of the three major tragic dramatists 496-406 B.C.

SPHINX
A winged monster with a woman's head on a lion's body who devoured all citizens of Thebes who failed to answer correctly a riddle posed by it.

STYX
The river across which the dead were ferried to Hades.

TANTALUS
Father of Pelops. For his murder of Pelops and for serving him up in a dish to the gods, he was condemned to hunger and thirst for eternity.

TARTARUS
The underworld where the souls of sinners went after judgement.

TEIRESIAS
A Theban blind seer.

TEUCER
Half-brother of Ajax, son of Telamon.

THEMISTOCLES
Athenian statesman and naval commander whose tactics defeated the Persians at the naval Battle of Salamis.

THESEUS
National hero of Athens. He was the son of King Aegeus and Aethra, though it was rumoured that his father was also Poseidon.

THETIS
A semi-goddess and sea-nymph, daughter of Nereus. She married King Peleus of Phthia and Achilles was their son.

THYESTES
Son of Pelops and Hippodamia, and brother of Atreus who became King of Mycenae.

TITAN
Pre-Olympian gods or demi-gods, the offspring of Uranus (the heavens) and Gaea (the earth).

TYNDAREUS
King of Sparta married to Leda.

XERXES
King of Persia, son of King Darius and Atossa.

ZEUS
Supreme god of the ancient world. He was married to Hera but had many extra-marital affairs with mortal beauties by whom he fathered children.

INDEX

Academy, Plato's 113, 119
Acharnians 82
Achilles 20, 23, 71, 87-92
Acrocorinth 49, 50
Acropolis 3, 9, 13, 15, 46, 47, 48, 60, 72, 73, 113, 114, 115, 121, 157
Admetus 150, 151-153
Adrastus, King 178-181
Aeacus 70, 72
Aeetes, King 50
Aegean 21, 126
Aegeus, King 30, 32, 37, 46, 56
Aegina 3, 10, 18, 27, 28, 66, 70-82
Aegina, river nymph 70
Aegisthus 39, 40-45
Aegyptus 169-172
Aeolus 81
Aerope 41,
Aeschylus 7, 8, 11-12, 14, 39-48, 59, 60, 61-63, 108-111, 116, 119, 133, 158, 163-167, 169-172
Aethra 29, 30, 177-178
Aithra (see Aethra)
Agamemnon, King 8, 23, 38, 39, 40-44, 77, 85-92, 94
Agamemnon 40-43
Agenor, King 100
Agia Marina 72
Agios Dionysos, monastery 148
Aigaia 133-135
Ajax 23, 24, 25, 71, 77
Ajax 23

Alcestis 151-153
Alcestis 150, 151-153
Alcmena 183
Alcyone 81
Alexander, the Great 6, 133, 134, 135, 137
Amazon 34
Amphipolis 77
Amphitryon, King 183-188
Andromache 20
Anthesteria 6
Antigone 111, 116-119, 173-175
Antigone 109, 111, 120, 153, 173-176
Aphaia 71, 72, 73
Aphrodite 30, 32, 33, 34, 49, 126, 163
Apollo 37, 40, 42, 45, 46, 51, 62, 70, 71, 81, 94-97, 150, 153
Archelaus, King 86, 125-127, 133, 135, 138, 145
Areopagus 47-48, 116, 157, 158
Ares 100
Argonauts 50
Argos 165, 166, 169-172, 173, 184
Argus, herdsman 170
Ariadne 19, 30
Aristophanes 3, 9-12, 18, 28, 63-66, 67, 70-82, 115, 133, 144, 145, 154, 158
Aristotle 138
Artemis 32, 34, 35, 71, 72, 85, 86-92, 92-97
Asclepius 37, 38, 151
Assembly Women 10
Astyanax 20-21

Athena 25, 42, 46-48, 60, 77, 96, 97, 100, 116, 121, 149, 157, 181, 186
Athens 3-12, 16, 18, 21, 32, 37, 46, 60, 63, 64, 70, 72, 73, 75, 77, 81, 82, 108, 111, 113, 114, 115, 125, 138, 144, 157, 158, 170, 177, 178, 179, 187, 188
Atreus 39, 44
Aulis 85-92

Babylonians 75, 81
Bacchus 6
Bacchae 6, 108, 126, 138-144
Bacchantes 7,
Beşik, bay 26, 42
Birds 77, 78-80
Boeotia 6, 85, 99
Brauron 96
Britomartis (see Aphaia)

Cadmus, King 4, 99, 100, 101, 138-144, 149
Calchas 86, 87
Cassandra 40-43
Castalian, spring 46
Castor 121
Cerberus 184
Choregos 8, 9
Chorus 7, 8
Christianity 6, 7, 49, 66, 67, 148, 153, 166, 167
Circe 51
City Dionysia (see Great Dionysia)
Cleon 73, 75, 77
Cleopatra 134, 135
Cloudcuckooland 78
Clouds 9-10,
Clytemnestra 39-45
Colchis 50, 51, 151
Colonus 111, 113-121
Corinth 37, 48, 49-56, 66, 101, 102
Creon, King of Thebes 102, 116-117, 173-175, 184
Creon, King of Corinth 52
Crete 21, 32, 100, 101
Cyclopes 151
Cyclops 8, 18-19, 22
Cyprus 26

Danaus 169-172
Darius, King 62
Delphi 39, 42, 45-46, 62, 102, 151
Delphic, oracle 5, 29, 30, 32, 72, 102
Demeter 59-67, 100, 101, 137, 138, 177
Demetria, St. 67
demones 170, 179
Diomedes 151
Dion 135, 137-145
Dionysios, St. 158
Dionysius 158
Dionysos 3, 4, 5, 7, 8, 9, 10-12, 16, 17, 38, 48, 61, 62, 70, 99, 100, 101, 108, 115, 119, 126, 135, 138-144, 148, 149, 150, 158
Dionysos Eleuthereus, 3, 7, 108
Dioscuri (see Castor and Polydeuces)

Eantio 15
Egypt 127, 166, 169, 171
Electra 39, 40, 44
Elektrai, gate 101
Eleusian Mysteries 60, 61, 138
Eleusis 59-67, 138, 177-181
Eleutherai 5, 107
Eleutherai, fortress 107, 108
Epaphos 169
Epidaurus 37-48
Epimetheus 163
Erechtheum 46
Eretria 85
Erinyes (see Furies)
Erinyes, Grove of 115
Eteocles 109-111, 116, 173, 177
Euboea 85, 99
Eumenides 45-48
Eumenides 116
Euridice 150
Euripides 6, 8, 9, 10, 11-12, 15, 16-22, 29, 30, 32-36, 49, 51-55, 64, 73, 82, 86-97, 108, 115, 119, 125, 126, 127-133, 138-144, 150-153, 158, 177-181
Euripides, Cave of 12, 16-22, 25, 66, 144
Eurystheus 184, 185
Europa 100
Eurotas, river 127
Eurystheus, king 151
Euripus, river 87

Fates 151
Frogs 10-12
Furies 45-48, 93, 116

Gaia 45
Galata 27, 29, 31, 37
Galilee 6
Gentiles 6
Glauke 50, 51, 52-55
Glauke's Fountain 51
God 38
Golden Fleece 50, 151
Greater Mysteries 62, 66
Great Dionysia festival 5, 6, 7, 8, 16, 32, 63, 75, 77, 82, 108, 114, 115, 119, 120, 138, 173, 188

Hades 11-12, 38, 40, 59, 60, 66, 118, 152, 177, 184, 188
Haemon 175-176
Harmonia 100
Hector 20, 23
Hecuba 19-21, 24
Hekademos 120, 121
Helen 38, 39, 77, 85, 86, 90, 94, 120, 121, 126, 127-133
Helen 127-133
Helios 51
Hephaestus 164
Hephaistion 144
Hera 4, 5, 38, 66, 165, 169, 170, 183, 187
Heracles 8, 11, 77, 150, 151-153, 166, 183-188
Hermes 166, 167, 170
Hermione 90
Herodotus 62
Hesiod 82
Hippolytus 30, 31-36, 151
Hippolytus 26, 29, 31-36, 49, 64
Homer 18, 19, 30, 59, 82, 138, 158
Hymn to Dionysos 21
Hymettos, Mts. 114
Hypermnestra 172

Ictinus 66
Iliad 138
Ino 5
Io 165, 166
Iolchos 50

Iphigenia 39, 40, 86-97
Iphigenia at Aulis 86-92, 126, 127
Iphigenia in Tauris 92-97
Iris 79
Ismene 111, 116-119, 173-175

Jason 37, 50, 52-56, 150, 151
Jesus 6, 7, 153
Jews 6
Jocasta, Queen 101, 102
John, St. 7
Joseph 4
Judgement of Paris 128

Kallichoron well 59, 60, 63
Kithairon, Mt. 101, 107, 108
Knights 73
Kolones 22,
Kore (see Persephone)
Kronos 167
Laius, King 101, 102, 108
Laomedon, King 77
Leda 128
Lenaia, festival 6, 73, 119, 173, 188
Libation Bearers 43
Linear B, tablets 101
Litochoro 145, 147, 148
Lycus 184-187
Lynceus 172
Lysistrata 10, 77

Macedonia 114, 125, 138, 144, 145, 147
Madness of Heracles 183-188
Maenads 8, 101, 108, 135, 140-143, 150
Marathon, Olympic 148
Mary, Virgin 4
Masks 8
Medea 37, 50, 51, 52-56, 151
Medea 51-55
Medus 56
Megara 184-188
Megara, town 57
Melos 21
Menelaus 25, 38, 39, 86-90, 128-133
Merope, Queen 101
Minos, King 51, 71, 72

Minotaur 19, 30
Mnemosyne 137
Muses 22, 137, 138, 157, 158
Mycenae 38-45, 48, 87, 92, 94, 184
Myrmidons 71, 167

Nauflio 38
Naxos 19, 30
Nazareth 7
Neoptolemus (Pyrrhus) 20
Odysseus 18, 19, 20, 23, 51, 87
Odyssey 18
Oedipus 46, 56, 101, 108, 109, 113, 115-119, 177
Oedipus Tyrannus 102-107, 108
Oedipus Colonus 111, 115-119, 173
Olympian gods 7, 167
Olympias 134, 135
Olympic, Games 121, 138, 148
Olympus, Mt. 137, 138, 145, 147-155
Omphalos 46
Orestes 39-48, 88, 92-96, 116, 157
Oresteia 39-48
Orpheus 150
Ouranos 167

Paloukia 14, 26
Pandora 163
Paris 38, 77, 127
Parnassus, Mt. 45, 62
Parnes, Mt. 114
Parthenon 13, 66, 72, 114, 153, 154, 157
Pasiphae 51
Paul, St. 56, 158
Peace 77, 154
Peisistratus 5, 6, 63
Pelasgus, King 170-171
Peleus, King 167
Pelias, King 50, 151
Pelion, Mt. 50, 152, 167
Pella 125-127, 133
Peloponnese 18, 26, 27, 49
Peloponnesian War 21, 70, 73, 115, 120, 144
Pelops 94
Pentelikon, Mt. 114
Pentheus, King 6, 139-144
Perama 13, 15, 27

Pericles 73, 115, 157
Peristeria 16
Persephone 59, 66, 118, 177
Persians 14, 16, 18, 25, 61, 62, 63, 121
Persians 14, 61-63
Peter, St. 140
Phaedra 19, 30, 31, 32-35, 49, 64
Phaedriades, crags 45, 46
Pherae 150, 151, 152
Philip II, King 133, 134, 135
Piraeus 10, 27, 69, 70, 114
Pittheus, King 30, 32
Plaka 4, 5, 9
Plato 82, 113
Pluto (also Plutus) 12, 63, 70
Plutonion 63
Plutus 63-64
Pnyx 64, 157
Polybus, King 101
Polydeuces 120
Polynices 109-111, 116-118, 173
Polyphemus 18, 19
Poros 27, 28, 31
Poseidon 18, 28, 29, 30, 31, 35, 69, 72
Priam, King 19, 42
Procne 80
Proitides, gate 101
Prometheus 8, 163-167, 169
Prometheus Bound 163-167, 171, 172
Prometheus the Fire-Bringer 167
Prometheus Unbound 167
Pylades 44, 93-96
Pythia 45
Pythian, Games 45
Python 151

Romans 6

Salamis, Cyprus 24
Salamis, island 13-26, 27, 57, 62, 67, 144
Salamis, Battle of 14, 16, 22, 62, 114
Salamina, town 25, 28
Salonika (see Thessaloniki)
Satyr, play 8, 20
Satyrs 4, 5, 18, 19
Scamander, river 20

Schliemann, Heinrich 44
Semele 4, 5, 38, 100
Sepphoris 6
Seven Against Thebes 108-111, 116
Silenus 4, 5, 18, 19
Skala Oropou 85
Socrates 5, 9, 10, 145
Sophist 9
Sophocles 23, 73, 102-107, 108, 113-119, 133, 153, 158, 173-176
Sounion 18, 72
Sparta 21, 39, 73, 82, 115, 120, 127, 144
Sphinx 102, 103, 107
Suppliant Women 177-181
Suppliants 169-172

Tantalus 41
Tauris 92-96
Teiresias 103-104, 139, 149, 176, 183
Telamon, King 22, 24, 71
Teucer 24,
Thanatos 151
Thassos 77
Thebes 5, 6, 56, 99-111, 138, 173, 177-179, 183-188
Theodosius, the Great 167
Themistocles 25
Theseus 19, 26, 30-35, 51, 56, 116-119, 120, 127, 177-181, 186-188
Thesmophoria, festival 64, 101
Thessaloniki 125, 137
Thessaly 71
Thoas, King 92-96
Thrace 150, 151
Thrasyllos 9, 10
Thyestes 39
Tiryns 183, 184
Titan 163, 164
Troezen 26, 27-36
Trojan War 8, 20, 22, 24, 38, 40, 77
Trojan Women 19-22, 127
Troy 19, 20, 39
Tyndareus, King 39

Vergina (see Aigaia)

Wasps 73-77
Women 8, 20
Women at the Thesmophoria 64-66
Wooden Horse 40

Xerxes, King 61, 63

Yahweh 7

Zeus 4, 7, 10, 38, 46, 47, 59, 60, 66, 70, 71, 72, 81, 97, 100, 135, 137, 138, 149, 150, 151, 157, 163-167, 169-171, 183, 184

ALSO BY JILL DUDLEY:

Ye Gods!
(Travels in Greece)

Ye Gods! II
(More travels in Greece)

Holy Smoke!
(Travels in Turkey and Egypt)

Gods in Britain
(An island odyssey from pagan to Christian)

Mortals and Immortals
(A satirical fantasy & true-in-parts memoir)

Holy Fire!
(Travels in the Holy Land)

Lap of the Gods
(Travels in Crete and the Aegean Islands)

Gods & Heroes
(On the trail of the Iliad & the Odyssey)

BIOGRAPHY

Jill Dudley was born in Baghdad and educated in England. Her first play was performed by the Leatherhead Repertory Company, since when she has written plays and short stories for radio. She returned to Iraq in 1956 when her husband was working out there and after the Iraqi revolution they came back to England where they bought a dairy farm. When they retired from farming in 1990 they travelled extensively around Greece, Turkey and Egypt and a number of her travel articles have appeared in the national newspapers followed in quick succession by her popular travel-writing books.

Website: www.orpingtonpublishers.co.uk